D0593458

PRAISE FOR ELISA NEW'S
Jacob's Cane

"In this poignant and wise study, New recreates that lost world for us, rebuilding it through memories, stories and archives, and presenting it through the prism of a single family."

—Edward Serotta, Director of Centropa.org,
a Jewish historical institute; author of *Out of the Shadows*,
Survival in Sarajevo and *Jews, Germany, Memory*

"Elisa New has managed to honor the past while also showing how the research to recapture it is done. Because *Jacob's Cane* is not only an historical detective story, but is also novelistic in its evocation of character and circumstance, Professor New's book is singular, poignant, and compelling."

—Stephen J. Whitfield, Professor of American Studies,
Brandeis University; author of *In Search of
American Jewish Culture*

"Here is a Harvard professor of literature, who goes in search of her family's Lithuanian Jewish story, and finds it, and brings back something that she may not have previously realized she owned: a rich poetic voice."

—Paul Hendrickson, National Book Critics Circle
Award-winning author of *Sons of Mississippi*

"*Jacob's Cane* is an intricate, beautifully rendered mesh of memoir and genealogical enthusiasm. New describes places, possessions, even the rhythms of business with vividness, even sensuality."

—Steven J. Zipperstein, author of *The Jews of Odessa*

"A lovely, fully grounded, yet lyrical family memoir . . . *Jacob's Cane* wonderfully transcends its 'back to my roots' genre; its narrative is loving yet objective, informative, beautifully written and a pleasure to read."

—Jonathan Wilson, Professor, Tufts University; author of *A Palestine Affair* and *The Hiding Room*

"Cultural history at its best. An engrossing exploration that reveals in its affectionate breadth the intimate ties between a Jewish family and major American manufactories."

—Susan Mizruchi, author of *The Science of Sacrifice*

"Elisa New's wonderful memoir adds a rich layer to the tapestry of American Jewish history."

—Suzanne Wasserman, Director, Gotham Center for NYC History / CUNY Graduate Center

"A family narrative of great fascination that includes in-depth social and economic history, all written with the pen of a poet."

—Henry Rosovsky, Professor Emeritus, Harvard University

"Elisa New's brilliant memoir prefers convergences to chronology. That 'history is a random business, made out of wanderings, guesses, and old glue' is the major idea—and also method—of the book, and its themes converge, surprisingly and pleasurably and emotionally—every which way. . . . A gorgeously written, marvelously structured memoir."

—Al Filreis, Kelly Professor and Faculty Director of the Kelly Writers House at the University of Pennsylvania, author of *Counter-Revolution of the Word*

"Like Andre Aciman's *Out of Egypt* and Rich Cohen's *Sweet and Low*, *Jacob's Cane* is a history of a Jewish family that is so much more—an imaginative recreation of two vanished worlds, Latvia and Baltimore from the 1880s to the 1940s; a natural, economic, and cultural history of tobacco, the product from which some of this family's fortune was made; and a moving personal quest. And it's a wonderful piece of writing."

—Louis Menand, author of *The Metaphysical Club*

Jacob's Cane

ALSO BY ELISA NEW

The Line's Eye:
Poetic Experience, American Sight

The Regenerate Lyric:
Theology and Innovation in American Poetry

Jacob's Cane

A JEWISH FAMILY'S JOURNEY *from*
the FOUR LANDS *of* LITHUANIA
to the PORTS *of* LONDON
and BALTIMORE

ELISA NEW

BASIC
BOOKS

A MEMBER OF THE PERSEUS BOOKS GROUP
New York

This book is dedicated
To my three great-aunts,
Jean, Myrtle, and Fanny,
Of blessed and beloved memory,
And to those members of the Levy family
Who perished between 1941 and 1945.

Published by
Basic Books, A Member of the Perseus Books Group
387 Park Avenue South
New York, NY 10016

Books published by Basic Books are available at special discounts for bulk
purchases in the United States by corporations, institutions, and other
organizations. For more information, please contact the Special Markets
Department at the Perseus Books Group, 2300 Chestnut Street, Suite 200,
Philadelphia, PA 19103, or call (800) 255-1514, or e-mail
special.markets@perseusbooks.com.

Designed by Timm Bryson
Set in 11.5 point Fournier

Library of Congress Cataloging-in-Publication Data
New, Elisa.
  Jacob's cane : a Jewish family's journey from the four lands of Lithuania
to the ports of London and Baltimore / Elisa New.
      p. cm.
  Includes bibliographical references.
  ISBN 978-0-465-01525-2 (alk. paper)
  1. Jews—Maryland—Baltimore—Biography. 2. Jewish
businesspeople—Maryland—Biography. 3. Levy family. 4. Barron
family. 5. New, Elisa—Family. 6. New, Elisa—Travel—Lithuania—
Anecdotes. 7. Jews—Lithuania—Biography. I. Title.
  F189.B19J56 2009
  929'.20973—dc22
                                    2009029941

10 9 8 7 6 5 4 3 2 1

CONTENTS

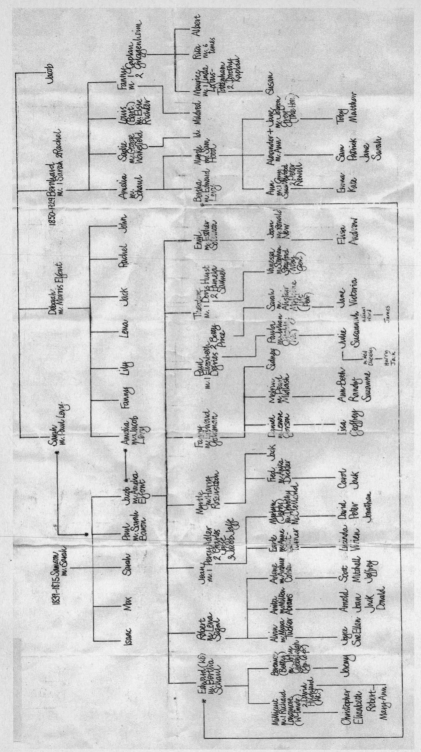

Levy–Baron family tree. Hand-drawn in London some time in the 1970s by Earle Adler (son of Jean Levy Jaffe) and Paula Baron (daughter of Paul Levy Baron).

Introduction

It was not until I held my great-grandfather Jacob's cane in my hands that all the hints and feints bestowed by those three sibyls, Aunt Jean, Aunt Myrtle, and Aunt Fanny, began to come together in this story.

Until the day I held the cane, my own proud Jewish family's history in America, and the history of many families like ours, remained to me obscure and hidden. Whenever I went looking for our story in the usual places, I found it missing.

Picturing my own ancestor—assuming him, like every Jewish immigrant, a Tevye—I imagined first catching sight of him as a barge neared the immigration center at Castle Garden. Rounding the bay, the boat would pull in and I'd be there waiting, beaming at this wan, disheveled bumpkin as he peered anxiously over the river's green chop. Or, I'd fancy myself meeting him in the Ellis Island registry room; I'd sympathize with his stumbling Yiddish phrases, his smell of steerage, his phylacteries.

This must be he, my relative, gesticulating over the official's stamp pad. This must be she, children pressed to her skirts, timid in her wifely modesty.

Not finding them there, I'd persist. I'd seek them out in the stalls on Delancey Street or up gray tenement steps to the workroom where they waited for me over their piecework. Seeking my immigrant fore-bears in the only Jewish story ever told to me, I wondered why they failed, for all my expectations, to appear.

We imagine every immigrant a transplant from the rutted *shtetl*, his background pious, his experience thin, his hopes fastened on the new land to which he makes his way. But with our gaze on the impe-cunious greenhorn, with our eyes straining after the rural milkman turned cloak maker, we may miss Tevye's more cosmopolitan cousin.

This is the cousin rendered worldly by centuries of transoceanic commerce.

A trader in timber or leather or tobacco, an expert in transport, storage, and the ways of officialdom, conversant with land routes from seacoasts to market towns, this cousin has for centuries known the feel of the deck, the bill of lading, the jumble of brokers at the port. Multilingual, versed in legal codes and his father's wisdom, he attended not *cheder* but Gymnasium, not yeshiva but the Polytechnic or even the university. He may have hailed from Prague or Memel, Riga or Novgorod, but his German is unaccented. His broadest boast is that he is a man of liberal, enlightened spirit.

Landing not in New York but quite likely in Baltimore, he lets his liberal spirit be his guide. He gives imaginative answers to certain questions on the immigration form. He was born not in a German land but in Shavli, Lithuania. But he deems such a fact a technicality. To write "Austria" on the form affords him the pleasure of renounc-ing an emperor and endorsing the modern in one stroke.

He grew up in, say, Rostov-on-Don via Brest-Litovsk, and was known round about as Ber, or Berel, or—who knows—even Baruch? But now he is Bernhard, with an *h*. Where would his native lands have been but for his own ambitious grandsires whose journeys to Danzig, Istanbul, and even Venice brought faraway traders, names, and contacts to river basins long neglected by Cossack horsemen? Would Brest-Litovsk or Rostov-on-Don have prospered had not his grandparents dug the ports and organized the customs houses? Where would Shavli be today had not his father stood patiently in line to buy stamps for the documents to convey goods on their way, thus tying rural depots to the globe's more glittering entrepôts?

To keep track of all the places the family has been, the languages spoken, the secrets for rebounding and succeeding, his family preserves certain artifacts.

A family tree, elaborately detailed, is written out from time to time, but a tree, mere paper, is easily mislaid when not burned up or destroyed. To be sure, certain generations produce their genealogists, persons attentive to history, who bestow keepsakes eloquent with meaning. But just as often, the generations history treats most generously are those most careless of the past. They leave artifacts less eloquent, objects simply too beautiful to throw away. A flowered dish in the style of Bavaria. A silver cigarette case, deco crosshatch on its lid. A photo, some clippings.

A cane.

The cane my family keeps was presented to my great-grandfather, Jacob Levy, in 1928. Today it stands in a closet in Baltimore, cushioned by the wall-to-wall carpet. Somewhere between cherished and disregarded, it has leaned against that wall for decades, the proud initials on it tarnishing. I have given years of my life to understanding this cane, to tracing its journeys, but the truth is: I was lucky to have been shown it at all. Only an accidental turn in the conversation gave it into my hands.

However accidental, I nevertheless know it was the weight of that cane on my palms, the raised touch of its carved initials under my fingertips that sent me looking for the Jewish civilization that had produced it. The proud, unmistakable elegance of that cane, its foreign appearance, its careful design, its Germanness, required me to throw out much of what I'd read and assumed about the Jewish world that produced me. But it was also something familiar, something of my past, closer to me than I would grasp for years, that required me to pay the strictest respect, if not the strictest credence, to everything my three aunts had told me long ago.

Nothing I've ever read revealed to me my Jewish civilization as this cane did. Nothing I've ever tried to write so taxed and worked me and filled me with a sense of tender obligation as did the story of this cane. For the true story of the cane could not be told through the mere gathering of facts and stories or through research, however ambitious or remote, through drafts and redrafts, new discoveries and their corrections. The true story of the cane depended, had to depend, on how truth looked, how it felt and sounded, to those who had to bear it. The story began, naturally, with my aunts.

The author's great-aunts (from left to right), Jean, Myrtle, and Fanny.

ONE

Initials

When I was a little girl growing up in the 1960s and 1970s, my great-aunts, Jean, Myrtle, and Fanny, would share stories of their father, Jacob Levy, and of his once bosom friend but later nemesis, the fabled London cigarette magnate Bernhard Baron. They called him "Uncle Baron" due to the multiple marriages he had engineered with the Levys.

Aunt Jean, the eldest of the sisters, would recount with pride the glory that her brothers Eddie, Paul, and Theodore Levy had achieved with Baron in London, and she would tell about how Baron had invited her young sons, Jerry and Earle, only ten and twelve years old, to come live with him. "Send me your sons and I will make them great men!" he told Jean. So she did. By 1928, when Baron's great Carreras cigarette factory was built, five of Jacob Levy's male progeny were living in London. There, Aunt Jean let it be known, they enjoyed a sort of Masterpiece Theatre version of Jewish success.

On the other hand, when Jean's younger sisters, Myrtle and Fanny, told of their brothers' (and then their nephews') defection to England, their foreheads contracted over their large powdered noses. They remembered their father's fearsome anger and still felt the effects of his sadness. Although they were cowed—who wasn't?—by their sister Jean, they also disapproved of her for letting their brother Eddie's uppity wife, Bertha (Baron's granddaughter), raise Jean's two sons while she moved on to her next, but not her last, husband.

I remember that when the subject of Jean's sons came up, my aunts would turn to look at each other, their heads shaking slightly and the silver and copper hairdos trembling in their coronets of spray. What but selfishness, their pursed mouths showed, could have moved Jean to send two young boys so far from home? Anyone who heard Jean's son Jerry tell the story knew that, even at seventy, eighty, or ninety years old, the memory brought him to tears.

Despite Myrtle and Fanny's ambivalence about the family's London adventure, when I was about six or seven the family albums they kept in their closets convinced me that the glamorous life their brothers and nephews had lived in England was far more interesting than anything else my relatives talked about. What other Jewish family could boast relatives who might really be called "aristocrats," an Uncle Eddie who had actually been knighted, or, as the aunts tended to say, "knighted-by-the-Queen," forgetting that Eddie's investiture took place eleven years before young Princess Elizabeth turned into a queen.

Sent off to play, I would go into the hall closet. I ignored the spinning top and the coloring books. Instead, I would drag out the heavy photo albums that were hidden under my aunts' furs and stacked against the card shuffler. Time had lent the photos and postcards a brown and satiny patina, the very texture of the high life my uncles had enjoyed.

Here was a photo of Baron's imposing Carreras cigarette factory as it looked in 1928, when it opened to lively architectural interest and much local acclaim. Immense, extending a long city block wide and one just as deep, with flags flying over its massive iron gate and two eight-foot black cats guarding the door, the building looked more like government offices, or even a museum, than a factory.

The Carreras factory shortly after its opening in 1928. Gift to the author from Fred Rosenstein.

Here too were my great-uncles in the 1920s, 1930s, and 1940s. First, Uncle Paul at Monaco or Biarritz, standing in front of an impossibly long roadster, a squiggle of palms in the background. And then a shot of Uncle Theo's wife before her presentation at Court, along with Dorothy Marks, of the Marks and Spencer department store dynasty, and then a panorama of Uncle Eddie's estate, Fulmer Chase, in Buckinghamshire, with its rolling lawns and large dogs. Yellowed clippings from the years after World War II showed Uncle Eddie just after he'd been knighted, and Aunt Bertha smiling as she hosted Mrs. Winston Churchill at the Fulmer Chase hospital. And there was a sheaf of letters, rubber-banded, bearing the return address "Ruthin Castle, Wales."

Just how we acquired relatives who had titles and wrote letters from castles, in addition to owning town houses, country houses, and racehorses, puzzled me. I was also intrigued by my uncles, so suave in the *carte postales* sent from Europe's pleasure capitals. And most interesting of all was our mysterious Uncle Baron, who had somehow started out in Baltimore with the rest of us but ended up in

London as our benefactor—though, of course, only in some people's eyes.

Invariably, after closing the album, if I asked Myrtle or Fanny a question about the brothers, or Bertha, or even Bernhard Baron, whatever answer I got began with the story of Jacob Levy's curse, often relayed in that delighted tone one keeps for events so utterly unlikely one cannot but love their coming to pass. The curse—pronounced by Jacob on the three sons who were leaving him—was "May you never have sons!" The tone an aunt used to pronounce the curse allowed that, as we were a modern family, we naturally did not believe in curses. Still one had to admire, the aunt's tone said, the splendid nerve, the grand sweep of this one. Especially since it *stuck*.

Jacob's sons Eddie, Paul, and Theo, who changed their name to Baron and broke their father's heart, had daughters only. For nought Eddie's careful provision in his *London Times* announcement of his change of name so that his sons, too, would become Barons. Not only were the prodigals denied "any lawfully begotten heirs to be known or distinguished by the name Baron," but also, by the mid-1960s, the great cigarette empire they had inherited was gone too. By the time I turned the pages of those albums, the fire sale of Carreras, arranged by Eddie, had already happened. According to Myrtle and Fanny, Eddie had revealed himself to be a person of compromised character, dealing behind his brothers' backs to unload the company quickly before some combination of the U.S. surgeon general's report, plus his own weakness for racehorses and fine wine, threatened to leave him not the head of a cigarette empire but someone with a cigarette millstone around his neck.

Later family discussions put the albums I found so alluring in an even dimmer light. I began to understand that the pictures of the young brothers grinning ear to ear must have brought distress to their father, Jacob. And I sensed that the brothers might not have turned out as well as Uncle Baron hoped when he invited Jean to send them to him. "Send me your sons and I will make them great men!"

One photo in the album shows Uncle Baron looking weary on his day of triumph in 1928, when the new factory was dedicated. Stoop-shouldered, wearing a top hat, he stands on the steps of "the largest factory in the metropolis" and looks somehow bereft. He seems to be bending one shoulder down to take the whole factory onto his back.

~~~

As I grew up, finished college and graduate school, and started teaching American literature, the uncles and all their glittering trappings continued to fascinate me. I grew curious about the great hopes and great disappointments of the generation before—of Jacob Levy and Bernhard Baron, Jewish immigrants from the Baltic States who had met in Baltimore, become friends, mingled their families through marriage, but ended their lives bitterly divided.

I wondered how these two young men had made their start in the new country that was so very different from their homeland. Who was this Bernhard Baron, called Uncle by Jacob Levy's family? Who indeed was my great-grandfather, the man who cursed so magnificently?

My interest in these characters was probably stimulated by the subjects I was teaching—early American settlement, regional literature, and Jewish literature of the city. I was especially fascinated by my home state—Maryland. Along with its slaveholding history and agricultural origins, Maryland also had an old and large Jewish population and a large city, Baltimore, that became a sort of cemetery for an earlier industrial boom.

Driving to the beach on the Delaware shore, my father, mother, brother, and I used to pass alongside tobacco lands and signs indicating these lands had once been farmed by slaves. On the way to the newly built Harborplace in Baltimore, we would go along avenues of six- and seven-story square brick buildings, now lofts and office suites but once factories, the Jewish or German names of their long-ago proprietors still sometimes visible in faded paint on the brick.

It was not easy for me, even by asking my aunts direct questions, to get a story of our origins that made sense, but in the years before they died, I tried to find out what I could about the family's early days in the city they called *Balt-ee-mewer*.

Aunt Jean, the sharpest of the aunts by far, was also the most motivated to help me understand. The three sons and two grandsons who had abandoned their father and grandfather for Bernhard Baron were a favorite topic of hers. Jean never tired of repeating the siren call he issued across the Atlantic, nor was she reluctant to share her own archives, more complete than her sisters', about Baron.

For one thing, Jean kept in her possession a sheaf of obituaries written about Baron in 1929, his death coming just months after the opening of the great factory and of the settlement house to which he gave his name as well as his money. Reading through these obituaries, I could tell that the narrative of Uncle Baron's life was quite a story, if corrupted (as I suspected) by mystifications both private and public. For instance, one obituary began by asserting that "no more romantic career can be imagined" than Bernhard Baron's, and it traced his rise from poverty in Brest-Litovsk. Another said he'd begun penniless in Rostov-on-Don.

Something about the hyphenation of both of these place-names inclined me to be skeptical of them, and to believe instead what turned out to be a fallacious account that traced the Barons, like the Levys, to Riga, in Latvia. Other extravagant claims in the obituaries also made me wonder.

All the accounts agreed, for instance, that Bernhard Baron had been a "benchmate of Samuel Gompers" in New York, and one went so far as to claim that "the association doubtless accounts for the sympathy with the Labour Cause the deceased so markedly showed in this country" before relocating to Baltimore and eventually London, where he became, according to the various obituaries and glowing encomia, that city's greatest philanthropist and most progressive employer.

The public record not only credited Uncle Baron with outstanding success but also marveled at his great humility. One obituary emphasized that he had refused a title, saying if "Mister" was good enough for his workers it was good enough for him. He ordered medals struck to celebrate the opening of the factory, stamped on one side "London's Most Hygienic Tobacco Factory" and on the other, to his workers, "My Thanks For ALL YOUR HELP." The rhapsodic accounts of his philanthropy went on and on. One paper called him a "Prince of Benefactors," bankrolling London's largest Jewish settlement house, building public tennis courts in Regents Park, funding North London hospitals, contributing to the cause of Palestine. The factory had apparently been a showplace for progressivism, a sort of laboratory for worker protection with vacation and retirement benefits, free education for the young, relocation for workers, subsidized meals, and theatrical societies.

It was in a reckless moment, therefore, that I queried Myrtle and Fanny whether any ambitious young man in his right mind wouldn't have followed Bernhard Baron. One had to realize, after reading the obituaries, that Uncle Baron had a career that our poor sire, Jacob, could hardly match. Still, pity the hapless grandniece incautious enough to say such a thing to Aunts Myrtle and Fanny.

Their steely, sorrowful, and baffled looks made clear to me that Bernhard Baron owed much to the brilliance, the vision, the generosity, the refinement of their father, who had arrived in Baltimore in 1886 while Baron was still in New York. For was not their father, as Fanny often pointed out, a brilliant inventor of machines, a holder of patents, who by 1900 had established himself in his own grand home on Baltimore's fashionable West Lombard Street?

Moreover—as Aunt Myrtle somewhat grimly informed me—didn't she, Myrtle, know better than the others? Wasn't it she who kept house for her father, Jacob, after her young husband died and her mother was sent to the place only Fanny would name—the "inst-*ee*-tution"? Jean may have worked with him at the plant and kept the family together early on, but hadn't she, Myrtle, dusted and straightened his "library," typed his frequent letters to the editor, and prepared his meals? She didn't need anyone to remind *her* of her father's books books books, papers papers papers, and of his many opinions on social questions or the fact that he was a Socialist.

That's *just* what he was, she said with emphasis, as if her discomfort were best managed with defiance: not just a member of the Socialist Party but its candidate for Congress in 1914. I'm grateful for the discomfort she let herself show, for the tone in her voice that let me see how the newspapers, typescripts, petition pads, and other paraphernalia of his public meddling must have weighed on her, a widow with two sons in knee pants and an irascible, glowering, chain-smoking, ink-spilling radical father.

Jean's perspective was different from Myrtle's, more worldly. But how did it happen, I asked Jean, that your father named his two factories—the first in Baltimore and the later one in Philadelphia—Levy's International Shrinking Company? Wasn't this a bit grandiose for two brick buildings—one on Front Street in Philadelphia, one on Redwood Street in Baltimore—and the latter only a few minutes walk from the original plant, which had been some dunking tubs and drying rods in a Lombard Street basement?

With that, Aunt Jean looked her sternest and sought the strength to show patience. Why indeed had her father called his company Levy's *International* Shrinking Company? Not just to be grand, she had me understand, not to put on airs. Rather, as he'd explained to her, it was to express those *internationalist* principles that were once the hope of the world. Like Uncle Baron, her father had been an inventor, a holder of patents, an *industrialist* of the *most* enlightened kind. He invented machines that did easy as pie, quick as can be, what used to take hours of handwork, and he did it to advance a cause—socialism you could call it—he did—but *she* called it just living decently, comfortably. Jacob, and Uncle Baron too, understood that machines—sponging and drying machines or machines to make cigarettes—were things that would free working people, help them live more civilized lives. But of course it had all been ruined, and her father's heart broken, when the unions pushed their way in.

Her father was a Socialist, yes, and so was his brother Paul, but this, in Jean's opinion, had nothing to do with unions—a bunch of thugs, that's just what they were. Same in America as in Europe.

And if I didn't believe her, I could ask my cousin Moshe, in Israel, to tell the story of his own father, Isaac, Jacob's older brother, and what he endured from the local thugs over there. Get Cousin Moshe to describe how back in Europe, as in America, the enlightened men, the intelligent Jews, struggled. Get him to tell me how his father had been sent to Germany by Frankel, the biggest industrialist in Shavli— their hometown—to learn modern techniques with leather, and how he came home only to be blackballed by the local tanners and their guild—just unions really, led by the gentiles, keeping the Jews out. When the Nazis came in, as Moshe could also tell me, the locals thought they'd have their chance to take over—except that none of them understood the machines or the modern techniques.

Nazis? I wondered. But Jean was now finished with that part of the story.

For years and years my aunts seemed no more affected by age than were the gloves and handkerchiefs they kept nested in original tissue in their bureau drawers. Born in 1894, 1896, and 1897, married and, in my Aunt Jean's case, already widowed before the end of World War I, from the 1960s into the first few years of the 1990s my aunts seemed almost to grow, if not younger, at least more freshly, luxuriantly, themselves.

At sixty-five, Jean had still to acquire the magisterial sinew she would show at seventy-five. At seventy, Myrtle was just giving bud to her most bountiful role, still learning the play of her fairy godmother's wand. And at eighty, Fanny was just coming into a waggishness, a drollery, that had been repressed—who knew how long? Their three brothers in London all died in the 1970s, as did their youngest brother, Emil, my grandfather. But Aunt Fanny lived until 1996, and her sisters Myrtle and Jean to just a year or two before.

Each within a year or two of turning one hundred, they gave out, and we went three times in as many years to the cemetery and then back to sit *shiva*, children and grandchildren, all squeezed into the aunts' jewel box—like apartments, eating off their crystal and sterling and trying not to cry at the end of an era.

※※

By the time they all died I was glad that I, at least, had done my due diligence. I had interviewed each aunt, tape recorder running, and had asked intelligent questions of all concerned, demonstrating interests not merely sentimental but historical and intellectual. I had written up what they told me in a college paper and stored my notes in a manila file.

In addition, I traveled to Israel in the 1980s and went to Givat Ram to meet the distant Israeli cousin, Moshe, born in 1907. I took careful notes of his account of my great-grandfather Jacob's departure from the Baltics. Truth be told, I rather enjoyed how Moshe's version of events seemed to put certain matters straight, and after returning to the United States I wrote up a version of the family story that emphasized his "corrections."

No one was anything less than completely tactful and gracious about what I'd learned from Moshe. Even though what he told me contradicted family lore and my great-grandfather's naturalization papers of 1891, which had been framed on the wall of the factory, no one argued. The naturalization papers said that Jacob M. Levy was a native of Austria, and that, moreover, he utterly and completely refused all allegiance to the emperor of Austria. Moshe assured me, on the contrary, that Jacob was born not in Austria but in northern Lithuania, near the Latvian border. As proof, Moshe showed me some of the same pictures I had seen in my aunts' albums, pictures documenting the trip that Jacob took in 1928 back to the land of his birth, taking with him my grandfather, Emil. Moshe had pointed out that these pictures were marked at the bottom with the names of towns— Riga, Siauliai, and Raseinai—and these towns were on the east, not the west, shores of the Baltic.

Moshe genteelly refused to enter into the question of whether Jacob had falsified the place of his birth or the relatives were wrong. His politeness and so much else about him reminded me of my aunts, who were his cousins not only in blood but in a certain horror of vulgar disputation. Back at home, they politely refused to enter into a silly argument with a relative so far away and over matters long past. For my part I'd have preferred them to insinuate that, even if Moshe did have the pictures, he must, somehow, be mistaken. But they didn't.

❧

It was not until I held in my hand the elaborately inscribed cane, my great-grandfather Jacob's cane, that all the hints and feints, the conundra and contradictions of our family saga, began to compose this story. From the very first morning I saw it and turned its pale engraved script into the November light, I knew this cane would exert a stronger, more persistent influence over my imagination than any one object ever had.

I first saw it on a bright morning in Baltimore shortly after the last of my aunts had died. I had just finished eating brunch with my mother, my daughter Yael, then just twelve years old, and our cousins Buddy and Anita, children of great-grandsire Jacob's son Robert. During breakfast, Buddy, bright-faced, amiable, had been talking about the old days of fabric shrinking in Baltimore, describing in detail the method of inspecting and treating the fabrics to be used in rainwear and umbrellas and fine haberdashery, and remembering too the labor struggles of the first half of the twentieth century, before he had finally closed the Baltimore plant. It was then, just as Buddy's wife stood up to clear away the plates of lox and bagels, onions and tomatoes on the sideboard, that Buddy mentioned, quite offhandedly, that he actually still had, if I wanted to see it, my great-grandfather Jacob's cane.

It was in his den.

Of course I remembered the cane as soon as Buddy mentioned it. I had noticed it many times in one particular heirloom photograph, beautifully mounted versions of which I'd seen in albums in Baltimore and London, Philadelphia and Washington, and also in cousin Moshe's apartment near Tel Aviv. The picture had been taken in 1928 when Jacob made his only trip back to Riga to visit the Levy family members still resident there, and then had visited for a few weeks in London. This had occurred, I understood, the same spring that Buddy's father, Robert, or Bob, had taken Aunt Jean's sons to England to be formed into "great men." There Jacob had visited with his grandsons and perhaps even had a reunion with his own sons, now bearing the name Baron, at the magnificent new Carreras factory on Mornington Crescent.

The photograph showed Jacob sitting among a large group of his relatives still living in the Baltics: his brother Max and his children and grandchildren. In the picture, Jacob's hands are folded over the cane's ebony crook, his vest front recedes lustrous behind the cane's scroll of filigree. Jacob looks like a man who'd waited long to come back to his homeland and had done so in the proper style. And yet, in the midst of this whole gravely dignified clan—tots soft-limbed on the foreground carpet; elders in chairs; the heirs apparent standing at the back—Jacob looks not the patriarch but the prodigal, the curser cursed. Among the unfamiliar relatives, his face clean-shaven, his eyebrows lifted, lips tight, he sits alone. No son, of five, stands by him.

Sadness leaks from the image. Like Bernhard Baron bearing the weight of his factory on his back, at the moment immortalized in this photo my great-grandfather Jacob, leaning on his cane, seemed to bear the sorrows of the world.

And now, here in a Baltimore ranch house, I was looking at the cane itself.

Leaned up against the wooden louvers of the den closet, it had a leggy, lounging gentlemanly look. Of elegant design, it conjured up topcoats and the flare of silk through a hotel door. Close up it looked like a *mezuzah*.

Putting on my glasses and walking the cane into the living room, I made out the beginning of the conventional German inscription, *Zur Erinnerung,* "in memory of," *from,* and then *our brother from your brothers*. And then this longish italic line followed by characters I could read, even without German: 1928, the date; *Siluva*, its place of purchase; *Loewensohn*, its maker; and then another city name, *Riga*.

Studying the cane further, I was nagged by questions. For instance, why was it that one set of initials, MPL, was larger than the others? This MPL, donor of the cane, might be evincing a certain modesty by placing his own initials second, a third of the way down the shaft. But contradicting this was the fact that the letters of his own initials were a good deal larger than the others. While the metal used in crafting the other brothers' initials was silver, this monogram, the second, had been executed in a brassy gold. Each set of initials presented itself in a dramatic twist of metalwork, and under each set a small metal frame, shaped like a shield, enclosed the name of a town.

PSL, the first twist of initials, was from Riga.

MPL, the second, from Raseinai.

And the last two brothers, *YRL* and *JML*, from Shavli.

But why this order? Why these particular towns? I noted that the cane confirmed Moshe's version of our family origins, not my aunts'. Not from Austria after all, I wanted to shout, but from Siauliai, the town the Jews called Shavli, Lithuania, not far from Riga! I felt tempted to grasp the cane like a baton, to lift its head and cheer for veracity's triumph over family legend. Not just a matter of invention and story, not made merely of feeling, history was a thing that *happened*. It could be known, discovered.

Yet this vindicating token had other cryptic, baffling intelligences to share, and these fractured what certainty my Moshe-stamped story provided. In seconds I found myself plunged into speculation, my thoughts scattered in all directions.

This PSL, Jacob's older brother Paul, who emigrated to America some years before Jacob, why was *he* first on the stock, and why identified with the city of Riga? Moshe had left little doubt that all the brothers were born in the town he called Shavli. What spell had the larger city cast that this man who'd emigrated in his early twenties to Baltimore might be called a man of Riga?

Similarly, MPL, the shield under which Raseinai was proclaimed. The eldest brother Max, Moshe had assured me, also started out in this Shavli. What version of belonging earned him the honor or duty to name Raseinai as his place?

Finally, what of the third town name written on the cane? It was the one Moshe had named as the family home, and yet it seemed odd that both his own father's initials—*YRL*—and those of my great-grandfather, Jacob, should have that name, Shavli, written underneath. Isaac had, I knew from his son Moshe, stayed in Shavli his whole life, dying there well before the Nazis came and killed most of his children. But Jacob had left Shavli as a boy of sixteen or seventeen. His life was spent in Baltimore and Philadelphia, not in Shavli.

From its German inscription—wrapping the grip like a silver cuff—down to the thick silver heel capping its straightness, the cane declared its bearer a person of parts, no Tevye at all, but someone more traveled, more sure—even cocksure. As I stood admiring it, swinging it down from under my arm, I caught the cane's tip where the carpet edge met the kitchen tile.

I felt the very plates of history shift.

Up the cane's length I seemed to feel the tremors of my great-grandfather's footfall and the thrum of machines. I sensed the din and buzz of parade grounds, the blue plume of smoke, and the seaside smell of wharves. Speeches rang out. Guns. Sound of stately music. Photographers' shutters opening, umbrellas opening, doors to a jitney opening.

How wonderfully suitable, I thought, to the study of a family's history was this symbol of a cane.

Supple in shape, sinuous in form, coming to hand in the form of a question, a cane is shaped like an inquiry—and puts its foot down with caution. Who knows the common yet divergent routes of history and story better than a cane? Accoutrement of a journey, and useful too as a probe or a pointer, a cane embodies the urge to go and find out.

Tool of tact, symbol of deliberateness, the cane bids slow going, bids faith, while the tale uncurls as it will.

≫ TWO ≪

From Shavli, in Lita

C ivilization! Progress! Enlightenment!
Such were the terms my great-grandfather, Jacob Levy, and my great-great-uncle, Bernhard Baron, used to invoke the world they'd come from, the ethos they had shared and brought with them from far-off eastern Europe to Baltimore in America.

"May you be to the world," my great-grandfather wrote in a letter to his infant grandson in 1915, "a leading figure of Civilization." Along the same lines, an entry in *Baltimore's Leading Businesses of 1899* described Bernhard Baron and his manager, Kraus, as "liberal, progressive and enlightened men."

Could it be that my great-grandfather Jacob's highly decorated cane would lead me to this civilization? From the stately German dedication *Zur Erinnerung* to its delicate silver engravings of names and cities, the cane hinted at a liberal spirit, a confidence in achievement, and a hope that, as I would learn, had nowhere been nurtured so carefully as in the lands along the western edges of the Russian empire, once called the Four Lands of the Polish-Lithuanian Commonwealth.

And of course, nowhere so fully traduced and destroyed.

Holding the cane in my cousin Buddy's living room, I already knew that the place-names on its shaft, along with the persons, were all names on the map of the Holocaust. My cousin Moshe had told me this long ago. Still, I'd not anticipated the impact of discovering my forebears' civilization through visiting the grave pits where it ended. Nor what it would feel like to make that discovery with my own child.

The first time I visited my family's town, Shavli, in Lita (Lithuania), was on the eve of Passover 1999, five months after I had held the cane in my hands. I was with my daughter Yael, who was three weeks shy of her bat mitzvah.

After our plane landed in Riga, Yael and I had made our way by train to Kaunas (the Jewish Kovno), where we hired a car and driver and a guide named Chaim. On our approach to Shavli, I saw fields on either side where men on tractors were cutting hay. Among the fields, boxy stucco houses, their shutters faded green, sat sidewise to the road. Twenty minutes ago we had come to a T at a slight rise. There a honey-toned sign, hand carved, pointed left to Shavli and right to Raseinai. Two names on the cane. And there was a third: Riga.

I looked down at Yael, her pale face turned to the light, and saw again how well, with her tilted chin and defined cheekbones, her wide-spaced eyes, light brown hair in a ponytail, she blended into crowds here. With her fine-boned, slightly Slavic features, she didn't look Jewish to me. But she was, of course, and we had both been aware of this since arriving—especially on the train from Riga, where we had met Chaim in the town with a famous ghetto, more famous than Shavli's. We'd scarcely slept on this leg of the trip, what with the train's spooky whistle and the fright of being awakened at the Latvian border by a conductor demanding "papers." And so I'd been all too glad to see Yael do as she'd done since babyhood—fall asleep twenty minutes into the ride, her knees drawn up, her shoes off. Who knew what we would see when she awoke. Now, though, I let myself breathe, taking in the passing scene, muddy slopes showing patches of green, the clouds piled in massive formations, cows browsing.

I felt a lift in my heart and remembered the first time I had heard the town's name as the Jews pronounced it—Shav-lee—fifteen years ago, by my cousin Moshe.

I had been visiting with Moshe and his wife, Tanya, at their flat in Givat Ram, Israel, following through on my promise to Aunt Jean. Across a damask tablecloth, the plates with the fishes, the cheese, and little rounds of tomatoes pushed to one side, Moshe slid a familiar photo across the table toward me.

Here, so far from my aunts' apartments in Philadelphia, were some of the same photographs the aunts had kept in a hall closet. Here was the photo with the cane, the one I'd looked at so many times before. My great-grandfather Jacob, among a group of unnamed persons in what looked to be an elegant setting, with the word "Raseinai" at the photo's bottom. Then Moshe handed me another photo, with a date and a place, Riga, and then another, in the corner a white scratch: Siauliai (Shavli). Again Jacob, seated, with his brother—"Yitzchak, my father," Moshe offered—while at each man's shoulder stands his tall son. And in the picture too, Moshe's brother Shlomo's family.

"That's Fanja, Shlomo's wife," Tanya says in English. Moshe nods and points to the woman with her feet in satin shoes, her ankles in silk stockings, one young daughter standing to the side and another at her mother's knee. "So beautiful, wasn't she?" Moshe tries in English.

"*Kol ne-elam, hutz me Shlomo.*" (All gone, except Shlomo.) Moshe looks up at me, oddly smiling, but in the quick, anxious way people do when something remains unexplained: "Disappeared." Tanya gently translates, furrowing her brow with the effort of English. "Vanished— all except Shlomo, Moshe's brother, and Max's granddaughter Riva, who lived with the partisans in the forest."

"*Kol n'hargru,*" Moshe says, letting his hands drop open, palms up.

"All killed," I say, looking at Moshe and then nodding to Tanya that I understand.

"Moshe wrote letter after letter," Tanya explains, "to get them to leave, to come to Israel, to Palestine, but they didn't believe they were not safe and wouldn't come. They had built so much in Shavli, had been there so long."

M'zman . . . M'zman . . .

"For a long time," Moshe adds again in English, and his tone takes on a slight formality, or the sound of gentle ceremony.

Earlier, Moshe had smiled indulgently and shrugged, as Israelis do, at hardships, looking—despite the short-sleeved polo shirt with the crease ironed down to his elbows—every bit the *halutz*, the rugged pioneer, who'd done what he had to do and expected others to do the same. Earlier, he had let his face register delight at the sheer nerve of Jacob—who told the American authorities that he was from one country, Austria, when he was in fact from another. Moshe didn't mind Jacob's creative genealogy. Who was to stop him, Moshe's look had said. What did it matter what he told them? The audacity of it made him happy.

But now Moshe's tone delicately shifted. Pointing at the picture of Jacob, Moshe said, "He was, we all were, from Shavli, in Lita."

When Moshe looked back at the photo, squinting over the pale white scrawl that spelled out the name of Jacob's hometown, his blue eyes looked fond. And when Moshe spoke the name, *Shavli*, he gave it a lyrical and lilting sound, drawing out the long vowel, the *ee,* as if he loved to hear it. Pronouncing *Lita*, he closed his palate gently over the t, as one closes a door, firmly but gently, on the past.

❦

I woke up Yael just as we were entering Shavli. The town was not what I had expected, for it reminded me immediately and unmistakably of Madison, Wisconsin. With a heartland feel, like Madison or other such towns between woods and pastures, Shavli had the look of a nice place to live. There was a large lake, the center deep blue and flecked with little frisking waves. Shavli's more noisome factories— leather, machine tools, dairy—were, along with the Soviet era apartment blocks, pushed out to the edge of town. My sense of Shavli's pleasantness increased as our car, now leaving the industrial edge, probed along the smaller side streets. Shoemakers and small stationery shops still opened in the old-fashioned way, through a door around to the side of the house. The sun shone brightly through large low clouds. I had been prepared for a place in black and gray, grim, muddy, a setting for tragedy, and I was surprised.

Gaining the heart of town, Chaim made straight for the Jewish Community Center, leaving the car and then returning to say that, perhaps owing to the holiday, Leibe, the man who'd said he would meet us there, had been detained. "Back after two," Chaim said, and urged a visit now to the ghetto sites—Traku or Vauclausko—before we went with Leibe to the mass graves at Kuzhai and Bubai.

This, we were quickly discovering, was the Jewish visitors' Shavli. Chaim, who had been born in the Kovno ghetto, and this Leibe worked together to shepherd "roots" tourists to the sites of their families' destruction. We were that. I couldn't deny it. But as I tried to signal Chaim, we had not come just to see the sites of carnage. I had a child with me, and besides, our family had lived in Shavli, this town, for generations.

I suggested a stroll through the streets, putting off both ghettos until after lunch. We walked along the cobbled alleys in Shavli and heard the sound of clothespins pinging in the air and, a way off, bicycles clicking on the gentle hills. Women in small backyards hung out the wash on wire lines. Passing tiny walled gardens, we caught the yeast and cucumber smell of lunch—whiff of pancakes frying, pungency of onions—and noted bowls of fuchsia beets on windowsills, cooling in sugared vinegar. I steered Yael and Chaim into a restaurant and we ordered lunch.

Whatever else you find in the Baltics, you will never find better cucumbers, nor sweeter peppers, nor better tomatoes, fat and lozenged with seeds like pomegranates, than you find in Lithuania and Latvia. That first lunch taught me that my great-grandfather's homeland is a veritable Provence of milk and salad.

You will not find more varieties of pancakes, lacy-edged or bulging with chopped filling or conserves, tart with a touch of honey, than in such towns as Shavli.

In the New World, a Jewish dairy meal—the "dairy" supplied by Breakstone or Land-O-Lakes—is improvised of supermarket tomatoes, waxed cucumbers, or maybe a frozen blintz. Half the savor is nostalgia.

But in the land of Jacob Levy's birth, the humblest breakfast board offers sweet and sour creams more fresh and varied than the traveler has ever eaten. Spooning them out, you taste a complex dairy culture, varietal, where cheeses bear the flavor of individual meadows, loams, and salt licks; where butter, rinsed in lake water, chills in hand-carved birch thimbles shaped like flowerpots. What New Yorkers call "Jewish rye" is in the Baltics just bread; one slice is jagged with caraway, its new crust so tough it tugs the bones in the jaw, the next nearly cakelike, like a rye brioche.

Lunch came. Chaim piled good things onto his plate with relish and explained that in Shavli, Jews made do with smoked fish while the gentiles heaped their plates with sausages. But both Jews and gentiles enjoyed the beets and dill and the delicious breads. Or they used to, Chaim remarked darkly, until . . . well, we would see for ourselves.

So we did.

After lunch, sun suddenly gone, wind blowing in from the lake in sharp gusts, we picked up Leibe Lifshitz. He confirmed Chaim's point. White hair blowing back from his hollow temples, Leibe pointed to the shacks of the Traku and Vauclausko ghettos. "They got our nice things and we got their *shmatehs*."

"Their rags," Chaim translated, not knowing *shmatehs* has entered English. Those who stayed alive in these hovels—as Leibe himself had done—were those with the skills to keep Frankel Leatherworks running. Shoes for the Wehrmacht, belts for industry, whips for horses.

And then, two or three miles out of town, Chaim and Leibe unloading us from the car and looking tired, we stood at a rutted site: just tractor prints and a farmhouse in a copse of birches where— Leibe shrugged—the Jews were made to leave their clothes.

It was August, Leibe said, and the women had walked in the fading light with their children. After they left their clothes in the barn, they walked to the edge of the pit that the men, now dead, had dug, and then fell in the rain of bullets.

With its stand of birches, white, delicate against the darker trees, the place was oddly beautiful. The fenced-in grave: Was it awful? Peaceful? I didn't know. Should I make my voice stumble through a *kaddish*, as Leibe and Chaim seemed to expect? I tried, and forgot some of the words.

Was our family buried here? Yael asked me. Were the people in the picture killed here?

❧

What kind of journey was this for a child? I was having second thoughts.

Three nights before, climbing down from my hard-cushioned bunk on the train, I had perched on the edge of Yael's sleeper and watched the woods fly past, so dark, with ghostly birches at their edge. Every river bend, every copse of trees marked a pit. Yael was sleeping, the small plastic butterfly clip she and her friends wore dangling from a lock of hair, her lashes quiet on her cheeks.

As night had fallen and we'd approached Kaunas, the Jews' Kovno, she'd stared out the window at the grasses burning on either side of the road, smoke licking in black curls from little pyres as the farmers prepared their fields in the old way. Kovno, its name more famous, or infamous, than Shavli's, was eerie, our hotel high-beamed, dark, empty of other guests. We'd taken a cab to find some dinner but found the town even more depressing than the hotel—its high walls flush to the streets, the dark roofs, scarred balustrades, gaping courtyards.

I'd grabbed Yael's hand and we'd run, forcing a laugh as we made for an open *Bierstube*, its cheery sign and simple square of light pulling us in like an assurance that, for tonight anyway, Jewish history was in abeyance. Yet earlier, at the first mass grave of the day, I had not prevented Chaim, stopping the car near Raseinai, from rolling the window down to ask a man on a tractor where they'd shot the Jews. Jacob's brother Max and his family, from the picture with the cane, were lying there.

Gray-stubbled, hunched in a windbreaker, the man pulled his gear and backed out of a dry rut. Shrugged. He wasn't sure. Over by the airstrip, he thought. And indeed, over near the airstrip we found a small new sign, post-Soviet, pointing in from the road to where a larger sign—in Hebrew and Lithuanian—declared that 1,100 souls, *zhidim*, had watered this spot with their blood.

Back at the Jewish Community Center, Leibe Lifshitz opened the ghetto register. Ah. Here. As his eyes followed his finger down the page, he nodded, yes, Salamonas Levy, Moshe's brother Shlomo, was still alive and listed as "metalworker" in 1942. This was in the Vauclausko ghetto.

And yes, here too in 1942 was Salamonas Levy's wife, Fanja, their daughters Tauba, 20, and Sarah, 17, and son Isaakos, just 11. Also alive in the Traku ghetto were Dora Levy, 16, Alisa, 8, Sora, 6, and Rocha, 2, presumably the children of some other Levys, already killed. They would have remained there in the ghetto until—and Leibe now took out a piece of paper—the *Kinderaktion*. After the *Kinderaktion* (he looked up at me, and at Yael), *November 5, 1943*, he wrote slowly, then all the younger children were gone too. And then next to the name Isaakos, he drew a symbol and then wrote:

Auschwitz. I remembered then that Moshe had told me all about this, had told me that his brother Shlomo never forgave himself for going to work that day. Like all the parents, he was gone when the trucks came for the children.

Well, Leibe said, looking stern, impatient, all the parents were gone that day and none of those who lived forgave themselves. But—and Leibe looked at me directly now, not with sympathy but with something like respect—he, your relative, must have had some skill, some special training, to have stayed alive through 1944. And—hadn't he said?—kept well enough to have made it to Stutthoff and then to Dachau. A lucky one, Leibe said with a bitter smile, he himself being another lucky one. But then he grew more animated, straightening with a pride that took us in, that he would share with us, for we qualified.

Who else but the Jews in the region knew the science, the engineering? Leibe asked. The local workers, Lithuanians, couldn't run Frankel's machines. The German soldiers, having seized the largest leather factory in the old Russian empire after being ordered to keep the Wehrmacht in boots, were helpless. Who knew how and where to get the special extracts that made the leather from Frankel Leatherworks so famous? As it had always been in these parts, it was the Jews who kept the Jewish factory, seized by the Nazis, in business. The Jews like your relative—Leibe gave me that—knew how to manage.

I remembered, at that moment, the way Moshe had said *m'zman*, *m'zman* and had emphasized, looking at Tanya for confirmation, that what had saved Salamonas, now Shlomo, was not luck at all, and not just that he was good with tools. It was, Moshe had implied with the same pride, that he had come from people who were modern, enlightened; who had done their part to improve, to *civilize* their town. I remembered Moshe's look of pride as he explained this to me. And I visualized Shavli's own prepossessing look. No muddy *shtetl* this but a place large enough for a chamber of commerce.

Shavli was, Leibe now stressed, no little burg, but the district center! By the time of the war it was a modern place. A place of culture, progress, enlightenment. I would have read, of course—and Leibe looked at me, testing—of Shavli's history. Did I not know of Shavli's role in the Jewish Enlightenment—the Haskalah?

⁓⁓

In his memoirs, the Russian Jewish poet Osip Mandelstam describes a woman, a stranger to his family, who, on the strength of having come from Shavli, demands that her parents find her a Petersburg husband.

Mandelstam marvels at the woman's confidence that this mere name, this shibboleth, Shavli, would give entrée to the metropolis. He reports, nevertheless, the self-same feeling of Baltic pride among his Riga-born grandparents. For such Jews of Russia's western edge, the fertile inland plains from Tartu down to Koenigsburg and even to the Black Sea, to Kiev, to Odessa, was all—though the czar might claim it—Enlightenment land. Which was to say: emancipated, or, in short, German.

In his classic study, *The Haskalah Movement in Russia,* Jacob Raisin singles out my great-grandfather's region in particular as fostering and promulgating the spirit of the German Haskalah. Go fifty miles in nearly any direction from Shavli and one finds the home or birthplace of a *maskil,* an enlightener, or a cluster of them, who had agitated for the full emancipation of Russian Jewry. At Zagare and Kedaniai, at Salantai and Raseinai, and in Shavli, the largest city of the region, throughout the nineteenth century Jews of idealistic and artistic temper struggled for emancipation in all its forms. Hebraists conjugated, novelists scribbled, poets lent their talents to societies for the freedom of the young, civic emancipationists lectured, and through it all, commerce grew and grew, and Jewish confidence with it. Farther north, crossing from Lithuania into Latvia, identification with all things up-to-date and Western was even more pronounced. "Few struggled so intensely for their intellectual and civil emancipation as those in the provinces of Courland and Livonia," writes Raisin. "A great many could be seen here dressed after the German fashion, speaking pure German, and having their whole household arranged after the German custom . . . the children visited the public schools, the academies and the universities."

This passion for emancipation, not just intellectual but also economic, was only enhanced as steam and railways shortened the distances between east and west. By the mid-nineteenth century, the roar of Germany's mighty industrial complex—its factories turning out new chemicals, new metals, new machines—sounded across the border and increased the traffic across the Baltic Sea. The railroads throwing their ties across East Prussia and into Russia brought ideas that had been developing in Germany for more than a century, ideas the Jews of the Baltics had been most eager to receive. Along with purely intellectual pursuits, there were practical advances—new techniques for growing crops, for mass-producing cloth and crockery, for emancipating workers from drudgery.

Not that the eastern Baltic rim hadn't fixed its gaze westward long ago. Before the age of transoceanic travel, during the twelfth to the fifteenth centuries, the Baltic had emerged as Europe's major trade basin. Commercial interests, too long hampered by highwaymen or, worse, the prohibitive tolls collected by every minor duke and feudal lord, established a league of free cities bound together for mutual protection and mutual interest. These German cities of the so-called Hanseatic League sent big-bottomed wooden cogs from Bremen, Lübeck, and Hamburg to run smartly along the yellow dunes of the Baltic coast. Nosing into the gulfs and lagoons, these coastal and riverine craft gave access to the granaries and timberlands of eastern Europe. At the south end of the Baltic, at the Gulf of Gdansk where the Vistula twists into Poland, and the Bug into Byelorussia, the Germans founded Danzig. At the north, they established Riga, where the river Dvina flows east from the sea toward Novgorod and eventually to Petersburg. Between the outposts of Danzig to the south and Riga to the north, at spaced intervals along the warm Courland lagoon the Germans built other cities: Koenigsburg, outpost of philosophy;

Nida, seaside haven for thinkers; Libau, splendid baronial capital; Memel, hub of trade and traffic. The river Neman from Memel dropped down first to Kovno and then as far as Grodno. It was a mighty artery.

Chronic incursions from all sides—now from Sweden, now from Russia, now from Germany—shifted jurisdiction over these rich meadows, from czar to grand duchy, Scandinavian queen to Baltic baron, through the ages. But the battles for control rarely halted economic activity. No conqueror wanted an interruption of the Baltic grain trade, nor of commerce in the maritime staples—hemp and flax, tar and wax—extracted from the meadows and especially from the oaks and the pines. The beamed cottages of many Cotswold villages, the half-timbered outer house walls of many towns in Alsace or Normandy, or the oldest buildings in the City of London, are Baltic timber. As architectural fashions of the late Middle Ages depleted the oak forests of western Europe, that region began to procure slow growth oaks from the relatively unharvested eastern timberlands. In high demand also were tall firs, useful for ships' masts and beams.

By the Renaissance, centuries of commerce between and among disparate peoples had diluted the tribal and linguistic homogeneity of these once fierce pagan lands. Large, fortress-like castles began to rise over the bends in the rivers, as second sons from Saxony came to colonize the vast open spaces of the east and Polish dukes established estates in the rich Lithuanian meadowlands. Some came only seasonally to hunt, remaining in the West but deriving fortunes from the Ostland. To protect their interests they sent emissaries who brokered and bargained, hauled and shipped and kept trade flowing from the hinterlands to the coast. Fanning out, these so-called Germans hired the reapers and the raftsmen, organized the work gangs from among local tribesmen. With tiny offices at river landings, with yards full of carts, contracts for horses, inns, taverns, these emissaries bargained wages down for landowners. In all the little towns, these "Germans" were the ones who moved the goods, dispatching logs and flax, butter and milk, cucumbers, fresh plucked down, and even live geese, over the sea to northern Germany and Scandinavia.

These non-German Germans with their foreign ways—Germany's and Poland's agents—were Jews.

❧❧

Two years went by before I could get to Shavli again, but this time my goal was to learn about the life of Shavli's Jews through the centuries. My informant was Vilius Puronas. A large, smiling man with a rough gray beard, Vilius was Shavli's chief designer and, locals told me, its most serious archivist. "Shall I tell you," he asked me, "how the first Jews were allowed to live in Shavli?"

Inside his cubicle in city hall, Vilius settled himself before a massive book, carefully homemade but huge and full of clippings. Looking over his beard, his pink face beamed as he opened the album to a picture of a figure that looked half superhero, half fool. Skull cap on his head, the figure held between his teeth a length of rope and, tied to the rope, a massive bell.

His name, Vilius explained, was Nurok the Diver.

As you know—and with this Vilius looked at me encouragingly—Christianity came late to Shavli, for the natives, the Samogatians, were loath to give up their gods of thunder and oak. They kept them, after all, longer than any other Christians in Europe.

But by the early seventeenth century, even the pagans of Show-Lay (this was how he pronounced it), fiercest of all, had been Christianized, had built themselves a church, and bought an impressive bell. Delivered to the edge of Lake Talksa, the bell sat neglected. How to get the bell across the lake? How to get it hung in time for Easter? As I had seen for myself, the terrain outside Shavli is hilly. In summer, the land undulates in grassy knobs hard enough to maneuver with a loaded cart. And in winter, the cart's wheels would sink and then freeze in the mud. Who would risk his ox or horse on such a dangerous task?

Nurok, the Diver. From the collection of Vilius Puronas, Siauliai, Lithuania.

Thus, Vilius relates, the village elders hatch a plan. When the river freezes, they will grab their chance. Centering the bell on a sleigh, they begin to drag it over the frozen crust. Others wait on the farther edge with ropes, ready to pull the heavy bell from the ice onto shore. The ice seems to hold, but then, in the very middle, it cracks, taking down sled, horse, cart, and bell into the freezing water.

Shavli's new Christians fall into despair.

Imagine then, their joy and surprise when they behold Wolf, the Jew, diving under the icy water, bell rope in his teeth, and swimming to shore. Wolf is a slight man, and the bell is many thousands of pounds, but this Jew nonetheless delivers the bell intact to Shavli.

"What can we do for you?" ask the grateful, joyful Christians.

"Nothing at all," legend has Wolf replying modestly.

"No," protest the townspeople. "We insist. What can we do for you? There must be something." At this Vilius shows me sketches of Wolf, a local folk hero, albeit a Jew.

Wolf ponders. Jews in increasing numbers have been moving to the city environs, residing in villages thereabouts. But they are not yet allowed residence in the city.

Wolf proposes, "Let the Jews who live outside the city be allowed to live inside."

So, as the legend goes, it was Wolf's service to the Christians that gave the Jews the right of residence in Shavli. For his valor, Wolf is given a new name, Nurok, which means diver. He and his kin prosper in Shavli. Eventually, when the Nurok family opens its shoe factory, its bank, and its companies for railroad development, the logo of Nurok enterprises features a picture of a diver, bell rope in his teeth.

Now Vilius will not deceive me. Show-lay, like all towns, had its share of those who did not like Jews. Many were the tales of Jewish greed and of the Jewess with her cackling laugh and wiles. Here she was—and Vilius produced another sketch—guarding the market, a warning to children straying from school to purchase sweetmeats on the sly. And here was her consort—the Jew who let his kinsman hang while he vaunted his patriotism. But for centuries relations were generally warm and cooperative.

"Another story?" Vilius asks with a confiding smile that makes me think of Moshe. "Another hero's story? This one of a Jew important not only to his co-religionists or even Show-lay, but to all Russia—and beyond!"

The year—Vilius tells me, setting the scene—is 1812, a hundred or so years after Nurok's feat. Jews comprise a quarter of Show-Lay's population.

The Jewish
Crone in the
marketplace. From
the collection of
Vilius Puronas,
Siauliai, Lithuania.

Napoleon, returning to the west through Russia, has stopped to
rest his troops in Shavli. Bored, the French soldiers quartered in the
town beseech their general for some entertainment, and so he turns to
Shavli's mayor, giving him to understand that his restive troops will
find their diversion, come what may.

The mayor wracks his brain. He calls his council. What will they
propose to amuse the troops?

A Jewish wedding! suggests a member of the council. Perfect!
What luck, marvel the Christians, that the Jews are to marry one of
their richest on the very next Sabbath, the festivities expected to last
a week.

To make a long story short, Vilius continues, Napoleon's men
enjoy the wedding immensely. They eat, drink, and cavort, and all
on the tab of the Jewish community. Nearby towns are stripped of all
their provisions, but the troops do not loot Show-Lay. Moreover, the
Jews, who have once again saved the town, accept in payment for a
whole regiment of guests nothing more than a token: one gold louis

d'or, stamped with the head of the king. And yet—Vilnius brightens visibly—the Jews will be rewarded!

In 1877 Chaim Frankel, a Jew laying the foundation for a small tannery, finds a huge chest of gold louis d'or, now worth many times their weight. With these gold coins, Frankel constructs not a simple tannery but a magnificent factory, the largest in the Russian empire, the products of which—at least through 1941—win gold medals at the Paris Exposition. And now look—Vilius says—at what Frankel built! With a flourish, he shows me etchings of this magnificent *fabrika*, and advertisements, their lettering in Lithuanian and German.

Of course, Vilius reminds me, tanneries had long been Jewish businesses. Jews of the region had made a specialty of silk-purse-out-of-sow's-ear trades. Furs, boar's bristles and goose feathers, gloves of ox hide and pigskin and kidskin, lambs' wool and lanolin—Jews were proficient at all the trades that took products sticky with mud or hair and blood and readied them to appear in drawing rooms. City people in far-away Bremen or Baltimore, London or New York, never thought, as they lifted boxes made of "Russia leather," of the tanneries along the riverways, or the stink of the tanning pits before the Jews made the leather smell like wealth and ease.

Yet as Vilius insisted, turning over a heavy page, this Chaim Frankel really was something different, something special. And now he points out to me again a handsome lithograph: a picture of the solid factory front, "Frankel's" in letters shaded to project dimensionally. Of all the men of industry, of all the region's innovators, none—Vilius swore—achieved what Frankel did. Not only had Frankel brought the techniques of modern industry to the town, but he also nurtured the tradition of Jewish-Christian cooperation that Nurok the diver pioneered.

The managers of Frankel Leatherworks had kept both Jews and Christians on their payroll. Clever Jews were sent to Prussia to learn the latest chemical processes and machine technology. Meantime, Frankel hired a greater number of Christians to work in his tanning factory. Jews were diverted into research and development, accounting and management, but the traditional functions of tanning were left to the Christians, who scraped, boiled, and stretched hides.

There were interruptions, to be sure, such as in 1915 when the Jews, Frankel included, were sent east on suspicion of collaborating with invading Germans. But Frankel came back, stronger than before. Later Hitler changed everything, but even then Shavli's surviving Jews owed their lives to the Frankel Leatherworks.

"Would we be wrong in believing," Vilius asked, smiling tentatively, "that had not Hitler come, and Stalin before him, such amity as existed between Christians and Jews would have perhaps lasted forever?"

❧

Standing in Shavli on a summer day after leaving Vilius, I, who had seen Moshe's fond, faraway expression, might be pardoned for believing so, for believing in the creed of progress so long nurtured by the Jews of Shavli.

The Christians raised the livestock and the crops. But the Jews made sure the butter arrived in the city fresh, the cucumbers unbruised, the flour free of weevils, meat fit for the table. The Jews refined beet sugar for the tea, and they procured the cattle and the church bells, proving adept at moving unwieldy goods, just as the legend of Nurok told.

The Jews brought in the comforts and amenities of urban life. From Riga and Memel and Libau, and from Germany beyond, they brought the elegant, narrow-toed shoes, the silver salt cellars and cut glass cruets, the wool of Swedish blankets boiled into thick felt to keep out the chills. They brought in all the "colonial goods": Maryland tobacco; cocoa, pepper, coffee, and tea from Brazil and India; nuts and seeds; wines and spirits from France and England; plus local distilled goods the Jews made and sold.

The Jews built workshops to turn wood pulp to paper, linen to lace, beeswax to candles, cocoa to bonbons, and tobacco to cigars. In town, their shop windows glowed with coal fires and then gaslight, and long past dark the Jewish salesmen purveyed bicycles and walking sticks, napery, and furs cut to more exacting patterns than local furriers knew.

In the shops, they lifted the boxes of shoes down from the wall with ceremony. Some of the shoe leather was tanned in Frankel's factory and some of the shoes were made by the Bata firm, owned by the Nuroks. These two families employed dozens of managers, sub-agents, craftsmen, and machinists, and many of Russia's railroad administrators settled in Shavli, filling its elegant three-story buildings. But none was larger or more elegant than Frankel's palace, wood paneled throughout, with plaster ceiling ornaments and furnishings in the latest Deco styles.

Farms ringed Shavli, as they still do, and in the town center the Jews multiplied and prospered. They called their synagogue the "White Swan."

Their children danced in rings around the broad lip of the town fountain.

❧❧

Such was the general nature of the place, this Shavli, this Siauliai, whose name was carved under Jacob's name on his cane. A civilized place.

And such the world into which my great-grandfather was born in 1867, a world holding out hopes to Jews of comfortable or even handsome prospects. Born in the days of the liberal Czar Alexander II on Smallprison Street in Shavli, Lithuania, Jacob was indeed well placed to hear the whistle of modernity coming straight his way.

"A shrewd location." Vilius nodded admiringly, drawing his finger along a map of Shavli in 1877 to show me the house's excellent situation—on a hill above the Frankel works but close to the lake. So picturesque. "These were, I think, people who used their heads, your relatives."

Which was more or less what Vitalija Gircyte had said to me and Yael two years earlier when she plucked a document of 1873—Max Levy's petition to His Excellency the Czar—from the file lying before her on the wooden table. Chief archivist of the still extant records of the Jews of the administrative district of Kaunas Guberniya, Vitalija tapped the folder with one crimson fingernail and beamed at me a librarian's smile.

Yes, these relatives of mine had had their chances and made the most of them. They were Jews on the move! These files—and she flipped the manila folder open with that red nail—were clear on this; for instance, here is the petition of one Meyer (Max) Levy to the czar regarding a house at the end of Smallprison Street.

What one did not immediately see—and Vitalija had smiled—is just why a young man so well situated as Jacob Levy would leave at all. Perhaps, just as the basis for the file, one might venture a guess? Perhaps it was pressure to compete?

THREE

From the River Bug to Riga

*U*nbearable.

This one word, *unbearable*, curls up toward me, sad, miasmic, from the black square of microfiche in the YIVO archive. It is an entry in a forgotten reference book, *Jews of Britain*. Every few months I journey to the YIVO Institute for Jewish Research in New York City to look at this entry again. Sliding a thin plastic sheet into the square reader, I find a checkerboard of images that mark page 39, where I locate the section devoted to my great-great-uncle, Bernhard Baron.

If I wanted to, I could probably see this square of microfiche with its one telling word, *unbearable*, closer to my home. Doubtless the microfilm collection at Harvard University includes this 1941 book whose proud title, *Jews of Britain*, and whose author remain ignorant of what was then befalling Jews on the European continent. But I go again to YIVO, for only there can I breathe the oxygen of those documents in which my great-grandfather and Bernhard Baron's idea of civilization sleeps.

There, amid the largest collection of writings by and about the Jews of eastern and central Europe, are documents still vibrant with the optimism of Europe's Jews that enlightenment would eventually prevail over Russian darkness. There too I draw close to the wild despair, the cyclic defeat, the pessimism, of those equally as hungry for civilization but barred again and again from achieving it.

At YIVO I can read Jacob's older brother Max Levy's own copious notes, in careful triplicate, purple carbons attached. These secretarial minutes of the Jewish representative of the town of Raseinai from 1919 to 1929 still sleep at YIVO in pebbled black file boxes. Here too I can look at the yellowing photos of Shavli's lakeside promenade, both before and after it was repaved with gravestones from the Jewish cemetery. The ephemera from the file box labeled "Riga" give glimpses into civilization at its proudest. Running my fingers down the typed pages, I note the elegance of the fonts, the play of the decorative in the proud nouveau printer's ornament, the unmistakable style and pride of that urbane city to which it seems every Jew seeking enlightenment made his way, including my great-grandfather's brother Paul, and including too Bernhard Baron's sister Sarah, whom Paul met there.

It is not surprising that a long-ago note in my Aunt Jean's hand, headed "From the desk of Jeannetta Jaffe," asserts that Bernard Baron was born in "Riga, Latvia." Riga was where anyone Jewish in the year 1850 would have preferred to have been born rather than where Bernhard actually was. Riga—a Hansa, or German city—was the place where a man could shed a crude, disenfranchised, cringing, or downtrodden mien in favor of a prouder one, a place where a boy from Belorussia by way of Rostov-on-Don might acquire the handsome German name Bernhard, the name itself signaling liberation from a place his father found "unbearable."

The microfiche clicks in, and seconds later the white print on black negative resolves: "As Bernhard Baron's father found life *unbearable* in his native town of Brest-Litovsk, he journeyed to Rostov-on-Don. But finding things no better there, the family journeyed to America."

History leaves little mystery of why a Jew raising a family in the town of Brest-Litovsk during the reign of Nicholas I would have found the place thoroughly miserable. Today the town is remembered, if at all, for the Treaty of Brest-Litovsk, which redivided Europe after World War I. The Poles were given back a much shrunken and nibbled Poland and, for the umpteenth time, Russia and Germany were reassigned their spoils.

But from the fourteenth through the seventeenth centuries, Brest-Litovsk was a proud Jewish capital, a jewel in the crown of the Polish-Lithuanian Commonwealth and a thriving center of commerce and culture. It was from Brest-Litovsk that pronouncements bearing on all Lithuanian Jews went out; its synagogue among the grandest in the commonwealth; its rabbis the most esteemed. Renaissance Brest was a seedbed for the intellectual culture that makes Lithuanian Jews so proud, even arrogant, about the superiority of the "Litvak." Brest's thriving intellectual culture was supported by real wealth. From Brest-Litovsk, Jews conducted trade with centers as far away as Venice. They conveyed furs and timber, leather and wax, filling a crucial role as stewards, managers, and transporters of resources from the east; the commerce made them mobile citizens of a multiethnic world and also brought them into contact with ideas. Like their brothers to the north, they moved goods; the river lanes to the Baltic and Black Seas connected them to the Vistula and Danzig, a port of the mighty Hansa, as well as to Turkey. Commercial trade became an avenue of culture—of books and luxuries, of ambition.

This Lithuanian golden age was interrupted suddenly, sickeningly, in 1648, when the Cossacks and Tartars, led by Joseph Chmielnicki, charged up along the Dnieper on horseback. Taking out their long-nursed resentment of Polish ducal control, the Cossacks vented their fury on the Jewish ducal managers, burning, raping, murdering. With their torn and baggy clothes, their belts hung with flasks of powerful spirits, fresh killed game, and sharp scimitars, they emblazoned themselves onto Jewish memory.

By the time the Cossacks arrived in Brest-Litovsk, the city's more prosperous Jews had fled to Danzig, where they would remain for the next fifty years. An epoch of optimism had ended, and those who returned would have much to endure. Catherine the Great expanded the Russian empire, and then the czars turned the border town of Brest into a modern front. After Napoleon's invasion, and with national feeling stirring in Poland, Nicholas I determined that Brest ("Litovsk" was shaved off to mark Lithuania's defeat) would become a Russian garrison. About 1830, Nicholas claimed the strips of land adjacent to the Bug River as the site of Russia's easternmost fortress. The whole town was to be torn down and moved three kilometers to make room for the fortified walls. Buildings of value to Nicholas and the holdings of select citizens were moved, but many monuments of the town's proud Polish and Lithuanian past, including houses of both rich and poor, were razed or carried off as building material.

With the fort completed in the 1840s and the anti-Semitic Czar Nicholas in charge, the Jews of Brest entered their darkest period until World War I. Jews kept body and soul together by trading second-hand goods on market day, which is to say goods "confiscated" from river rafts by underpaid customs officials and then sold to Jews for pittances. This pathetic trading occurred only once a week. Or the Jews moved timber. When the weather held it was a better livelihood than hawking black market booty from the rafts, but the weather seldom held. It was dangerous work, dislodging timber from the yellow mud. Workmen were trapped there, grown men and children too, as the riverbed shifted and logs burst out of the sucking mud as if shot from a cannon. Particularly able or clever Jews, swept up in an ironic push to "industrialize" the Jewish people, might pursue a craft of some sort. Brest had a factory for leather and another for the one product which, no matter how depressed, nearly every hamlet needed—tobacco. But conditions in those workplaces were grim.

All this was miserable enough—the familiar tale of *shtetl* life—but "unbearable"? The word suggests something more. True, conditions in nineteenth-century Brest were considered so terrible that the rabbi—in a town renowned for piety—permitted the eating of dried peas and beans on Passover. Also, the decades-long construction of a brick fortress five kilometers long would have turned this town into a sort of Egypt, for who would have made and hauled the bricks, dug the canals, risked (and lost) life and limb on the ramparts built to protect the cream of Nicholas's army? Who but the Jews? All of this could have made life unbearable for a Jewish family. But there was, I think, something else. It was finding the name "Beron" on the "Registration" rolls of the town of Brest-Litovsk that planted the question, for to be on the Registration rolls at all might augur the "unbearable."

Thus, while I gloried in locating Uncle Baron's actual family in Brest-Litovsk, I knew that the Registration rolls of the Russian empire were the equivalent of wanted posters. Jews were registered so that they could be hunted down for conscription. These rolls were instrumental to a policy of rounding up boys—5 to 18—to serve as "cantonists," or cadets in the Russian army. Nicholas's bellicosity required a constant flow of draftees. To be drafted in the Russian army as a cantonist was a life sentence. Only after finishing a term of eight to ten years as cadets would these boys begin serving twenty-five-year terms as regular soldiers.

No Jew was completely safe from the threat of conscription, not even those merchants technically exempt. My cousin Moshe recounted with no little delight the derring-do of his own grandfather, Avraham Shimshon, in evading the *khapers*—the catchers. "Our sire kept three steps ahead of these *khapers*," Moshe told me. I can still see the smile lines around Moshe's blue eyes deepening as he conjured for me the sight of Avraham Shimshon's stout-wheeled cart maneuvering through roadblocks and musket smoke. "As a boy in the 1840s, our sire, Avraham Shimshon," Moshe declared, "had been too fast for them, and as a man, too valuable." In his stout cart he traveled long distances, filling contracts for army supply. And he used some of the profits to offset the lesser morality of other Jews, bribing officials to overlook one or another scrawny neighbor.

Not so lucky, apparently, poor Beron of Brest. With the fort only three kilometers away, Brest-Litovsk's Jewish children were perhaps the most vulnerable in the empire. One day a little boy built mud castles in the yard. The next, he was slung over a horse, booty of the czar's kidnappers, bound for military reeducation. More *unbearable* still, Jews were part of the process.

Hard put to provide the czar the number of soldiers he demanded for his Crimean adventure and desperate to protect the many, the rabbinic council of Brest-Litovsk in 1851 appointed its own *khapers* to prey upon the few. Recruited from the ranks of the Jewish dregs, these *khapers* "caught their brethren of any age and any status and handed them to conscription centers."

Various sources date the Baron family's departure for their new home in Rostov-on-Don, at the Crimean front, to around 1853. They were not alone. Families betrayed by their own co-religionists sometimes hoped that by trailing the troops down bloodied roads they might find the small cadet who had been taken from them. Many families like the Barons left native towns behind to become an accessory to Europe's first modern war. The czar learned that no matter how many men and boys were poured into a battle, no matter how cheaply human lives were held, Russian glory was outmatched by modern armaments. The dead seen on the roads or piled by doorways, the soldiers on litters moaning their last, had wounds such as Russians—armed with the firelocks used against Napoleon—had never seen.

Was there among these boy soldiers a younger Beron, lost brother of so many lost brothers?

If so: *unbearable.*

❧❧

This narrative of Uncle Baron's early years is one I have cobbled together out of scenes from Tolstoy's Crimean works, biographies of Belorussians such as Chaim Weitzmann and Menachem Begin, placenames from the atlas I keep on my desk, its pages cracking open to the entries "Baltics and Belorus" and "Poland, Danzig, and Lithuania."

In the 1870s and 1880s Brest once again emerged as a busy capital of trade. My own journey to Brest, which included a long walk along the brick fortifications and the streets of the Jewish quarter, afforded me glimpses of that civilization (as hope, as memory, as legend, as realized fact) that led Bernhard Baron to become so outspoken a champion of "enlightenment."

And yet all my patient siftings, guesses, and outright confabulations do not, in the end, get me as close to Bernhard Baron as my great-grandfather Jacob Levy's elaborate cane gets me to his brothers and his world, his "civilization."

The cane conducts me to a world with great confidence in civilization. Fashioned in one country, purchased in another, its inscription written in the tongue of a third, the cane proclaims a Jewish way of life—liberal and enlightened, attuned to competencies and chances not available to provincial persons. The cane, accessory of a person out and about, hints at hotels and long travel routes, ambitious itineraries, and reliance on a servant sector. Its sleek, traveled look, the prints it bears of persons and places long since lost to family lore, point to a life elevated above subsistence, to a life lifting itself into modernity.

❧❧

Hanging three high, finial to ferrule, clamped in little springs up the vaulted walls, canes were displayed by the score. Before Yael and I ever met Vitalija, Kaunas Goberniya's colorful archivist, we spent an hour in the cane chamber of the Kaunas Ethnographic Museum. The museum's roomful of canes showed us the choices, the chances, that Jacob Levy, unlike his future kinsman Baron, had been raised to enjoy. The cane room in Kaunas tells the story of the progress of industrial civilization in the Baltics through walking sticks.

Standing in barrels, splayed open like wild bouquets, the early folk canes are more like cudgels. True, their grips may be carved to resemble small-eyed swine or hares, beaked birds, bears, or—with a bit more craft—carved to imitate a noose of hempen rope, or the pebbled

teardrop of ripe wheat, or beet and turnip tops, homely onions. But
the craft bestowed on these whimsical heads ends at the ferrule. The
stocks of these rustic canes, though stripped and scraped to form rough
dowels, show knotholes and the natural curvature of tree boughs.

One step up, then, arranged on shelves along the walls like wine
bottles, are the canes of the rising classes. With decorative crooks
and handles, these are not shillelaghs. Mahogany or ebony, not oak,
their grain invisible beneath a coat of stain, these canes boast metal
ferrules between head and stock. Among those lying on the shelves
are some boasting a bit of gimmickry, like a little door that opens to
reveal a tightly whorled map, or a set of pens, or a ring for keys.
There are canes with a stock carved like a pistol, or that have a working trigger that releases a flag. Such canes, by their style or ingenuity, declared their bearer a person of parts. Produced for a volume
trade, those canes were bought by town dwellers—merchants of the
second guild, professionals, midsize manufacturers, students with
well-heeled fathers.

And finally, last along the walls and displayed like trophies, are the
rarer specimens of a cane maker's art. The finest ones, German made,
disdain cheap gimmickry in favor of luxe materials—malacca, ebony,
or rosewood; silver, gold, ivory. By such exquisite artifacts as these
life was imbued with ceremony. Bestowed on dignitaries, travelers
from afar; ordered for birthdays, special days of triumph, anniver-
sary galas—these presentation canes honored both giver and receiver,
stamped the estimability of both.

And it was this quite subtle kind of message, I began to see, looking from the canes in barrels to these on shelves and then to those
along the walls, that was written on the cane Max Levy gave to his
youngest brother, Jacob Levy, on the occasion of Jacob's return visit
to the homeland in 1928. Observing all the conventions, the cane reminded its recipient just whom he had to thank. The names of the
four Levy brothers and their associated towns were arranged on the
cane in age order, but the giver's initials were in a different metal.

Place-names were given in their local spellings, but the cane's inscription, in German, supervened like a transposition of local manners into the most ideal terms. Nothing about the cane signaled anything but the utmost respect.

Vitalija the archivist confirms such surmises and more. An hour after we viewed the museum canes, Vitalija pushes the enlarged photograph of our cane back across the table to Yael.

Yes, Vitalija says, beaming, this was *just* the kind of thing that relative of yours, that Maksas Levy, would have gone to trouble to order. Not only to show his brother, visiting after so long, the proper welcome but also—and here she cast a knowing glance at us—to show the *kind of man* he was.

Not ordinary, not without status. Vitalija pronounced the word sta-*Toos*. The cane might well have been ordered in Siluva, a village near Rasainei, a provincial place. But it was made in Riga, by a proper German cane maker whose prestigious imprint "Loewensohn" went on every one of his handcrafted canes. A distinguished man, this Maksas!—Vitalija nods in approval—clever, and making the most of his chances. For instance!

And with this Vitalija flips open the file, not thin, in which she has gathered extant documents of the family of one Max Levy, Advocat, of Raseinai, born 1860, son of Avraham Shimson Levy, of Shavli, born 1839, died 1873.

Under Yael's curious eye, Vitalija now traces her fingers, line by line, across a solid block of Cyrillic script. Translating as she goes, she leans toward us to signal her excitement at sharing this precious paper with us. He was just a bit older than you are, Yael, Vitalija says, when he prepared a document on his mother's behalf in 1873.

What Vitalija had to show us was a petition written on behalf of one Sarah Levy by one Meyer Levy, age 14. Addressed to the Esteemed Officials in the fortunate service of His Most Excellent Czar, Alexander Nikolaevich, with a stamp affixed to indicate seventy kopeks duty paid. Written in a flowing Russian hand, Meyer Levy's

document inquires the following: Will the authorities kindly send his
mother a paper confirming that the family house on Malutremnaya
(Smallprison) Street indeed belongs free and clear to Sora Rivkah,
widow of the late Avraham Shimshon. And Vitalija shows us, attached to this same document but in a different hand, the reply that
came six months later from the officials of His Most Excellent Czar.

"Owing to its location just outside the town boundary, said house
and its wooden annex on Smallprison Street are entirely the property
of the wife and heirs of Avraham Shimson, no fees or city taxes due.
The Jews are free to live or work in it as they please." By settling outside Shavli's plat and thus off the city rolls, Vitalija explains, the family of Avraham Shimshon lives in a place not worth the czar's
attention.

"And look at this!" Vitalija exclaims as she pulls another typewritten sheet out of the file, pointing to an entry recording taxes paid
by one Marcus Levy (Jewish taxpayer 144 and presumably Avraham
Shimshon's father): his 1846 "candle tax," one of many devices that
Czar Alexander's father had deployed to force assimilation of his Jewish subjects. Though the dwellers on Smallprison Street managed not
to pay it, these nineteenth-century candle taxes supported the Jewish
schools young Max attended. It was this very program of compul-
sory Russification that Max's mother, Sora, had to thank for her son's
accomplished Russian letter to the czar. At the same time, what a very
wicked, what a very *Russian* device it was, Vitalija now explained.
For how did the czar fund the Jews' Russification? By taxing Sabbath
candles, the very candles the rabbi's wife sold out of her kitchen, making the *rebbitzin* not only the czar's tax collector but also his own dep-
utized agent of Russification.

Jews like your relatives—Vitalija explained—beat the czar at his
own game, extracting the benefits and avoiding (with houses off the
city plats) the penalties.

Now once again Vitalija flips the file open, extracting a document.
Two years later (*flip*, and a rustle of paper), Max is now sixteen years

ВСЕПРЕСВѢТЛѢЙШІЙ, ДЕРЖАВНѢЙШІЙ,

ВЕЛИКІЙ ГОСУДАРЬ ИМПЕРАТОРЪ

АЛЕКСАНДРЪ НИКОЛАЕВИЧЪ,

САМОДЕРЖЕЦЪ ВСЕРОССІЙСКІЙ, ГОСУДАРЬ ВСЕМИЛОСТИВѢЙШІЙ!

ЦѢНА 70 КОП. СЕРЕБРОМЪ

Max Levy's correspondence with the czar. From the collection of the Kaunas County Archives. Reprinted with permission.

old and (excitedly, Vitalija shows me a page, its script Gothic, its language clearly German) is living in Riga. This page is from the Riga business digest. Below one Adolph Levy, his business, *Getreidehandel*, she points out the name Max Levy, *Getreidehandel*—the grain trade. She slips the page back into the file, taps her nails on the manila cover. Her hand on the sheaf of pages is momentarily still. Then, not without a flourish, in one rapid motion she pulls out and fans open a sheaf of photocopied packets.

Neatly stapled here and here and here, Vitalija points out with satisfaction, are entries representing the activities—civic, philanthropic, professional—of the now grown, now prospering Maksas Levy, with privileges to practice law along the whole length of Kaunas Guberniya, in Kurland, and at the ports of Memel and Riga. Meyer, Maksas, later Max Levy, now settled in the agricultural town Raseinai, has come into his own.

Distinguished jurist, Maksas Levy; county representative, Maksas Levy; library committee; fire prevention delegate; liberal delegate to the Sejm. A man to cast a long shadow, to set a high standard, was this Max Levy.

❧

Back at home with my young children, Yael the eldest with two younger sisters, the passage of years began to show me what effect an older brother like Max Levy could have had on his younger siblings and eventually on his children. Vitalija's take on Max seemed obviously right and ever more shrewd.

A few years later, when I returned to Shavli and Raseinai without Yael, I met a man in Raseinai who actually remembered Max Levy. *Mister* Lawyer Levy, Victoris Andrekaitis called him, emphasizing the honorific *Mister*. He used his hands to draw down two imaginary tufts of beard and then settled an imaginary hat on his head. Victoris bade me imagine Independence Day sometime in the 1920s. Raseinai's one broad avenue lined with citizens, half Jewish, half gentile. Down the middle of the street who comes marching? *Mister* Lawyer Levy. And just after pronouncing that exaggerated Mister, Victoris Andrekaitis pantomimed something else. Balling one hand into a fist and lifting his knees, he thrust an imaginary cane under his arm and strode his driveway's length. Max Levy.

Even without an older brother who was something of a prodigy and something of a martinet, Jacob would have had, in Max, a high standard to meet. A picture began to form for me of my great-grand-father's early life as the youngest of four brothers. It could not have been easy for Jacob to make his mark.

Born to the first generation of Jews afforded real opportunities, Jacob had little excuse for not succeeding, if not brilliantly then at least by making the most of opportunities the new times offered. Enlightenment! Emancipation! Shavli, a stronghold of both, was home to cultured but also practical men, keen to kindle ambition and drive as much as cultivation. The Society for the Promotion of Enlightenment, with active chapters in Shavli and Raseinai, discouraged the purely intellectual in favor of credentialed competencies; the society's mission was to "assist the young in devoting themselves to the pursuit of science and knowledge." Formerly, a Jew of northern Lithuania would have been a scholar, an agricultural middleman, or a craftsman serving a local market. Now the scholar was to become a jurist; the grain trader, an agronomist; the locksmith or saddle maker, an engineer or manufacturer. Fathers pressed sons, and brothers pressed younger brothers, to go beyond occupations and to claim professions. Civilization would follow auto-emancipation.

Simply growing up on Smallprison Street gave Jacob a front row seat on the modernizing world, as well as plenty of stimulation. For instance, the north-south railroad connecting the Baltic port of Libau with the wheat fields of Ukraine was finished in 1872. (Jacob was then five.) Two years later, the north-south line connecting Riga further north to Koenigsburg in East Prussia was also completed. The rails of both lines crossed at Shavli. Then the Petersburg to Warsaw line was built, with stops in Vilnius and Kaunas, via Brest, and Shavli was its major central Lithuanian station.

Young Jacob could thus watch from his own backyard as a new industrial world was born, could glimpse all the apparatus and paraphernalia of modernity being unloaded from the trains. Out with the cauldrons and the rusty forges. Out with the workshops that went up in smoke when stray sparks licked wooden walls. In with steam-powered jennies, pulverizers, tension rods. On sunny days, the carters and draymen unloaded the new steam boilers and wheeled them on dollies into the brick-walled factories.

Delicate controls on the new machinery moderated temperatures and produced novel varieties of everything. When heated to a precise temperature, ordinary beet sugar could be turned into bright lozenges flavored with lemon, sassafras, and peppermint; into fondant colored creamy pink and violet. At lower heat, the chocolates that Shavli was mad for were produced in the factory owned by a Jew, Kagan.

Local flax and creased linen still had a place in any bride's trousseau. But now cotton from England and America came in via Germany, and the bride might smooth out marriage bed sheets of a finer, silkier feel. The workshops were full of spinning bobbins, the thread drawn out thinner and thinner until, satiny and shining like glass, it gleamed on a spool. The new mercerizing process made the fiber stronger and improved its ability to take the aniline dye. Other processes could turn hanks of oily wool or wiry horsehair to gleaming, supple dry goods, fit to smooth onto a divan or turn into gentlemen's trousers. The old weavers, tanners, and blacksmiths did not have the skills or materials to fashion such modern goods. The new products needed experts who understood how a roller kept even tension, how a mangle turned stiff things supple, how dyeing was more than pigment. Chemists, engineers, inventors, machinists—persons with knowledge of cold versus hot water baths, caustic agents, air pressure, revolutions per minute—commanded high wages and respect. Each new product or process created new realms of possibility and a demand for skilled persons to make them work. In short, the more innovation, the more opportunity, the more of what everyone now called "progress."

Of course, the opposite was also true. With the older products, the more established their traditions and methods, the more resistant their craftsman might be to mechanization. In Shavli it was just the same as across the industrializing world, for even as machines saved labor they inspired terror in the laborer. And one product in particular seemed to exemplify all the injustices workers had to struggle against to earn their bread.

Was there ever a product in the history of the world so hungry to burn human labor for the sake of human pleasure? Rapidly consumed, yet desire for it nigh unquenchable, this was a product for which demand, ever rising, only pressed down prices, ever falling. The more refined and sophisticated its mystique, the more wretched were those who produced it. The many exacting steps that went into its cultivation spread slavery across the Western Hemisphere. The abuse of its workers would be a spur to progressivism worldwide. But in Shavli (as in Brest and Rostov, as in Raleigh and Shanghai, as in New York and Aachen) its mid-nineteenth-century victim was still hunched over a workbench, rolling rolling rolling, his daily quota ever rising as the pay for every unit rolled fell. The product was, as the young Bernhard Baron, now in Rostov-on-Don, knew from the pain in his hands and wrists, along his bent spine, and in his throat—tobacco.

❦

I wonder if any of Jacob's brothers would have been around in 1880, when tradition dictated that Jacob Levy, on turning thirteen, would be called to the Torah as a bar mitzvah. Had Jacob's aging mother, Avraham Shimshon's widow Sora, managed to get her youngest, her most rebellious son, the dark, slight, intense, and restlessly intelligent Jacob, to stand before the gray heads in synagogue? Would this Gymnasium student—already, I'd guess, prone to passionate declarations, to standing on principle—be willing to go through the ritual?

If the tales told of my great-grandfather's extraordinary library—a collection including not only Engels and Lasalle but the King James Bible and *Don Quixote*—tell me anything, they say that this recipient of an enlightened education may well have objected. On the other hand, I know that Jacob's education had not omitted ancient Hebrew, along with Russian, German, Lithuanian, Latvian, Yiddish, and, later, accented but flawlessly grammatical English. Many years after his death, his daughters, Jean, Myrtle, and Fanny, recalled that in Baltimore and then in Philadelphia, he led a Passover Seder, reading the Hebrew from the Haggadah at top speed and then discoursing on the book's political aspects—the Jewish people's flight from oppression. Thus I think that he would, despite the Enlightenment curriculum he and his brothers followed, have gone through his day in synagogue, perhaps not fretting that his brothers were not around to hear him read or join him for an *aliyah* on the *bimah*.

Max would have been unlikely to attend. In 1880 he was completing his law degree at Tartu, or as the Germans called it, Dorpat, in Estonia, where many Jews attended the university. Tourist brochures of the period commend Tartu's "remoteness from noise" and its "picturesque situation," but I doubt Max would have much noticed this. With its Lutheran charter and a governing board of Baltic German barons, it was the university's reputation for turning out modern doctors, lawyers, and scientists that drew its high percentage of Jewish students. They soldiered on at Tartu, despite the mean, small homes that boarded them, the beet and fish diets, and isolation. A Russian university whose language of instruction was German—one of the czar's many accommodations to the tax-paying, port-managing Baltic Germans—Tartu was a magnet for multilingual Jews. Willing to study Russian law in German, or German law in Russian, they endured privations as long as accreditation followed.

Probably also absent when Jacob was called to the Torah as a bar mitzvah was his brother Isaac, who at sixteen had been sent to Freiburg in Germany, sent by the richest, greatest, and eventually most famous industrialist in Shavli—Chaim Frankel.

Sharing Jacob's interests if not his temperament and a few years older, Isaac was a gentle, kindly boy, one gifted with a wrench and curious about machines. The boys had grown up together near Lake Talksah, within earshot of rail yards and close by the rising brick pile of Frankel's magnificent leatherworks. The southeastern edge of town would have been full of interest to growing boys. Near the train yards they could put a coin on the rails and see it flattened to a satiny disk when the train roared by. They could play at the edge of the lake, building dams of wood and brick discarded as the Frankel factory was constructed near the shore. And in the late afternoons, as darkness crept out from the trees, the spooky sound of a train whistle allowed a boy to recall battles of long ago: the Teutonic knights fallen in these same marshes, "cut down like women." They would have read the phrase out of the *Livonian Chronicles* in school. Then by morning all was hammer and clamor again.

What interested both boys most was the scale and ambition of the leatherworks. Whether funded by Napoleon's retreating soldiers' louis d'ors or German investors, this was no ordinary backyard tannery with a slaughterhouse and manufacturer cheek by jowl—men in bloody aprons skinning pigs and calves hanging from hooks—but a real manufacturing plant. After first bringing in experts from Germany, Frankel soon realized the advantages of training his own, of sending local boys abroad to learn how to stabilize dyestuffs, to moderate steam, to learn factory layout, fire protection, first aid. Some he sent close by, to Kaunas or Riga Polytechnic. But the most promising were dispatched west. When he chose Isaac from among Shavli's boys, it would have shown all the family that, despite Avraham Shimshon's death, the boys would make their way.

I think that the only brother living close enough in 1880 to see Jacob stand up and read the Torah would have been the second eldest, the sweet, idealistic, dreamy, awkward, waggish brother who, born Pin-chas or Perel, at a certain point became known as Paul. By 1880 Paul was in Riga, the metropolis, which was now within a day's train travel from Shavli.

It would have taken a lot to get Paul to go there. Shortly after Max took himself to Riga to study *Getreidehandel*, grain trading, he would have begun urging Paul to follow him to the city. To get out of Shavli. To not let grass grow under his feet!

Problem was, though, Paul loved grass. He was a country boy through and through, who grew more sentimentally rustic as he aged. Many years later, from Glyndon, Maryland, where he owned the town's largest individually held plat and was its only Jew, Paul wrote to my aunts, "When the boys are finished school, send them out to me. Mother Earth will do them good." Those who showed up at his farm he'd take to the coop to feed the chickens, to the barn to squeeze the teats of cows. He named the cows so lovingly, Rosh Hashanah and Yom Kippur, and my aunts remembered how they'd sometimes find him murmuring to these friends, his skinny neck near their flanks.

Yes, young Paul would have been loath to leave the plains of Shavli for Riga, to bid farewell to the milk cows, pastures, and breezes with their scents of hay and cucumber. Eventually, though, he must have gone, for the name Riga on Jacob's cane says so. He'd have been per-suaded that a lover of Mother Earth had best learn to care for her properly—to gain intimate knowledge of feed and fodder, the proper potash levels, electrification. Plant hybridization, livestock breeding, machine maintenance—these were the essentials of the practical cur-riculum embraced by modern Jews of the soil. In the 1870s this newer agriculture was called agronomy. Paul's teachers at the Riga Poly-technic, all recruits from Germany, had social ideas to impart as well. Collectivization was sweeping across Europe. What agronomy stu-dent did not do his stint on a model farm?

An old photograph—gray, grainy, fished out of a suitcase of Paul's personal effects—suggests that the experience changed him for good.

The photograph shows three rows of boys and girls in a forest clearing. The boys wear overalls or peasant blouses, with knotted kerchiefs on their foreheads. The girls, a half dozen out of a group of thirty, wear their headscarves tied up more fetchingly, the knots pulled over their ears like flowers, and on their legs what must be bloomers. An outing of the Jewish Agricultural League? A summer week in the Rumbula forest spent cutting wood?

When I hold the magnifying glass up to the grayish photo I see the young Paul Levy in a back row. Between two older teenage boys, he is the skinny one; the flanges of the family ears protrude from under his cap. Now I scan the rows of girls once, and then again, but do not see her. Though I strain to find the dark browed girl with a statuesque figure and full, kissable lips, she is not there.

I want to find this girl because she, Sarah Baron, had a romance with skinny Paul in the city where he came of age, making her the only romantic heroine in my family history. Sarah was, I'm guessing, the tie that first bound the Levys to the Barons, the reason why it is the name of a city, not a county or rural outpost, associated on the cane with dreamy Paul. Putting the inscription on the cane, Max would have known that it was really the girl, and not where he met her, that mattered to Paul. Nevertheless, Max put a Baltic city's name on the cane. The city was Riga.

In 1799 Peter the Great, having routed the Swedes, pronounced Russia's reign in Riga to be as perfect and permanent as the goblet he then dropped from the tower going up in his name. Yet the Riga to which Paul arrived sometime late in the 1870s was a thoroughly German city.

Established as a beachhead by Teutonic Knights and the bishop of Bremen, Riga was the Hansa's eastern jewel, its key role in Baltic trade making it the Russian city with the best claim to being, in the German sense, "free." In the 1870s the ambitious Alexander II was not disposed to leave Russia's most important gateway in the hands of backward Russians. In exchange for the brisk trade Baltic Germans could maintain with Bremen, Hamburg, Danzig, and Lübeck, he let the city's culture, language, and architecture remain German.

All the side streets in Riga today are built in a naive style recalling the Latvian folk past, but the clustered domiciles also bear resemblance to villages along the western Baltic coast in Germany and Sweden. In summer, these cities of the Baltic rim turn their faces to the yellow northern sun that warms the bricks of the city squares and ripens the shadows on the stucco. Winter scours this northern sun to a dull throb; the walls of the cities roughen with gray frost. But in Riga, as in Lübeck and Sassnitz, tucked under the steely cobbles are cozy *Bierstuben*.

In the major squares and along the avenues, handsome high-fronted residences in the style of Bremen and Lübeck rise above the cobbles, not far from the docklands that used to swarm with agents and factors, inspectors and moneychangers, for Riga's wealth came from the polyglot, raucous flow of trade between nations. By the nineteenth century Jews had finally, fully arrived in Riga.

Until Peter the Great's triumph in the eighteenth century, Jews in Riga had suffered the same restrictions on residence and mobility as their cousins in the Latvian countryside and farther south in Lithuania, and would see these rules tighten under Catherine the Great. In the years before Peter, Jewish raftsmen, conveying logs or grain from the interior, sailed the Dvina to Riga. But they were forbidden to sleep overnight inside the city limits and lodged three to a room at a *Juden Herberge*: a Jews' shelter. Many a Jewish raftsman preferred to make his bed on the Dvina, falling asleep with the breeze in his face, than in an odorous dormitory with a stigma of his unwelcomeness blazoned on the door.

As time went by, however, the Baltic barons and their Russian trading partners began, little by little, to accommodate their Jews. At the port of Libau, southern Jews became so indispensable that "temporary" arrangements with more permanence were devised to accommodate the Jewish brokers, conveyancers, shippers, translators, and warehousers who maintained the grain, timber, leather, and other trades. Technically excluded from residence in Libau proper, Jews nevertheless made up Libau's tax base.

Thus the duke of Kurland arrived at a clever method to palliate the sting of their presence; he issued expulsion orders attached to a hefty schedule of fines: "Jews continue to be present in the country contrary to the Law. Steps shall therefore be taken to assure that all Jews leave within six weeks from this day, and if any Jew shall be found within the borders of the Duchy after that date, he shall be imprisoned and be released only upon payment of one thaler for each day."

One thaler was not, for a Jewish businessman, an impossible sum to pay. But one thaler per day for every Jew in the city was a tidy sum for a duke to collect. Thus Kurland's expulsion order, perennially unenforced, allowed the region to absorb useful Jews in number and, as with the czar's candle taxes, tax them for their own exploitation.

In Riga, when the proprietors of the *Juden Herbergen* sought more regular arrangements for the temporary billeting of Jews, they asked the city to compel Jewish boatmen, technically forbidden to stay in the city, to do just that. In time, Riga's prosperity so depended on Jews that the restrictions cramping Jews throughout the Pale, the vast area of restricted residence, were lifted for the Jews of Riga.

A Jewish resident of Riga by the 1850s could believe himself living in a German city. Osip Mandelstam described the world of his grandparents living in old Riga as ineluctably German. Isaiah Berlin's father, a native of Riga, embraced German culture as his own. Morris Hillquit, Riga-born chairman of the Socialist Party of America, recounts that "the language of [Riga's] courts and administrative offices, its theatres and schools, the language of its business and social intercourse," was German. Coming of age in the 1870s in Riga, Hillquit considered himself "bilingual and cosmopolitan, without any marked national traits."

No wonder, then, that from all the provincial districts of Latvia and Lithuania, from as far away as Vilnius and beyond, young Jews

flocked to Riga to escape the Pale of Settlement and to become something higher than Jewish, Russian, or even German—*civilized*. The
ribbon of road crossing the Lithuanian border to Riga was the road
for people with places to go. Jews of means beat dirt tracks to
macadam, bought slips in Riga harbor, hired Riga agents, and set up
pieds-à-terre near Riga's baroque hotel.

By the 1920s, when Jacob Levy returned to Riga from America
and had his photo taken there, Jews lived in handsome residential
blocks, designed by Jewish architecture students returned from Germany. In the late nineteenth century the city had begun to explode
with architectural invention.

The buildings lining Riga's new Jewish neighborhoods had soaring facades with stem-like window apertures. Tendrils of iron curled
around bay windows lined with silk organza, and from the balconies,
in rows, young girls looked down, just as they looked down from their
perches in Munich, Berlin, and Vienna. The German-educated children of timber wholesalers and glove manufacturers built curving
staircases, gilded facades, doors and gates for the new German-style
synagogues, hotels, and theaters in the style of art moderne and art
nouveau.

From the provinces, from as far away as Byelorussia and Poland
and from the nearer cities of Lithuania, modern children might be
sent to live together while they attended the Polytechnic or began ca-
reers in law or medicine or engineering. In dockside offices some children apprenticed themselves to uncles, who, by steady application,
had made themselves known as reliable in all the relevant ports. There
was a romantic logic to it as well. While billeting the likely boy in an
upstairs room for the course of three years at the Polytechnic, one
would not be shocked if the young man, in the course of learning a
profession, also fell in love.

Riga was then, as it still is, a young person's city, where girls from
the provinces gathered the hair off their necks, frizzing it at the temples, and put on high lace collars. Strolling the square on the golden
cobbles before the Cathedral of Peter and Paul, the girls swung para-

Modern-day Riga. Photograph by Fred Levine.

sols as young men quickened their pace to join them. Free from mocking younger brothers and clucking, fussy mothers, the young men let hair grow on their upper lips, bought walking sticks, began to smoke.

Nothing like this had ever happened to Jewish boys and girls penned inside the Pale of Settlement. But this happened frequently in that grand and established city on Russia's western coast, the Free Hanseatic City of Riga.

Which is why an image of Jacob's first meeting with a Baron—Bernhard Baron's sister, Sarah Baron—eventually formed in my mind along with a scene that goes something like this. The image and the scene provide a tender rationale for why the initials on the cane—PSL—have a little plaque under them reading "Riga." Although he was born in Siauliai, Lithuania, as his brothers were, it was in Riga that Paul came of age in all important ways. In Riga he changed from a moony country boy into an agronomist and in Riga he grew to love Sarah.

I like to envision the day when Jacob, visiting the city for the first time, bounds out after Paul from Uncle Adolph's flat near the docks. Who is more boyish looking—the younger brother, Jacob, with his intent and searching eye, only thirteen—or the older Paul, loping, almost running, along the golden cobbles for a glimpse of his beloved Sarah?

With his bar mitzvah behind him, Jacob has been permitted to board the train with his brother Paul and stay with him in the city. The train had sped across the green plains, its engine huffing rhythmically as they clicked across the border. From the second class compartment, now raucous with laughter, Paul and Jacob had burst out onto a street in Riga. What new sights the city offered! The depot itself was majestic, the skyline lit. In the morning, the city was somewhat less impressive yet more conducive to a lift in the heart, with its colored facades drinking in the sunlight and an impossibly blue sky bracing the spire of Peter and Paul.

"There she is," calls Paul over his shoulder to his brother. He hides nothing of his joy at seeing the girl, whose beauty I study many years later in a tintype I find at the Jewish Museum of Maryland. Sarah's high lace collar and tight sleeves tell me that she and Paul must have met and fallen in love sometime between the late 1870s and early 1880s. Sarah's sleeves and the frizzle of hair at her temples date the first blooming of love with Paul to just before he set sail for America, and thus the first rendezvous of Levys and Barons took place in this prepossessing city.

◆

Did Sarah know then that even when her bosomy softness turned to solid fat, even when her richly colored skin sallowed, Paul would love her as he did the morning he ran after her in Riga? Perhaps she did, for on that day I believe she had already delayed departing for America for more than a year, putting off the brother now urging her to join him in Baltimore. This brother Bernhard's epoch of penniless struggle in the New World was now definitely past. "Baron and Company," he had written to her, was now a strong and expanding establishment, with a training school for boys, a wide and popular inventory of cigars, cheroots, and hand-rolled cigarettes, and prospects of future mechanization. Baltimore, unlike New York, was a city she need not feel lost in, for its German streets and German names would remind her of Riga. Still, I think it was not until her brother Bernhard wrote to say why not bring along her beau—he would pay the passage for them both and help the young man make something of himself—that Sarah agreed to leave Riga for Baltimore.

I know with some certainty that Uncle Baron was not "from" Riga anymore than my Uncle Paul was, but came originally from the muddy slough of Brest-Litovsk and later from Rostov-on-Don. I do not even think it was Riga where he deposited his sisters, Deborah and Sarah, before he left for America, but rather, Jewish Zagare, Lithuania. It was a poorer place, and Deborah, along with her sister and her Zagare-born husband, might have moved to the city with others. Zagare's connection to Shavli, as well as to Riga, would draw me and eventually bring me to stand in the woods where Shavli's Jews lay with Zagare's. But this was later, and another story.

On the question of why and how Paul and then Jacob came to Baltimore, I believe that sometime in the late 1870s or early 1880s, Sarah met my great-grandfather Jacob's brother Paul in Riga and fell in love. By then her brother Bernhard had passed through his difficult early years in America and had begun to build something—a vision as well as a machine—in Baltimore, and he brought Sarah and Paul to join him there. Then he brought Jacob. And then, a few years later, he brought his other sister Deborah, whose eldest daughter, Amelia, eventually became Jacob's wife and the mother of my three great-aunts, my great-uncles Eddie, Bob, Paul, and Theo, and my grandfather Emil.

For as long as she lived, however, nothing stopped my Aunt Fanny from insisting her father was from both Austria and Riga, handling the discrepancy thus: "My father came," she insisted, "from Riga—in Austria."

So distracted was I by the fact that my aunt sounded the *i* in Riga like the *i* in "fig" that, except for thinking that it sounded somehow wrong, I didn't pay much attention to the way she'd moved Riga out of the Russian sphere of influence into the German, with as little regard for geography as if Bangor could, on someone's say-so, turn up suddenly on Lake Michigan, as Chicago. When I knew better, I just assumed, not without some smugness, that sweet dear Aunt Fanny was rather muddleheaded. Latvia? Austria? Six of one, half a dozen of the other. But geographic boundaries, after all, existed.

These things kept countries mired where they were planted.

Except, as I was to learn, as the cane later taught me to understand, when they didn't.

FOUR

The Free Hanseatic City
of Balt-ee-mewer

W hy *had* my great-grandfather used the occasion of his naturalization in Baltimore in 1893 to claim Austria, rather than
Shavli, Lithuania, as his place of origin? And what *was* the reason for
my aunts' insistence on places of family origin vaguely, if not actually,
German?

Weren't Riga and even Siauliai sufficiently proud and prosperous
not to have tempted my great-grandfather to lie about them? When
I visited there they seemed presentable enough, and Jacob had gone
to no trouble to cover evidence. The passport tracing his return from
Europe in 1928 was stamped England, Germany, Latvia, and Lithuania, without even a stop in Austria. And of course the metalwork
plates on the stock of Jacob's cane specified, in addition to Riga in
Latvia, only Lithuanian towns, Raseinai and Siauliai, which no one
looking at a map would ever find in Austria.

Was it shame, then, at not hailing from western Europe but from the
Pale of Settlement, that cordon sanitaire established by Nicholas I of

Russia to solve the Jewish "problem"? After returning from meeting my cousin Moshe, this is what I thought had to be the case: My great-grandfather made the not atypical Jewish decision to claim a German pedigree rather than the more common eastern European one. But this guess was wrong.

For when I found and then used Jacob's cane to guide me around the streets of his adopted American city, Baltimore, I came to see that while Jacob's claim to have come from Austria may have been a fabrication, it was an imaginative and a telling, rather than a trivial or shamefaced, fabrication. Moreover, little in his subsequent experience in Baltimore would contradict that fiction because his Baltimore almost fancied itself as Vienna, an outpost of Germanness, though one less parochial and more enlightened than Germany itself.

The gesture of using a line on his naturalization papers to declare himself quit of the emperor of Austria told a truth about Jacob perhaps more telling than mere birthplace. The scorn he expressed for Austria and its ruler stood for his general scorn for every king, pharaoh, or potentate, and indeed for every imperium the world over. Jacob's renunciation of the emperor was a sign of his universal, liberal spirit.

꿍꿍

Baltimore. A city rivaling Vienna? A place of cultivation, cosmopolitan grace, and European grandeur? It was hard to credit. Certainly the Baltimore I'd seen, or thought I knew because my relatives lived there, was no Hapsburg capitol.

The Baltimore I visited as a young girl was a dingy, smelly, sketchy-seeming place. My family lived outside Washington, D.C., in Maryland, and we drove though Baltimore regularly on our way to Philadelphia to visit my three aunts. Rusty, drab, its residential streets lined with liquor stores and Polish seafood joints, the Baltimore I glimpsed from the car was down at the heels. A pervasive burning smell—diesel fuel overlaid with cheap, sweet pleasures (hot dogs, crab shells, cigarette smoke) drifted out to the highway. From the backseat my brother and I clowned that the letters on the derelict-looking railcars, B & O, stood for body odor. When my father told us they stood for Baltimore and Ohio, the once proud railway that took thousands of newly arrived immigrants west, Ohio suffered by association.

My brother and I were amused by the way people from Baltimore, or at least our relatives, spoke, exaggerating long vowels and accentuating consonants in an accent that struck me as odd but certainly not "European."

My Aunt Fanny's way of turning any silent, half silent, or even short vowel sound into a long one (as in "don't you look just bee-ooo-tee-ful") and at the same time, of changing random consonants (voicing the final *s* of "gas" to make it "gazz") was an extreme example, but all of my relatives had similar ways of emphasizing and improvising sounds. My uncles, who called themselves man-*ahfack*-chrs, would lament the end of man-*ahfack*-chring, remembering the heyday of all the *may*-jer man-*ahfack*-chrs. My aunts traced Balt-*ee*-mewer's decline to when the fine *dee*-partment stores started to close down. Once it was no longer possible to spend a Sat-ur-*dee* in town—too dangerous, too dingy, and even the best downtown hotel, the Lord Balt-*ee*-mewer, had closed its tea rooms—the city's best days were over.

End of an *eee*-ra in Balt-*ee*-mewer.

As I said, it was hard for me, hearing these sounds as a child, to understand them as intentionally cultivated. But this is what they were, for my aunts and uncles had been raised in Baltimore, where slurred letters signified low class. Their exaggerated ee-nunciations were their generation's retaining wall against the argot of the South and also a bulwark against a host of merely American, that is to say, *gentile,* habits of speech and manners.

These could all, in some way, be represented by the local pronunciation of the city's name—Ball'mer. Ball'mer was a place where the gentiles took bottles right from the icebox and placed them on the dining table. Balt-*ee*-mewer Jews knew to put their condiments in proper condiment trays, bestowed on brides.

Ball'mer was a place where girls sat on stoops in sloppy bobby socks, men visited taprooms and went to work without proper coats and ties. But not my relatives in Balt-*ee*-mewer, where nice people, Jewish people, knew how to live properly.

So it was represented to me by my three elderly aunts—who lived in Philadelphia, where they moved to be near the second branch of their father's company, Levy's International Shrinking Company. Each in her one-bedroom apartment sanctum, my aunts cultivated this weltanschauung—old, exacting, fine—without ever mentioning, or acknowledging, the more casual American ethos it stood against. This was a weltanschauung not unkind but strict, one that took for granted prompt arrivals, clean babies, monogrammed guest towels.

Fundamentally urbane, their weltanschauung also took for granted the superiority of a Saturday "in town" over any of the laxer amusements of home. It exacted workmanship in haberdashery and upholstery. It believed family life was properly regulated by a cycle of clubs and card games, dinners and coming-out parties, engagement luncheons and other charming *fêtes*. The rhythms and ceremonies of the life cycle were maintained by orders of stationery—announcements, invitations, thank-you notes.

This weltanschauung assumed the superiority of a taxi over a carpool, a trunk over a carry-on, and regarded as only suitable such functionaries as the driver, the porter, the caterer, and the waiter in the club car.

"I can tell you," I remember my aunt's voice rising with emphasis, "trains were certainly different in those days—none of these plastic cups and 'self-service.'" From Aunt Fanny's tone, I was to understand that for a Jewish lady of Balt-*ee*-mewer, service was not something of which a self was strictly capable.

Given all this, it was ignorant on my part and tactless, I now realize, to ask Aunt Fanny if she remembered any Yiddish.

"Yiddish?" She laughed nervously.

I persisted: "Your father began, didn't he, in East Baltimore, an immigrant. He must have spoken some Yiddish, didn't he?"

I could see she found the question in bad taste. I ought to have known Jacob Levy was as likely to speak Yiddish to his children as they were to mistake fork on the left for knife on the right. The language of the household was English, although her father's background would have permitted him to converse in German, Russian, whatever they spoke in Riga, Austria, and maybe Yiddish as well.

Aunt Fanny was trying to answer my inquiries, but I was not to take advantage. Which left the whole matter entirely confusing and mysterious—until Jacob's cane led me from his Baltic origins to his own little Austria in Baltimore. As my aunt implied, Jacob, arriving in Baltimore in the mid-1880s, made a claim true to the spirit of both his place of origin and of destination. The Baltic regions of his origin had been, for centuries, little Germanies once removed.

In 1790, when George Washington created the first United States consulate and dispatched the first trade envoy, no insider would have been surprised that the city he chose for this honor was the Free Hanseatic City of Bremen. In addition to thumbing America's now independent nose at Britain's king, his action embodied commercial good sense as well as poetic justice. As uncowed by England's royal prerogatives as by any German prince's, the cities of the Hansa had long conducted themselves with perfect indifference to royal monopolies and imperial claims.

Since the Middle Ages, the kings and queens of England had no choice but to deal with the Hansa, whose emissaries, installed in their Guildhall in London, controlled not only Baltic but North Sea trade as well. The German Hansa cities of the Middle Ages bankrolled some English ventures, blocked others, and generally exerted an influence on trade across Europe exceeding England's. As kingdoms dissolved and empires rose and fell, through wars of roses and wars of succession and wars of seven, thirty, and one hundred years, the Free Hanseatic Cities traded on.

Even after the league itself dissolved, Bremen, Hamburg, Danzig, Memel, Libau, Lübeck, and Riga went on trading. As Germany, perennially disunited, had its boundaries drawn again and again, the Hansa merchants kept the wine and cloth going east; the flax, hemp, timber, furs, and grain going west.

From the late seventeenth century to the end of the eighteenth, Britain monopolized all the major ports along the Atlantic colonies and made the rest of Europe pay for the goods England imported from America and then reexported. Cities like Bremen and Hamburg, free since the eleventh and twelfth centuries, knew how to bide their time. These international cities were accustomed to long business cycles.

The tobacco trade, carried on to Bremen's disadvantage from the founding of Jamestown through the American Revolution, provides the quintessential case of Bremen and Hamburg's patience. For two centuries, these free cities paid the substantial markup on tobacco exported from the Chesapeake to England and then reexported to them. They hoped to profit eventually.

What a boon it was then for the Hansa! What fine repayment of the free cities' patience when, the guns of the Revolution echoing their last, Bremerhaven harbor began seeing American ships laden with tobacco. In the year following George Washington's agreement with Bremen in 1790, only 4 of the 478 ships entering the Weiser River were from America. But in the next hundred years the flow of tobacco to the east increased exponentially. Between 1800 and the 1850s, the sea lane connecting Bremen to Baltimore became one of the busiest in the Atlantic. The U.S. Civil War interrupted the flow, as the sea war of 1812 had, but by 1868 Bremen had reestablished itself as the main tobacco port in Europe, followed by Rotterdam. Baltimore was the main port shipping tobacco from America. For every hogshead going to England, Baltimore now shipped six or seven to Bremen.

Beginning in the middle of the nineteenth century, ships discharging hogsheads of tobacco in Bremen and Hamburg began to take on a new kind of freight. The siftings from the fragrant barrels of tobacco now pillowed the heads of an equally lucrative but more lively cargo. Ships from Baltimore conveyed tobacco to the Free Ports and returned to Baltimore carrying immigrants.

Before that time German immigrants to America landed at Havre de Grace on the Susquehanna River, bypassing the noise and dirt of Baltimore on their way to quieter places. Religious pietists, provincials, country people, these Germans sought farmsteads a hundred miles away in York and Lancaster counties, Pennsylvania, or farther west in Ohio. Disembarking from schooners, they spent their carefully saved hoards on wagons and then, fitting German harnesses on American oxen, lumbered out the next day. Steady people, traditional people, they evinced little interest in cities.

Nor was Baltimore in the 1820s to 1840s an irresistible place to be. Indeed Baltimore was a city hard on the nerves.

Travelers steering out of Chesapeake Bay toward Fells Point between 1790 and the 1830s still found Baltimore's docks higgledy-piggledy—now a pier, now a marsh, now a handsome jetty, now a mire. Construction projects were mounted in bursts, abandoned when exports did not get expected returns or when labor trouble erupted. Piles of lumber stood in all weather. Ships in all stages of completion shifted in the sucking mud. Slaves were hired out by inland masters, and their mistreatment was obvious to any who paid mind.

Just inland from the busy harbor, sailors unloaded fine teas and eaux de cologne, silks and cheeses and mailbags full of letters. And then they reeled drunkenly through Fells Point, where the streets were ankle deep in flood water and emptied slops. European merchants, encouraged by Baltimore's smart well-rigged ships, recoiled at the city's crude accommodations. In Baltimore, one supped on corn coarsely ground and meat butchered in the alley outside. The supply of vegetables from the fertile hills above was irregular; the stink of animals in the city center was pervasive. Baltimore was, one visitor sighed, a place of "many luxuries and no comforts."

Farther out from the city's populous center, things were often worse. If central Baltimore sometimes steeped in a bay broth rich with sea life, ordure, sewage, and disease, the city's edge endured chronic mudslides, not to mention frequent tangled accidents with horses and carts. The same geography that made the city a noisome hole catching refuse from the heights also hampered the delivery of fresh goods from the countryside.

To Baltimore, along with their crafts and their ethos of craft, immigrants from the Hansa towns brought ripened notions of social good and of the dignities accruing to social roles. They brought not just luxuries but comforts; not just progress but modernity; not just the adrenaline high of life among crowds but a set of well-developed beliefs in civil life and the city.

What this new immigrant brought to the Chesapeake was the word my great-grandfather used and his daughters Fanny, Myrtle, and Jean embodied and impressed on us all, merely by how they stood, walked, and stored their many pairs of gloves in their bureau drawers in original tissue. That word is *civilization*.

Imagine the new immigrant arriving in Baltimore circa 1880. On disembarkation, he is greeted by a welcoming party from the local Mechanic Society, German chapter, or if he possesses a trade in local demand (say, cigar making) he may even be met by a member of the local German manufactory. Perhaps this old European concern has now opened a branch in Baltimore, the better to select its own leaf at auction in Danville. Whichever it is, having departed from Bremen or Hamburg, the immigrant coasts into the city along with the weekly mail.

As he adapts to his new setting, the newcomer finds Baltimore as fertile in *Gemütlichkeit* as any city on the globe. From the Locust Street dock, he may be led to a neighborhood where members of his own church or synagogue pray from the prayer books of home and hold the picnics and festivals familiar to him. If he does not already have employment, he may be helped to find it, seasonal or permanent, in one

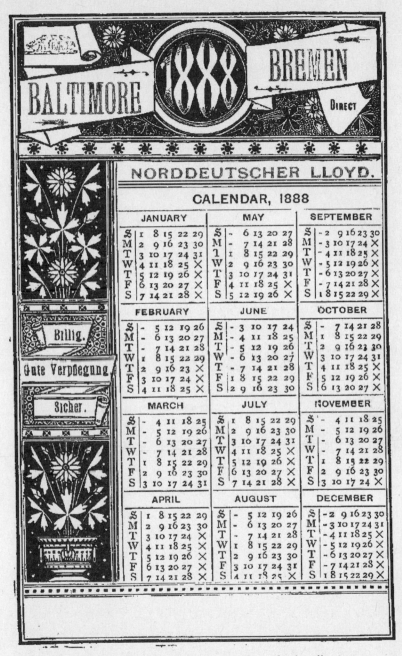

Calendar, 1888, Norddeutscher Lloyd. From the author's collection.

of the manufacturing workshops springing up all over the city. And if he has a wife he will be encouraged to look to her. Perhaps she ought to make herself useful? Make a decent contribution as the family gets on its feet? Every Thursday the Norddeutscher Lloyd docks see many German country girls bound for service up Charles Street, making their way to the kitchens and nurseries of the rich.

In the unlikely event that our immigrant is slow in understanding the Americans' unorthodox ways with headgear—casualness about hats on or hats off, their penchant for straw—he will be admonished not to be distracted by sloppy American mores. A man sets the right tone in business in a coat and collar. Has he not yet joined a club, a workingman's group, some association of mutual aid and recreation? Has he not yet learned to keep his countenance, to remain equable in proximity to slaves or ex-slaves? He will be reminded that he is a worker of a proud tradition, one drawing on the oldest guild ways and the newest social theories. Yes, many people have started out in America poor. And look at them now.

Look at them now—smoking, sipping beer, and debating the world's affairs with no one to interfere. In their own clubs, the Germania and the Concordia, they are speaking the German language.

Certainly Baltimore's men to watch in the 1850s, 1860s, 1870s, and 1880s were the busy Bremen and Hamburg traders who traveled the seas and then repaired to these clubs to discuss business. The men at the Germania and similar clubs comprised a striking subculture. Enthusiastically German and enthusiastically American, they would be likely to characterize themselves, if asked, as simply enthusiastically Baltimorean. Like the Hansa's London emissaries of centuries back, the Bremen and Hamburg traders owned the place.

The smoking room of the Germania, well stocked with latest news of local commerce—the *Baltimore Sun*, the *American*, *Niles Register*, *Prices Current,* and of course *Tobacco Leaf*—was also where a man found conveniently posted the last-minute changes in the schedule of the Norddeutscher Lloyd. He would want to know when the ships would pull in, for then the smoking room would be restocked with papers from all over German-speaking Europe. The local German sheets—the abolitionist *Wecker*, *Deutsche Correspondent*, and others were stacked conveniently in the magazine stands.

Yet any who mistook the members of the Germania Club for reluctant Americans—or for sentimentalists, throwbacks, or greenhorns—would be wrong. They threw themselves wholeheartedly into their new country's politics. It was not nostalgia for what was left behind that the members of the Germania Club nursed in Baltimore. It was *Gemütlichkeit* and *Kultur* they fostered there. They had a talent for not being alien.

Baltimore's famous son H. L. Mencken recalled his grandfather August's spasms of identification with a wide range of authentic but wholly inconsistent Germanies. A penchant for submitting himself to theological discussion did not, in Grandfather August's book, ill comport with also affecting the dialect of the Pennsylvania Germans from whom he bought tobacco. Nor did the fact that he, like most of the German businessmen in those days, came from people once traders in Oldenburgh, inhibit him from scorning those from the Hansa towns. H. L. Mencken's grandfather's adopted pedigree as a "Saxon," a pedigree acquired in Baltimore, entitled him to "disdain them Plattdeutschen" when the whim struck.

What August Mencken might have meant by Plattdeutschen was Jews. The coastal, cosmopolitan trading zones of the northern Hansa towns were more likely than inland regions to host their share of Jews. Baltimore German Jews were not immune from the prejudice to which Jews worldwide had long been subject. And yet it is fair to say that Jews enjoyed in this port of entry, as in so many others, privileges accruing to Germanness frequently in excess of penalties levied on Jewishness.

Historian A.J.P. Taylor once pointed out that it was trade that spread Germanness across Europe. In places where Germans had "no concrete national home and little expected one," they were unmistakably German. Meanwhile, as Taylor continued, "Where Germans did not penetrate, their influence was carried by Jews."

It cannot be literally true that nineteenth-century Baltimore gave the Hansa its last hurrah, but to many of German extraction in Baltimore it seemed that way.

This protean, as opposed to purist, Germanness, so detachable from national identity and *volkisch* rootedness, struck strong roots in Baltimore and its preservation carried no threat to ardent American patriotism, nor to what was just as common, ardent love for the adopted city of Baltimore. This Germanness embraced English as the language of the home and coined key terms for its liberation from the parochial or ancien régimes: "Liberal" was one. "Enlightened" was another. Business in nineteenth-century Baltimore was ecumenical. At the Germania, it was hardly worth remarking that some among the smokers had learned Polish or Latvian from their mothers or that some mixed Hungarian loanwords with their German.

In Baltimore, for those properly liberal, neither country nor ethnic origin outweighed the bond of the common language. Spoken by Baltimore's rising business class, German carried with it *Kultur*—the common love of music, reading, and the edifying lecture.

Nor did religious affiliation present insuperable barriers. In 1869 the bride of Rabbi Benjamin Szold wrote to her mother, "We have made many friends, Jew and Gentile, German and American." Henrietta bids her mother imagine that her husband, the rabbi, not only "delivered a speech in English on the subject of 'Charity' before an American Gentile audience in the Masonic Hall in Lynchburg Virginia," but that his speech "was printed in all the English language newspapers."

Even more striking examples of the ecumenism of the 1880s are provided by H. L. Mencken, who recounts that at his Gymnasium, the famous German-English Knapp School, there was no "enmity between the Chosen and the Goyim in the old professor's establishment, and no sense of difference in the treatment of them."

In the 1880s, Mencken notes, there was "still a class in Hebrew" on which he himself sat in "long enough to learn the Hebrew alphabet." True, Professor Knapp might discharge his own Prussian spleen by "bursting into a classroom that was disorderly, to denounce it as a Judenschule," and yet, Mencken recalls, the Prussian schoolmaster was also "fond of using a number of Hebrew [!] loan words, *tokos* (backside), *schlimiel* (oaf), *kosher* (clean) and *meshuggah* (crazy)." Not to be outdone in liberality, Mencken points out that the Jewish students helped themselves to the whole sideboard, clean and unclean. About the pork eating of his Jewish schoolmates, Mencken writes, "I must add in sorrow that the Jews at Knapps's were unanimously *chazir-fressers*."

Mencken's Yiddish usage reveals how easily, how promiscuously, "Germans" of all kinds mixed in 1880s Baltimore. I say this knowing that my aunts would have found such mixing quite unfortunate.

As well as I can remember Aunt Fanny's response to the question of whether she remembered any Yiddish, it was to be offended that I could picture her so Ball'mer. She thought of Yiddish as an earthy, casual language spoken by persons of haphazard upbringing. For Jews who knew no better, Yiddish was fine, but the language of Balt-*ee*-mewer Jews who hailed from "Austria" was naturally *English*.

And if Aunt Fanny had looked mournful at my lack of understanding, Aunt Jean did not scruple to hide her strong indignation. Did I imagine, her stern look challenged me, that her brothers, Eddie, Paul, and Theo, and then her sons, Jerry and Earle, would have been *invited* to join Uncle Baron in London, to inherit what he had built, had they not had the *proper* upbringing, had not come from the finest sort of Jewish home? Not a Yiddish-speaking but a *nice* home, full of her father's books, with proper furnishings, and children brought up carefully to know exactly what was what?

Admittedly her father, Jacob, had regarded his sons' name change from Levy to Baron, their employment change from cloth shrinking to tobacco, and their departure from the country of their birth, America, to England, as a betrayal. The subsequent departure of his grand-sons, her sons, he also regarded as a knife thrust at his heart. Jean herself chose to see the transfer of the Levy men from Baltimore to London as destiny.

What my Aunt Jean did not tell me, and what I did not begin to understand until I followed Jacob's cane and let history guide me back to Baltimore, is that these seeds had been planted well before either her formidable father or good Uncle Baron ever sailed into Chesapeake Bay. Generations before they came to the Bay, a full century before George Washington established the trade relations with Germany that would crowd the shipping lanes, these seeds were planted.

Long before Bernhard Baron struck wealth from his invention so prodigious, so marvelously productive of pleasure and well-being, young men had been reaping rewards in London that had sprouted from seedlings on the Chesapeake.

Like my great-uncles, like Uncle Baron himself, what seeded all their fortunes was tobacco.

FIVE

That Bewitching Vegetable

It really was a pity, in Aunt Jean's case, that the United States of America decided not to confer titles on its distinguished citizens. For I think she was as formidable a lady as her sister-in-law, Lady Bertha Baron of London, who also was raised (though she hid it) in Baltimore. Or if Jean could not have an actual title conferred at Court, then she should have had one of those epithets given to sovereigns and conquerors. *Jean the Unswayable.*

Jean the Indomitable.

Imperious over her steel rims, queenly behind her city balcony, Aunt Jean resembled Bette Davis's Queen Elizabeth in a Bonwit Teller dress. Part diva, part dragon, opinionated but wholly indifferent to opinion, Aunt Jean, all the family agreed, was great.

Not nice. Or considerate. Or warm, or any of those pleasant things her sisters Myrtle and Fanny were. But *great.*

❧❧

Just like appearing at Court, calling on Aunt Jean meant meeting the highest standards of sartorial care. Jean wore, of course, whatever Jean liked.

Unlike Fanny and Myrtle, who believed that a lady, even an old lady, should remain au courant, Jean was above truckling to fashion or observing the protocols of dress dictated by occasion and hour. Sometime in the 1960s Myrtle and Fanny started having their hair cut, colored, and teased into one of the silver-or gold-blond or copper-blond coiffures in favor with the ladies of their card club. Sharing one cab to the hairdresser, having lunch out, they made a day of it, sometimes even wandering from the salon and into Lord & Taylor's for a bit of shopping, looking at the newer styles. Myrtle never went very far, but there was a three-year stretch in the 1970s when Fanny, inspired by the racks, was known to appear in pantsuits. "Whoo-*hoo!*" her son Dan would say, stretching out his long legs. "Pants for company, Mother? But of course you'll change for dinner," he teased. "Should we call Jean to ask what she thinks?"

As she had done since roughly World War I, in the mornings Jean swept her thinning brown hair into a French knot. Then she put on the elastic hose. And then whatever dress and cardigan, or satin quilted housecoat, went best with her arthritic back and state of mind. Arrayed by eight o'clock in what she'd wear (barring a "function") all day, she'd stretch her legs out on the stool before the damask chair and brief her housekeeper, Leona, on the day's visitors: delicacies to offer, accoutrements required.

Weekdays: coffee. Cake plates stacked, percolator at the ready. Dried fruits and nuts heaped or fanned artfully in the Limoges, chocolates in gold paper in a crystal dish.

Weekends: brunch. Vinegar cruet. Pickle forks. Platter of tuna, salmon, tomatoes, lettuce frills. Bagels, defrosted, sliced, toasted, and presented on a crisp napkin. Pie server raised on silver tiptoes on the cloth, ready for its Pyrex insert (piping hot).

Ice bucket (sterling) furred with condensation and thus assigned a little table of its own. A child desiring a refill stood up quietly, filled the glass from the frosty bucket (*tongs* not fingers, please!), and ducked into the little kitchen where Leona poured. Coke, ginger ale, and such in cans were kept strictly out of sight. The procedure was a delicate one, so children learned to slide their hips around the folding kitchen door and to slip back to their chairs with all dispatch.

Aunt Jean's glance was sharp. She did not countenance childish interruptions to her flow of talk. It took all her patience, all her intelligent resolve, to straighten out, to set right the acts, to get in the proper order and perspective the family story that others could be relied on to miscarry. For what she offered was not just anecdote or gossip, though they were included, but *History*.

I can still see Aunt Jean, light from the terrace slanting onto her speckled hands. Sitting under the portrait of herself bedecked in pale blue satin, she would chronicle the life and times of the Levy family. Jean knew well, for instance, as Fanny somehow didn't, that Riga was in Latvia, not Austria, and that despite his German-sounding name, Uncle Baron was of "Russian or Polish extraction." The thick file Jean kept was full of documents to that effect. Inconvenient facts were twisted or altered as occasion required. But she understood history's continuities and causations, its force and sweep. Beyond dispensing discrete factoids, Aunt Jean was the one oral historian in the family, the only one who knew how to knit the decades into a proper saga, to launch our heroes—Jacob and Bernhard—with the proper pomp.

If she steered clear of the actual content of her father's politics, she was a strict disciple of its forms. Jean's narrative of Jacob Levy's progress had a kind of brilliant teleological dynamism—leaping toward the future, retouching the past—that would have made her father, that old Marxist, proud.

It helped Jean's momentum somewhat that both her father, Jacob, and her uncle, Bernhard Baron, had made their breakthroughs courtesy of the roller, the oblong turning cylinder of polished steel that speeded up and smoothed the progress of anything fed into it. This cylinder, turning at so many revolutions per minute and then so many more—symbolized progress. Thus Jean gave her visitors to understand how, from 1900 and into the halcyon 1950s, when she had been at the helm of Levy's International Shrinking Company, what had been slow became quick. The cloth for rainwear, suiting, sails, and canvas awnings which, in 1900, Jacob had lifted from dunking tubs and hung on wooden rods, turned into another stuff entirely, courtesy of the new roller machinery. Now it was a *textile* that leaped and rippled in waves of sheen and fiberglass.

This same roller, Jean implied, revolutionized tobacco too. Whether fabric and tobacco were related in fact, they certainly were in Aunt Jean's mind and came, in turn, to be related in mine, so that when I imagined Levy's Shrinking and Carreras Tobacco, I saw them rolling together on one great bolt, blurring into one product.

Jean's narrative also held together what others thought betrayal drove asunder. The affinity between Jacob Levy and Bernhard Baron, the continuity of Jacob's Baltimore cloth-shrinking enterprise and Uncle Baron's cigarette-rolling juggernaut encompassed the whole chain of inevitabilities that had taken Jean's brothers and then her sons to London and made them principals in Carreras cigarettes and then Baron's. Those who saw it otherwise, Jean implied, lacked vision.

As Jean had it, the fact that our own Uncle-Baron-had-invented-a-cigarette-machine-in-Baltimore-sold-it-in-England-went-on-to-manufacture-there-summoning-nephews-grand-nephews-making-them-great-men was the happiest of inevitabilities, decreed by history, destiny, and the intrinsic excellence of the persons concerned—with, she allowed, a little help from tobacco.

One could see, listening to Aunt Jean expound on the great epoch when the family had owned Carreras, that just thinking about tobacco made her very happy.

Taking pleasure in tobacco was hardly unique to Aunt Jean. By the 1960s, when we used to visit her, tobacco's reputation had began its steep decline, but for nearly four hundred years prior (from tobacco's discovery by Sir Walter Raleigh in the 1590s to the U.S. surgeon general's report on smoking and health in 1964) tobacco had been producing a global glow in the lungs only augmented by happiness in the international pocketbook.

It was the tobacco of Maryland, Virginia, and the Carolinas, shipped from Baltimore, that launched Bernhard Baron in the 1880s. The role he played in busting the tobacco trust and renewing the Anglo-American tobacco trade established him in London as a Jew to reckon with. And it was tobacco that made the fortunes of my great-uncles Eddie, Paul, and Theo who, after joining Uncle Baron in London, gained wealth, influence, and for one of them, even a title.

Generations before my great-grandfather Jacob or my uncle Baron arrived in Baltimore from Bremen or Hamburg, the sea lanes between Europe's major ports and the oozy inlets of the Chesapeake were crowded with ambitious hopefuls, crisscrossing the oceans, perfecting vessels of transport.

The young men began coming in the seventeenth century, as news of endless fertile lands was brought back across the ocean. Anchoring at some moist inlet of the Chesapeake, a landless second son from Sussex could set himself up for life, the proceeds reaped from the first year's crop paying ship's passage for the laborers required to farm a larger swath of acreage. For each passage paid, London investors topped off his holdings with fifty more acres. In short order, he would be in possession of a country seat.

And what, really, was sweeter than sitting pretty in a seller's market? A young planter set up along one of the Chesapeake's many inlets might cross his boots and await the Sovereign's coming to fetch his own fields' produce. From the Bay's deep basin, the King's ships let down little tribes of boats. So desirous was the King to pick up and transport the besotting weed, or sotweed, he would call at one's very back gate.

No one sums up the first century of tobacco commerce better than the first William Byrd of Virginia, who looks out on his world, likes what he sees and pronounces it good. Marveling at the wonderful popularity of the crop he calls "that bewitching vegetable," Byrd in 1730 describes a life "abound[ing] in all kinds of provisions without expense." Established amid his thousands of acres of cultivated tobacco (the original Byrd estate now contains the entire city of Richmond), Byrd epitomizes planter insouciance: "I have a large family of my own, and my doors are open to everybody, yet I have no bills to pay, and half a crown will rest undisturbed in my pocket for many moons altogether."

Nor does Byrd suffer undue rustication. Each year he sails to London for the "season." Tobacco's European devotees are city people—patrons of coffee houses and counting houses; readers of papers, members of clubs—and so are its producers. Tobacco's travels make it, and everyone who touches it, more urbane. Sliding his ship into Liverpool with his crop battened down beneath, Byrd strikes the template for a transatlantic type: the tobacco cosmopolitan.

Fifty years later, Britain's heavy hand, including a chokehold on credit to tobacco planters, compromised the lifestyle Byrd loved. But tobacco itself was no less bewitching or profitable a commodity. The market for Virginia and Maryland tobacco easily survived George Washington's curtailing of tobacco exports to Britain, and the trade sprang back. The growing worldwide market—and slaves—kept profits up.

America's first profitable region, the Chesapeake, had been born in tobacco, but its industrial and commercial development was promoted by tobacco too. Hard to grow, tricky to preserve and package, tobacco nevertheless provided technical challenges and scope for innovation that an ambitious young man could turn to good account.

Cured tobacco spurred advances in greenhouses and smokehouses, in coopering and caulking, in sailcloth and tar and thus, in contemporary terms, in heating, cooling, packaging, preservation, containerization, and waterproofing of all kinds. Inelegant in its less processed forms—stuffed into a pipe or, worse, into a cheek as a chaw or under the nose as snuff—tobacco's social climb from saloon to salon, from exclusive use by men to common use by women, forced developments in fine papermaking, in filtering and advertising, as well as advances in belts, rollers, and precision knives. By the first decades of the nineteenth century, tobacco had made Baltimore not only America's largest shipbuilder but also its biggest agricultural exporter and the country's second largest port of entry for immigrants. Ships emptied of tobacco took on cargoes of immigrants; ships emptied of immigrants filled up with cargoes of tobacco, and the ports organized for its shipping—Port Tobacco, Annapolis, Danville, Roanoke, and Baltimore—grew in complexity and opportunity. Baltimore shipped its tobacco to the world.

"The relation," writes H. R. Billings in *Tobacco: Its History, Varieties, Culture, Manufacture, and Commerce* (gold tooled, handsomely illustrated) in 1875, "existing between the balmy plant and the commerce of the world is of the strongest kind. . . . The great herb . . . has gone on its way . . . ever assuming more sway over the commercial and social world, until it now takes high rank among the leading elements of mercantile and agricultural greatness."

Tobacco's ascent up the ranks of products had, of course, been accelerated measurably by war. Billings, who published his book not long after the U.S. Civil War and only twenty years after the Crimean War, would have seen the commerce take a sizable expansion. "*Tabac bon*," says a "soldier in the red shirt" in Tolstoy's work on the Crimean War, *Sebastopol*. "Yes, good tobacco—Turkish tobacco," answers the Frenchman, "and with you Russian tobacco good?" "*Rouss Bonn!*" repeats the soldier in the red shirt.

Mid-nineteenth-century battlefields were great cigarette clearing-houses, with new blends and new smoking fads being taken back home after the war. The cigarette, which in Tolstoy's works symbolized nationalist antagonisms, attained international standing and became a universal token of world commerce. Inevitable accessory to any worldly scene, part of business and of leisured life, the cigarette traveled across the Atlantic, up the Black Sea and the Dnieper, and down the Elbe and Bug, out from Bremen, out from Hamburg. Billings quotes a Russian correspondent:

> Everybody smokes, men, women, and children. They smoke Turkish tobacco, rolled in silk paper—seldom cigars or pipes. These rolls are called parparos. The ladies almost all smoke, but they smoke the small delicate sizes of parparos, while the men smoke larger ones. Always at morning noon and night come out the inevitable box of parparos, and everyone at the table smokes and drinks their coffee at the same time. On the cars are fixed little cups for cigar ashes at every seat. Ladies frequently take out their parparos, and hand them to the gentleman with a pretty invitation to smoke. Instead of having a smoking car, as we do, they have a car for those so poky as not to smoke.

Now, of course, we are all poky. Except for the two cigarettes I smoked for "research" purposes (working my courage up with half a bottle of wine on a porch in North Carolina), I have never smoked. I have done my part in coaxing one father, one daughter, one husband, several cousins, and assorted friends to quit the habit, and I do not wish that anyone I love should start again.

And yet it is a lie to say tobacco does not make me—like Aunt Jean—happy in a mysterious way, and I would probably mourn the disappearance of certain peculiar, irreplaceable forms of well-being associated with centuries of tobacco use.

Erotic? Aesthetic? Sublime? One writer has called cigarettes these names. I would not disagree. Cigarettes are, whatever else they may be, artifacts of the subtlest instincts of humanity, the urge to confect, concentrate, and distill; to risk, to deny death; cigarettes are *civilized*.

Which is why one of my most cherished possessions is a box top full of bright tobacco, now dried and nearly odorless, from a curing barn in Wilson County, North Carolina, one of the places my great-great-uncle Baron went every year between 1875 and 1895 and where, in his stead, my Aunt Jean's youngest son Jerry went too.

꧁꧂

"Pretty, isn't it?" asked Joey Scott, tanned, modest, as I stood with him in August 2001 in a Wilson County tobacco field. After I had spent the previous day at the Tobacco Life Museum, the Wilson County curators sent me to Joey, whose father, grandfather, and on back beyond the Civil War had raised the choice bright leaf tobacco my Uncle Baron had bid top price for at the local auctions.

Joey was right. Tobacco ready for cutting *is* pretty to look at. Especially on an August morning, with the dew on. The tiers of tobacco's spiraling leaves make a pleasing picture against corn's silkier verticals. And where cotton also grows, as it does on Joey's farm, where the pink and white blooms of the unopened boll toss for three days before the cup of cotton froth appears, tobacco makes a handsome backdrop, complementing with its straight green the riot of pink nearby.

And out of the curing barn, bright-leaf tobacco is even prettier. A hand of cured tobacco set against the sky is a dazzling matte gold, like a child's thick-crayoned round of sun; cured hands being loose piled are the color of luxury. From out of the velvety looking shadows of the barn waft besotting, bewitching odors natives call "sweet scented." As if the earth itself came up in a fire of honey: That is the look, the smell of bright-leaf tobacco.

No wonder, as one of Uncle Baron's biographers put it, he made a "lifetime study of tobacco culture in all its branches, from the planting of the seed to the manufactured article." Every spring brought him from London back to the tobacco belt. "From 1871–96," this source continues, "there was not a single year that Bernhard Baron did not see for himself the growing and cutting of the finest crops of Virginia and other tobaccos." Uncle Baron took these trips not just for the pleasure of it; those who would make a success of tobacco had better know it and all its idiosyncrasies. Tobacco defeats casual cultivation and rewards only those who tend it devotedly. From February through June, tobacco is like a child in need of patient nursing; there is no end to the care the plant exacts.

Around December in some climes and by early February everywhere else, the seed is started in a protected place—a barn warmed by the heat of livestock, a sunny woodland clearing sheltered from wind, or under a cabin floor. The seedlings sprout and send up stalks and leaves. In late March or early April, when a spring thaw warms ground a spade can break, a young boy takes a crate of bright sprigs outside, pokes down and digs out and opens new holes to replant the seedlings, keeping the hills equidistant, giving each seedling space to broaden.

The six- or seven-year-old boy is brought back in May or June to pick the grubs off the lower leaves while his father suckers the plants, pulling off the top leaves to encourage bushy second growth. The nine- or ten-year-old boy walks the fields in June, sack around his waist, tossing in both grubs and narrow leaves that are forcing out the best growth. Then come weeks of waiting. After the last suckering, the leaves are left to fatten undisturbed in the moist heat of midsummer.

At least for a while in the cooler days of September, tobacco is not the worst crop in the world to pick. Unlike rice, which grows in malarial swamps; unlike sugar, which requires a machete to cut it; unlike cotton, which tears the fingers with its woody burrs, tobacco is a crisp and supple plant. Tall, its prime leaves growing at a man's hips or a child's shoulders, its leaves, though sticky, break off the stalk with a sharp snap.

Nor is the curing always miserable. Arranged in tiers in a curing shed, each hand on its own dowel, the crop is barn cured—leaves placed where air through the slats can lift their edges and brush their central ribs.

On a day with a breeze, a boy can slip away, find himself a nicotine bower, and doze in the coolest spot around. And in the early morning dew, who would not enjoy lifting down a fragrant, cured hand and inhaling its breath: *sweet scented*.

Problem is—most places—the weather.

In most places, August is brutal.

In August a boy working tobacco awakens with a headache. He will have spent the night curled near the opening of a shed, its rough door unhooked to admit what breeze might come. As the day's picking begins, the temperatures in the Chesapeake or the Crimea are already high. By one o'clock the sun burns through sweat soaking the boy's neck; pools of standing water from last night's rains grow fetid. It is hard to imagine lifting a finger in weather that loves tobacco but hates mortal comfort.

Picking and flue curing both happen in August and September. A boy picking by day may also be assigned the task of tending the flue at night. Sent to sleep on a pallet next to the hot walls, the boy's job is to wake the men in the event of a stray spark. The smoke tugs at his lungs all night, not altogether unpleasantly, but he wakes blinking in an acrid, intoxicating haze. Early mornings, on the hottest days of the year, the job may fall to him to restoke the fire, pushing lengths of dry wood into the flue to keep the heat constant.

The person tending this fire, setting these plants, pulling these worms, his face a smudge, his hands a cracked and blistered mess— who was he? A fixture of the trade. Unmentioned in Byrd or Billings, he was indispensable to tobacco culture through the end of the nineteenth century.

From William Tatham's classic *Tobacco Culture*, 1800, London.

Page through ledgers of Maryland planters or old tobacco sales accounts; watch the loading docks of Annapolis and Port Tobacco, of Norfolk as it suddenly appears on maps. Turn the leaves of Tatham's classic *Tobacco Culture* (1800) or browse the glass cases and etchings of the Maryland Historical Society.

You will see pictures like this. In the double dugout (two canoes with a hogshead lashed between), a boy leans back. His oar lifts in a stroke of ink. The object he rows or pushes, a hogshead of tobacco, is many times larger than he is. It weighs about a thousand pounds. He weighs, perhaps, ninety.

He is fourteen or fifteen years old.

On this boy, a slave, American tobacco culture depended.

❧

Arriving in America in 1868 or 1869, a few years after the Civil War ended, Bernhard Baron was just in time to catch and ride a great crest of industrialization and modernization that would eventually carry him out of New York and Baltimore to glittering London. The last decades of the nineteenth century saw a demand for affordable, rapidly produced luxuries of all kinds. Demand for tobacco kept rising, and so grew the need for more efficient and viable ways of producing it.

Baron arrived, in other words, in a country without a theory of labor adequate to this modern demand, and in a region in shock from the loss of its slaves.

As a child traveling in a car through Baltimore and its environs, I always found it incredible to consider that the places we passed by had a mere century ago been the "slave south," a phrase I would pronounce under my breath as we drove. I think it must have been during those drives that I began to grow curious about tobacco and about our nineteenth-century relatives who made their fortune in it. During these drives my father sometimes skirted I-95, going Route 29 from the D.C. suburbs to Baltimore's, and we'd drive through farmlands. Old houses—white, the porches sagging, sheds akimbo—stood back from the road. How old were they: Eighty? Ninety? One hundred? In late summer, the crops along the road were mostly familiar. I recognized corn by its height, also the spinach, tomatoes, and other summer vegetables growing in what our social studies books called "truck gardens." But what was this tall plant, firm leafed, spreading, as high as corn but broader?

It was tobacco.

The road to the seashore, to Bethany in Maryland or Dewey in Delaware, was lined with tobacco. Even in the killing heat of August we'd see workers plucking the top leaves. Many of the towns on the way to the Ocean Bridge had national landmark signs near stoplights. These relayed the information, fascinating to me, that the sweltering fields we passed through had once been worked by slaves.

Slaves! It seemed unimaginable, outlandish, and yet fascinating. The unremarkable look of the lands we passed through—so close to our modern suburban life—was part of History, that far foreign country, inaccessible to modern people. But these drives taught me that I could get to History by stepping over the margin of the familiar as easily as over a crack in the sidewalk. I could step into the past, out of the narrows and into the broadness of time, simply by looking out the window. Certain sights give up eloquent stories to those who know where to look and how to listen. Open barn doors were evocative, their black squares full of floating dust. Evocative too were lyrical little creeks, the bridges we passed in the blue dusk serenaded by cricket orchestras. Absent a highway to travel down, there were pages—books—full of the same lyrical chirpings. Reading a certain book or poem might put you there, in History.

My youthful fascination later propelled me on my life course. This perception of history, sometime while I was in graduate school, made me shift my scholarly specialty from the study of poetry to American poetry, and eventually to American literature before 1900. As a young professor at the University of Pennsylvania, I felt moved every semester when teaching, say, Frederick Douglass's *Narrative* to remind my students that the Mason-Dixon Line was only forty minutes away from our classroom. Once I brought in a map to show them that not forty-five miles from their seats in West Philadelphia, Route 13 branched toward Odessa, Delaware, from I-95—and this was the slave South.

I remember once, searching for a way to convey the uncanniness of it, that I told students about the golf club, a mere twenty-five minutes west of my parents' suburban Washington house, in which I'd worked as a cocktail waitress during a summer vacation. Out Route 270 from Potomac, this too had been part of the slave south. The club's regulars, from families resident in the area for generations, now found more time for golf and drinking and less for work as they sold their farms bit by bit to developers. They were the closest I'd ever been to southern cavaliers, courtly and never rude to college girls who worked the bar, and I count the summer I spent bending with my tray over tables billowing with their cigar smoke a crucial installment in my education. Whether the families of some of these men would have once held slaves I could not tell, but it seemed plausible to think so. There were no blacks who belonged to or worked at the club, not even a caddy, and I myself felt a little swarthy. My Jewishness was not something I advertised.

Once I'd begun to research Bernhard Baron, his career and that of my uncles, not just permitting but requiring me to follow the history of tobacco, my passion for the bewitching vegetable flared up in eccentric ways. Every year, when I taught Byrd or other Chesapeake characters, I began to bring in my large box top full of yellow tobacco, collected from Joey Scott's garden, and during vacations I sought out ways to immerse myself in tobacco history. By the time I drove up to the big white gabled farm in Glyndon that my great-uncle Paul, Jacob's brother, purchased in 1911, I had already discovered that these acres had once been owned by one of Reisterstown's most notorious slave-owning families. The whole town of Glyndon, including the farmstead where my mother had played, had once been the property of a slaveholder, Thomas Worthington. Files at the Maryland Historical Society made clear that my Uncle Paul's street, Bond Avenue, was named for the bondsmen—slaves—who were once penned down the rise from his chicken coops. Like all the slaves in the area, the Worthington slaves farmed tobacco as well as corn and wheat and then sent it by rail or wagon to Baltimore.

One May, I drove the back roads near the Bay Bridge until I found the Great House Farm where Frederick Douglass toiled in tobacco. I got out of the car to look at the little creeks. Another year, on my European trip to Belarus, I sought out and gazed at the massive brick pile of the tobacco factory in Grodno, now as then the largest in the district where Bernhard Baron was born, and where his father might well have worked. Back in the United States, I took myself to Maryland's Port Tobacco Courthouse ("once listed on world maps!" its website boasts). Later I lost myself in the George Arents Collection of the New York Public Library, on the history, literature, and lore of tobacco, with its pamphlets, broadsides, engravings, royal decrees, and slave bills. And of course at a certain point, I taught myself to smoke.

It was at the end of the day that I visited Joey Scott. Joey had asserted adamantly that he didn't smoke, of course not, and, moreover, that he'd taught his children to view the pretty acres he farmed simply as agriculture for export. Philip Morris had *nothing* to do with his family. Still, late that afternoon I decided that my probity as researcher required some sampling, some firsthand taste of this bewitching vegetable, and so I bought a pack of the local product.

Lighting my first from the gas burner in the kitchen, I went out to the porch, cigarette in one hand, large glass of wine in the other. How fast the weed burned down as I took my puffs, how full and plump the sensation along the lungs and up the sinuses to my very brainstem! I felt brighter, smarter, calmer, my chest a little ragged to be sure, but pleasantly so. Bewitching, indeed, the delicious vegetable. I felt like another and lit one from the red end of the first.

One more and I'd be a smoker now.

SIX

What Is to Be Done?

It is said that the immigrant's fondest wish is a better life for his children.

If this is true, then my great-grandfather, Jacob Levy, and my great-great uncle Bernhard Baron were aberrant, or at least uncooperative, examples of their kind, for the comfortable lives their children achieved gave them little apparent pleasure.

Late photos show both men looking vexed and frustrated, frowns drawing down their mouths, as if disappointment long resisted had finally landed full on them and there was nothing to do but carry it. In these photos they look like brothers more than rivals, both attired impeccably. Surrounded by the glossy and thriving members of their families, posing for photos that framed and ratified their great successes, both men drooped.

No one ever told me that both had died as saddened men. Even less did anyone let on that what made them look so disconsolate was a common disappointment in the children they "shared," Jacob's by birth but Bernhard's by name.

I had to gather this understanding bit by bit, building on stray, nervous hints my relatives dropped about a certain eccentricity of Jacob's or a crotchet of Uncle Baron's. The theme that united their peculiarities was the socialist politics espoused by both.

A memorable anecdote concerned the time Jacob dragged his daughter Jean's little Earle—only six years old—out of bed on a frigid winter day. Why would he disturb a little boy's rest? And worry his mother so? Going into his room to wake the boy, she found him gone, the door to her father's room open too. Where had they gone? To 30th Street Station in Philadelphia. There, with motley old socialists for company, the little boy shivered while his grandfather and comrades stood at attention for the hero-felon Eugene Debs, just released from jail.

Then there was the perplexing matter of Uncle Baron's refusing a British title. Had many other men of Hebrew extraction been so honored by the king? "Plain Mister is good enough for me," Baron had said, charming his interviewers but exasperating his children. And his perverse choice of residence—not in London or even in the country near his children, but in plebian Hove, near Brighton. With all his money ("Richer than the Rockefellers, that's just what he was!" my aunts would emphasize), what was his point in eschewing the luxuries—a townhouse in Belgravia such as Eddie occupied or even a modest flat off Park Lane—unless, perhaps, to make a point of his humility.

Jacob had a passion, shared with his brother Paul, for the elevation of the Jewish people through physical labor. "Return to the land! Hand *and* brain!" he would thunder, cribbing from Debs. His belief in the salutary effects of bucolic exertion led him, late in life, to propagandize for Stalin's brainchild, the Jewish homeland in Birobidzhan. And his favored punishment for errant juveniles was a spell of summer labor pulling up carrots on Uncle Paul's scraggly farm.

Uncle Baron invariably produced effusions for his workers, those sentimental encomiums delivered at the conclusion of every shareholder meeting and duly transcribed each year in the *London Times* city page.

Dispatched to the family in America by Paul or sometimes Edward, the clippings made clear that no meeting of Carreras ended without a peroration by the Old Man to his able, loyal, skillful, sacrificing, meritorious, and beloved workers in whose debt he, they, nay all England, stood always. Which debt, certain younger members of the family intimated, was most handsomely discharged—not only in such extravagances as three thousand sterling silver medals on velvet ribbons (each engraved "MY THANKS FOR ALL YOUR HELP") presented at the factory's grand opening, as well as the free canteen, the vacations, the paid education, sport facilities, yearly theatricals, and immense bonuses of turkeys, hams, cakes, and cigarettes the entire Carreras staff enjoyed.

In our family, no one expressed open disloyalty to the two old men. To their great credit, my aunts and uncles, great-aunts and great-uncles would stick by the official family story that these were *good* men, loving, kind, providing for their families and striving always to do right. But in more unguarded moments they also let slip how these old fellows certainly did have their *ways*, their *quirks*, and certain topics on which they were—truth be told—a little nuts.

Once they got on these hobbyhorses, try to stop them:

The intrinsic virtue of the worker.

The dignity of labor.

The betterment of humankind through cooperation, innovation, and efficient address of worker grievances.

Through reform if one sought to avoid redistribution; through redistribution if one wanted to head off revolution.

Which was to say through judicious, liberal progressive management.

Their children humored them as best they could, but they were a hard pair to please.

This humoring, I surmise, would have been a large part of what gave Jacob and Uncle Baron their look of constant vexation, the telltale squint or wince before the camera, worn like part of a uniform they donned along with a silk tie or formal cutaway. They were not stupid. Both were more learned and experienced in the world than any of the younger ones. They would have been maddened to know their children winked behind their backs.

"Just a snap of the Guv'ner," writes Paul jauntily from England, dashing off a note in 1928 to his brother Emil, one line of slanting scrawl filling the whole back of the picture of Uncle Baron taken on the day of the great factory's opening, when Baron looked so weary.

Had Jacob picked up the card, his forehead would have puckered too, his jawline tightened. "Guv'ner" was a new locution for Paul, who had arrived in London just two years earlier from Baltimore, where he had worked as a delivery boy. It was a good term, one well adapted to the young man's need to be offhand about the elder who paid his way, a good term for the person to whom he owed his natty suits and cream-colored coupe.

See Paul with roadster. Paul at races. Paul in morning coat. Paul striding, tailored, sleek. Said "snap" was one of many Paul dispatched from Europe's pleasure capitals; his new job was making sure Black Cat and Craven A cigarettes were found at every corner newsstand, on every boulevard.

What *tone*, Paul found, delighted, in the English phrase book, such a fine compendium of usages ready to hand for an Englishman still wet behind the ears. He had been relieved to observe that mastering the English accent was not, as he'd feared, crucial. Learning on the job from brother Eddie, he noticed that the vowels of old Baltimore would at times escape, with no harm done.

Not if one had the touch. The way, at a shareholders meeting (members of the press in the front row) if no one else struck up the cheer for the Old Man, Eddie, standing modestly at the dais, darkly handsome, struck the ringing, rousing vocal salute:

Hear! Hear!

Eddie, Paul noted well, did not attempt to draw the *r* out overmuch. His "Hear Hear" brought the accent down firmly on the hee,

"Snap of the Guv'ner" sent from London by Paul Levy to his brother, Robert Levy, in Baltimore, 1928.

the r's flying straight and unabashed off those long Baltimore vowels. That *r*—along with his ingenuous American grin—begged the room's indulgence for crimes of elocution. If his simple "Hear Hear" did not do the trick, Eddie might then essay the even more adorably English "Hip Hip Hooray." The charm of it was at times sufficient to raise the room and so head off one of the Old Man's lugubrious lectures. It was known, and much appreciated, that Edward took it as his office to watch out for the stockholders. Men leaving their desks in the City were without infinite leisure to listen to lectures.

No fool, the Guv'ner was aware that his presumptive heirs took him for a throwback. He let them laugh. In his will he had safeguarded his principles, giving just enough but no more than was necessary to those who winked, and found a worthy, charitable purpose for every last dime that might otherwise be spent on cocktails or thoroughbreds. By means of a complex set of trusts, he effectually skimmed millions off his fortune, bestowing on worthy causes—his workers, first; then the pioneers in Palestine; North London's foundlings, plus Brighton's and Hove's; diseases of the lung and heart; researches pulmonary, ophthalmological, and gynecological; the Baron Cottages in Sussex; the athletic fields in Regents Park; the Park Tennis Courts; the Liberal Synagogue; the Liberal Party; the Bernhard Baron Settlement House; and only then his son, Louis; and only then his sister, Deborah, in Baltimore, along with her husband Morris; his deceased sister Sarah's husband Paul Levy; Myrtle, Fanny, Jean, Emil, and Robert Levy; and only then, the three boys, brothers, who had taken his name.

For their stewardship, their business acumen, and their sense of honor, when Baron died in 1929 he left to his one son, Louis, and then to his adopted sons Edward, Paul, and Theodore, the magnificent Carreras cigarette factory as well as rights to the patents on the Baron continuous cigarette rolling machine. They might build or wreck as their talents permitted. It was, he would have reckoned, far more than they'd ever have gotten in Baltimore. Jacob's sons were hardly expected to rise to be directors of Carreras cigarettes—with thousands of employees, standing orders around the world, and the largest factory in the metropolis under their supervision. If the Old Man's will came as a surprise or shock, their good English manners would have kept them from breathing a syllable of disappointment in the final disposition of their great benefactor toward them.

Just as Baron's late sense of having miscalculated, having failed to predict the outcome of his generosity, kept him from ever telling them that they had not turned out as he hoped.

⁕

Jacob, who died ten years later, felt no such constraints.

Jacob made sure his last will and testament, written sometime in the spring of 1939, was a masterpiece of acidic pointedness, a document that would bring a laughing *bon vivant* up short.

For a prodigal son could not—even from across an ocean—read the document that arrived in late August 1939 without a pang. "As each of my sons," the abandoned father writes, "is prosperous in his own right, I, Jacob M. Levy, bequeath to my son Paul the sum of one hundred dollars. And to my son Roosevelt Theodore, I bequeath the sum of one hundred dollars." The third son, reading the will, could only feel worse for being singled out: "And to my eldest son, Edward Samson, as he is prosperous in his own right" (again that phrase) "I bequeath the sum of ten dollars and my Morrocan Bound Bible."

In this volume Jacob had placed for Eddie's discovery the clipping dated 1915, in which Edward Levy announced to the world that he "utterly renounced, relinquished and abandoned the use of my said surname of Levy . . . so that I and my heirs lawfully begotten might therefore be called known or distinguished by the surname of Baron."

At the clipping's bottom, Jacob had written: "My first born son, named after my father, Abraham Samson on June 22nd, 1892 at 3 PM."

Edward never collected the Bible. And it was not until 2002 that anyone else saw the clipping Jacob had left in it. Sixty years after Jacob's death, more than twenty after Edward's, I am the one who turns the pages. The clipping slips noiseless from between the Bible's pages, brittle, flat, its fold sharply creased from being pressed inside the book of Exodus for more than half a century. At first I think it is something cut in half, a bookmark perhaps.

But it isn't. It is the shocking clipping preserved whole, and the answer to why Jacob had added an extra bequest for Edward. I see that the note in the Bible was meant to leave his son with the sense that his father had died still grieving over the son's defection, so fundamentally terrible as to alter the family tree itself.

When I spread the clipping out on the desk I can see how significant, how full of import and reproach, Jacob meant his gesture to be. Reading the sad, carefully penciled postscript, I feel—for the first time—the grandeur of my great-grandfather's anger, and how the literate, civilized means he used to express that anger perhaps exceeded the capacity of the persons he was angry at to understand. I thought then of Jacob's cane, its inscriptions long unread, with certain sardonic hints in its correct but telegraphic inscription intimating the inevitable incommunicability of one generation's core beliefs to those that followed.

I see something else. Perhaps I wanted to see it so badly that I have claimed an inheritance never meant for me. Holding that clipping, I see my great-grandfather as the scholar, the bibliophile, the thoughtful polymath he was. He eased his moods, his anger, his discontent and disappointment by sitting at the desk and typing, typing, typing. Just as I do.

He was a man who wrote.

I was, I hope, not so foolish as to think myself in any occult sense his addressee, or even to imagine that he'd not have traded a great-granddaughter in love with his precise, sardonic ire for a son who would simply keep his name.

Yet in studying the documents, the clipping, and the will, I feel closer to him and fancy him closer to me, due to the fact that this man seems to have typed his last will and testament himself. The font of this document is the same as I find in others—all those indignant, rueful missives on the letterhead of Levy's International Shrinking that he dispatched over the years. He would not have been too sensitive to send a grandson to fetch a book on probate, a template for wills, from the public library, and then, on the same typewriter used for so many animadversions to The Editor, the typewriter on which he'd schooled himself in perfect written English, to compose a parting rebuke to sons.

Learned, solitary, scholarly; impatient, rude, in love with ideas, Jacob is naturally the ancestor I hoped to find—and so I am not to be trusted in claiming him as such. And yet, holding the clipping and then holding the photocopy of it up to the pages of the will and testament, I still feel the quality of ardent *will* he made his will convey, and I admire and approve the writerly means he used to make this will known.

The sin of my great-grandfather's sons, the crime they had committed, is a simple, primal one: betrayal, for which he must have held himself at least partly responsible. His will is not only an angry and hurtful document but a self-wounding one. Rather than simply disinheriting his sons, it guarantees their refusal of inheritance in bequests too poor to be worth accepting. A man does not board an ocean liner to collect his father's spite. Sparing the sons the trouble of collecting his blame, yet blaming them because he spared them, Jacob's anger at his sons becomes anger at himself. His anger at Bernhard Baron had a more poignant source.

It was not for luring his sons to give up their birthright, to leave their father, their sick mother, and their widowed sisters. The sons had decided to do these things themselves.

It was not just for Bernhard's enticing them from the New World back to the Old, back to the lands of kings and emperors. No respecter of nations, Jacob knew the United States was as liable to favor the powerful and rich as any princely state or kingdom.

It was not even that Bernhard took away his own workforce, his own future, leaving him alone in Philadelphia and Robert alone in Baltimore to manage the larger plant. It was not just that Baron took the sons in and made them his heirs but that he made them *heirs* at all.

Worldly persons would not doubt that his sons were fortunate. Their handsome offices; their outrageous Egyptian boardroom; the drivers waiting by their cars; the honor they enjoyed owing to the founder's own spotless reputation—all these showed them to be world cynosures of commerce, notables of Europe's Hebrew elite. Their wives (handpicked for them by Bernhard) meanwhile kept themselves busy with decorative and philanthropic offices.

But this was not what either Jacob or Bernhard had meant when they spoke of *civilization*.

May you be, Jacob had said in a letter to his grandson Earle, a "leading agent of civilization." Earle was now Bernhard's agent, the "civilization" he guarded was Bernhard's Canadian, Australian, and South African interests. Was this what Jacob and Bernhard wanted, this what they struggled in Baltimore together to advance—to produce fine examples of the ruling class?

Well might Bernhard look disconsolate in the photos Jacob saw of him. The world might deem him a success but the man who knew best, Jacob, could see his failure. For had he not failed in doing what he wanted to get done?

Lionized the world over for creating the first truly global luxury by putting Black Cat and Craven A cigarettes in the hands of rich and poor, men, women, and children, Bernhard had also surpassed whatever the unionists had done in helping those who worked for him lead better lives.

But having sworn, having promised on his heart to make Jacob's sons Great Men, he made of them something far more meager: rich men.

Having set out to perfect the very machinery of civilization—using the cigarette as his tool—what had Bernhard produced in the end but an excellent machine?

❧

Today it strikes us as strange that Bernhard Baron would ever have imagined the cigarette to be a vehicle of progress or enlightenment.

But it is a fact of American, and indeed world, history that between the American Civil War and World War I no product, no industry better exemplified the struggle and gains made for social progress than tobacco did. Toxic and intoxicating, lethal and luxurious, tobacco's complex history parallels the history of American social progress.

Tobacco's effect has always been to concentrate power in the hands of the few and enslave the many. The "bewitching vegetable," the tobacco that brought the first colonists to America, also established the colony's first leisure class and forced its first labor shortages. Tobacco precipitated the importation and breeding of American slaves. Tobacco's power to line pockets, and thus the influence it exerted in favor of colonial dependence, strengthened the loyalist cause and deferred the struggle for American independence, while the model of land use tobacco farmers pioneered before independence—break new ground, use it up, push westward—provided a template for the antebellum Cotton Kingdom's spread to larger and larger tracts of frontier.

None of the above could be called progressive. And yet the same tobacco debt that bound Americans to British colonial power eventually, in the late eighteenth century, fostered a growing commitment to revolution. The spread of slavery from coast to tidewater, to Appalachian rim, to the Mississippi and beyond, spurred the development of free labor, and free soil, ideology. With the Civil War over, tobacco culture once again became a staging ground for shifts in attitude and policy, fresh evaluations of industrial, social, and specifically labor policy.

Between the 1860s and World War I, developments in tobacco culture mirrored the development of modern standards of access, of protection and justice. Tobacco's rising popularity counterpointed struggles for:

- Equality between the sexes—and exploitation of women
- Unregulated industry—and workplace safety
- Accessible luxuries for the masses—and the concept of public health
- The growth of advertising—and investigative journalism

Tobacco became the symbol of monopoly—and trust busting. Mostly, though, tobacco had become the talisman of the parlous situation of American labor and, in particular, the twin labor crises brought on by emancipation and mechanization. The fundamentals of extracting profit from tobacco without using slaves exposed the relative primitiveness of homegrown labor theory, making America face the futility of its old commercial and labor practices and requiring new ideas, symbols, and even new heroes of American labor.

It is a largely forgotten bit of history, but the American labor movement found its first modern leaders in the cigar industry, its cynosures and vanguard in the bookish agitators of the International Cigar Makers 144th. The first truly national labor leaders were German speakers who hailed from the cigar towns of central Europe. Accented, argumentative, intellectual, the cigar maker was the aristocrat and cynosure of progress. And if, among his fellows, the cigar maker was known as the most cerebral of workingmen—the vocation of cigar maker an alias for social theorist—he had a reputation too for intelligence of craft, for hands that not only rolled tobacco but knew it. An internationalist in politics, the European cigar maker in postbellum America was nevertheless a hot commodity. He had a skill backed by centuries of craft tradition, and this was worth something to an industry suddenly without captive labor.

In the hands of men with names like Gompers, Strasser, and yes, Baron, rested American tobacco's world market.

That begins to explain why, from the first day he arrived in America, Bernhard Baron would have found himself in some demand. He did not have much money, but what he did have—a thorough knowledge of tobacco—was worth a lot to an industry trying to lift itself out of a Civil War past and get onto a more solid footing.

One thing to remember is that in 1870, tobacco in America was ubiquitous but also déclassé. In England tobacco had traveled straight from Sir Walter Raleigh's pocket to Elizabeth Regina's court. And in Europe, centuries of ingenuity, art, and science had been lavished on finding a market niche for every smoker's taste and pocketbook—from the paper-wrapped, rapidly consumed smokes popular with soldiers and workingmen, to the silk-wrapped "parparos" rolled for ladies' fingers; from the carefully compounded mixtures whose elegance derived from "purity" of leaf (the exclusive use of choice "Turkish" or other

"Oriental" strains), to blends that made up in smoothness, steady burn, or complex flavor what they might lack in pedigree. Moreover, Europeans had created ever more elaborate devices for the enjoyment of tobacco (cloisonné snuff boxes, gold cigarette holders, carved cigar boxes, silk embroidered pouches, meerschaum, amber, ivory) and had developed a genuine tobacco culture, including a polite literature extolling the charms of tobacco in many languages.

In America, tobacco's uses were crude, its signs visible in stains on walls, inside and out, and the sight of men—cheeks bulging—expectorating long ribbons of tobacco juice. The "chaw" was the preferred form of tobacco in the New World. Marketing tobacco to the better classes was an uphill battle. For a long time Europeans had been remarking the American fondness for the spittoon, marveling both at its ubiquity and its inutility. Why provide the revolting cuspidor, they asked each other, since, as Charles Dickens was hardly first to notice, few used it.

Where then, after the Civil War, could hungry American tobacco entrepreneurs go to find examples of refined tobacco use? To whom did rising tobacco magnates Duke and Liggett, Kinney, Lorillard, and the Ginters go to recruit their talent?

Where but to the workshops up and down the coast, from New Haven to the Carolinas, where German (Jewish) émigrés were employed. Hailing from the river towns and industrial ports of German-speaking Europe, where every hamlet with a slimy dock had its tobacco "factory," the German immigrants of midcentury brought to the west the talents of the tobacco-using east.

Brest, the town from which Uncle Baron hailed, was not quite as large a tobacco center as nearby Grodno, but circa 1850 it had five factories within the city limits, four of them devoted to the processing and manufacture of tobacco products. Moreover, the very first factory to open in the raw frontier town of Rostov-on-Don (where the Baron family moved in the 1850s) was—what else—a tobacco factory, opened to meet the demand of soldiers fighting in Crimea.

From such a place my Uncle Baron, and many other immigrant Jews like him who had worked in the tobacco factories, brought ripened talents and a sense of dignified vocation. They brought their long-nurtured pride in craft and their esteem for the product, as well as the adaptability of persons accustomed to living with and through disruption.

Ten, twenty, forty Jews might be brought to Carolina to teach the locals refinements of rolling and curing, the proper way to strip a leaf, and then sent back on a third class car, one way to Baltimore, where every second immigrant had relatives. Some manufacturers recruited whole villages of rollers from muddy Bohemian or Belorussian sloughs. Agents would land at Bremen or Hamburg and send scouts down the riverways, and then the manufacturers would raid each other, stealing the cream of the cigar makers and spiriting them from city to city.

The late-nineteenth-century émigré cigar maker was perceived to have qualities that made him valuable indeed in newly corporate America.

❧

The only problem with these émigrés: their ideas.

Along with their talents, the European cigar makers brought habits of thought. They brought ideas about feudalism, serfdom, radical socialism and syndicalism, anarchism, trade unionism, craft unionism, Marxian and Lasallean communism, and every other ism filling the journals of the day. They brought conceptions of the workingman more nuanced than those of "slave" or "free" that had engrossed American labor thinkers hitherto. With their knowledge of blends and growing conditions, stripping, and the crucial matter of the wrapper, they also brought outrage at risks a tobacco laborer was heir to, all the toxic syndromes and economic inequities of the trade.

They had expertise in the muscular limits of the human hand, the vertebral column, the nerve tunnels running from wrist to shoulder.

They knew the vulnerability of the human lung to fine particulates.

They knew the long-term effects of an unlit workspace on the eye; the contribution of unventilated workshops to the spread of the scourge, tuberculosis. They knew too that TB (along with grippe, bronchial ailments, influenza) spread from producer to consumer through the saliva on a cheaply sealed cigar.

They realized the impacts of child labor on juvenile growth, education, and opportunity.

They recognized the effects of child labor on an adult breadwinner's livelihood.

They saw the effect of falling prices due to overproduction or increased demand on a cigar maker's income.

They saw the insult to craft, craftsmanship, and product quality in the breaking up of tasks once performed by one craftsman into mechanical operations.

They witnessed the insult to manliness, family, and domestic peace in employing women and children to replace the skilled craftsman.

They endured the insult to manliness in replacing the craftsman's delicate intuition and dexterous hands with the cigar mold.

They suffered the atrophy of mind and spirit in a workday reduced to repetitive motion, and the atrophy of hope in a workweek without Sabbath or any surcease.

To all of these risks the German cigar maker who had seen everything now saw something new—the effect of slavery's abolition on the price of labor throughout the United States. Wages in the postbellum South depressed wages everywhere, for the tobacconist now hired free men but still needed to make a profit. The shift from slavery to sharecropping meant that the man who had picked tobacco at someone else's pleasure, poorly fed, badly housed, now picked tobacco as a free man. What was the difference? In 1869, the "Tobacco Factory Mechanicks of Richmond and Manchester" wrote to a newspaper, "Our masters hired us to the Tobacconist . . . the tobacconist furnished us lodging food and clothing." Now these same employers offered a wage, but from this wage workers had somehow to pay for bed and board. The workers wrote, "They say we will starve through laziness this is not so. But it is true we will starve at our present wages."

To compete, northern tobacco manufacturers cut labor costs to the bone, developing various schemes to keep the workforce stable and cheap, especially the system of urban sharecropping that became the cause célèbre of the Cigar Makers Union. "Cigar makers," Samuel Gompers explained, "paid rent to their employer for living room which was also their work space, bought from him their supplies, furnished their own tools and received in turn a small wage for completed work, sometimes in scrip or in supplies from the company store." Gompers warned that such a system would eventuate in the circumstantial destruction of both peaceful homes and dignified labor. Jacob Riis devoted a whole chapter to this situation in *How the Other Half Lives*. Riis found hovels where "a man and wife [are] working the bench from six in the morning until nine at night. She strips, he makes the filler; she rolls the wrapper on and finishes the cigar." For a thousand cigars they earn 3.75. They manufacture 3000 cigars a week. This is one a minute on a two person assembly line.

In postbellum America the gap left by the abolition of slavery opened new vistas of degradation for the tobacco worker. But he also had ideas.

⁕

"We chose someone to read to us," explained Samuel Gompers, "who was a particularly good reader, and in payment the rest of us gave him sufficient of our cigars that he was not the loser." A quiet task, requiring dexterous hands but leaving the intellect unoccupied, cigar rolling afforded long hours for conversation and brought a man of thoughtful bent into contact with like-minded others. Cigar factories up and down the Atlantic coast were sites of lively seminars in social thought. Debating in both German and English, habitués of these cigar salons viewed their workshops as satellites of London and Vienna, outposts of internationalist thought.

David Hirsch's shop, for instance, where Gompers worked, was, as contemporary accounts suggest, less a cigar factory that happened to employ men of intellectual bent than a sort of reading room for socialists. There the German intellectual tradition blew strong day and night, émigrés keeping themselves and families in groceries at the bench but keeping their minds—and hopes—alive with Marx, Lasalle, Bernstein, and Owen. German speakers like Adolph Strasser and English speakers like Samuel Gompers exchanged labor theories and language tutorials. The 1870s were, as Sorge, the American head of the International Workingman's Organization, called them, "the period of highest accomplishment . . . when real true wage earners and craftsman of all possible trades . . . competed with each other in learning economics." It was generally agreed that the cigar rollers set the tone and held the center, their eloquence preparing the ground for the next generation's leap into progressive reform.

They might work with their hands, they theorized, but this did not make their work brutal or unintelligent. Between "manu-facture" and mere "manual labor" was the skilled worker, whose dexterous (rather than automatic) motions, his diligent (rather than coerced) industry, whose mindful (not absent-minded) agency conferred human value on mere matter.

❧

In the New York Public Library, scrolling year by year through the microfilm of the city directory, I find Uncle Baron's first actual address in America.

Living on Broome Street in 1873, he is not yet Bernhard but Bernhardt. He lives a few streets south of his famous bench mate, still

Gomperz, Samuel, occupation also listed as "seegarmaker." I surmise that as I find no trace of him in New York before this date, he probably lived for a few years in the basest poverty, flush days allowing him a flop in one of the dormitory "hotels" in which single men, for three or four cents, could buy the use of a canvas hammock.

Later pictures of Uncle Baron tell me what he would have looked like in 1873, age twenty-three, rolling cigars on his bench and listening to the philosophers of the 144th union spin out their debates, perhaps even adding a thought of his own. From the pictures of the mustached older man, vest buttoned over his squarish torso, I summon up a solid youngster on the edge of manhood. Not tall but robust looking, with a strong nose, narrow nostrils, brownish hair, and dark brows, he tilts his head as he listens to the dialogue, drinks in the rhetoric.

What is to be done? (This is what they ask each other.)

What is to be done to ameliorate the suffering, the ignorance, the poor health, and the hunger of the working man?

What is to be done to free the textile worker, the man in the field, the hauler, the stevedore, the grimy factory operative?

What is to be done to feed his belly, to nourish his brain, to realize for him and his fellows the intrinsic dignity of the worker?

With eloquence, with learnedness, with disputes sometimes so heated that a man throws down his work, stalks out, and is not seen again, the cigar makers among whom my Uncle Baron spent his first years in America asked always the same question, in many forms: "What is to be done?"

Sometime in 1873 or 1874 Uncle Baron disappeared from the Broome Street address.

David Jeremy, in the entry for Bernhard Baron in his volume *Business Leaders of England*, places him at that time in New Haven, the tobacco center of New England, selling cigars to Yale College students, and then has him in New York working through 1875 or 1876 for F. S. Kinney, who produced the Sweet Caporal cigarette, the first European-style parparo produced in the United States.

Kinney would have done well to hire Uncle Baron; he was among the most aggressive Americans hoping to make the cigarette sell. A more interesting possibility, though, is that in 1875 none other than James Buchanan Duke spirited Baron away from Kinney in one of his many raids on Kinney's workforce, taking to his bosom the man who would, twenty years later, foil Duke's takeover of the European cigarette business. This would explain my Uncle Baron's claim to have spent many of his early nights in America in "tobacco sheds," as well as his frequent reminder that between 1875 and 1895 not a year went by that he did not see for himself the cultivation, harvest, and cure of the tobacco grown in Virginia, Maryland, and the Carolinas.

Perhaps it begins to explain as well the pity, the sentiment, the passion that inspired Baron as, in his last bent years, a scion of London with every comfort, he seemed unwilling to allow himself or anyone to forget the world's unfortunates, so that he sometimes appeared gripped by memories he could not keep down, his voice on the speaker's platform going reedy with urgency.

He had himself seen the epitome of human exploitation in the lot of the tobacco workers of Brest and Rostov. There he had seen the haze of golden dust disperse, the fine brown particles settling on the sleeve, and had cocked an ear to hear the telltale cough. He had observed fetid alley homes and the cramped planks where men and women slept, immodest, filthy, hungry. He felt indignation that anyone should be forced to work in hard or unhealthful conditions, felt with conviction that the duty of the fortunate is to assist the unfortunate.

It was then that he fell prey to a tenderness—this perhaps more than anything else—for the poor mother's child who, at the end of a long day, made his bed in a tobacco shed.

In the Baker Library at Harvard University I first see Uncle Baron in high resolution, as he was when Jacob Levy first met him in Baltimore.

The original ledgers of Dun's Baltimore credit inspectors, now held at Baker Library, contain long entries on Uncle Baron. The inspectors reported on him twice a year, noting his energy and success in building a growing tobacco concern.

In careful, close handwriting the inspectors note (November 1879) the establishment of Baron and Company Cigars in Baltimore, headed by one Bernhardt Baron (of Russian Jewish extraction), whom former employers call an "honest reliable man: prospects excellent." After the next visit, observing that Baron is said to be "upright in all his transactions," the inspectors also describe him as "an active, pushing man doing a good cautious trade." In June 1880 his capital is estimated at "3 to 4 thousands," but a few months later they round it off to 5 and note, approvingly, the acquisition of a partner, one Bernhard Heinebach, who adds $12,500 to the capital. Inspectors on February 7, 1881, report that while Baron has been burned out of his former factory space, he is insured, and that by March, with working capital of $10,000, he is moving into new larger spaces on East Pratt. By 1884, "encumbered by a ground rent" he has "15 or 16 thousand in capital, is in good repute at his bank and works with comparatively light expenses." The handwriting of a new inspector notes the acquisition of a new investor and partner, Hy Krauss.

He notes too that Baron is now "employing a number of the boys at St. Mary's Industrial School." Krauss attends to financial matters, the inspector notes approvingly, while Baron shuttles between the Pratt Street factory and spending time with the Negro boys of the Industrial School.

In 1884 his business is estimated to be worth "30,000." He works 150 hands, sells to the best trade, to "first class parties."

It is clear that Dun's inspectors like and approve of my Uncle Baron.

❧

I am swept up in the excitement of his rising success.

Uncle Baron has been dead for 90 years, and it is almost 120 years since he left Baltimore, but as I read and reread volume 9 of Dun's I feel proud of his honesty, his good sense, and his exceptional kindness. The boys of the St. Mary's School, the poorest of the Negro unfortunates, have few patrons like Uncle Baron, the man I see more and more clearly as solid, serious, with a warm face under his bristling hair.

I see him in various scenarios—journeying by streetcar to St. Mary's, returning to his red brick house—a whole house, large enough for a family—on Sharp Street, writing letters in his cubby of an office, in a firm and careful hand. By this time, summer 1884, the Dun's inspectors note that though "burnt out again" he is again rebuilding. My great-grandfather Jacob would have arrived in Baltimore by then and met the man who would profoundly affect his family's destiny. I cannot picture Jacob yet, but his mentor, his patron, his new marvelous friend holds the center of scenes fully formed in my mind.

One scene has lodged in my imagination so long that I believe it happened.

A summer's day in August 1884. The closeness of the inland town unbearable, heat like a lid on the fetid streets, Uncle Baron sits under the fan in a pump room on Thames Street, Fells Point. There is a breeze, if a somewhat noxious one; the moist air off Locust Point brings the stink of oysters, tomatoes, and beans rotting to mush on cannery floors.

Leaning forward at the wooden bar, Uncle Baron pushes his stein across the slick bar, buffs the wobbly circle dry with the tail of his coat. Then he draws a pack of oblong papers from his pocket, then a little chamois pouch, breathes its sweet moisture, and shakes something out on the precious slip of paper.

The tobacco is warm and moist from the humidor of his trouser pocket, but the paper is so dry and silken he can't catch it on his calluses, can't roll a smoke of uniform length and bulk with any reasonable consistency. If Bernhard Baron can't roll a perfect cigarette more than two times out of three, who can?

What option is there, he thinks, what choice for a man of advanced views, but to use some machine, some device for rolling the cigarette.

Not, he thinks (now experimentally pressing the cylinder into the bar's guttered lip; bracing the roll on either end with two matchbooks) to do away with a manly craft. Not (and this would be worse) to visit on little hands of children the burning, the numbness, that he and every cigar roller sometimes suffered.

But somehow, rather, to preserve and also to humanize this more delicate work for men of craft—while also making it pay for one such as he, one devoted (as his circulars promised, and as he told Dun's adjusters) to "liberal and progressive" enterprise.

He would never deny that the cigar mold had brought on deepening troubles. Through the 1860s and 1870s cigar rollers had pronounced the cigar mold the weapon of capital, and what's more, the end of the rollers' manly independence. A device that made it possible for any "colored" woman, any Russian Jewish child, to roll a cigar was a threat to the old guildists and the New World protégés alike. Their arguments had merit.

But he knew too, in his own fingers and wrists, just how damaging the manly craft of cigar rolling was to hands. Late in life, if in sleep his right hand should curl a certain way, reflex would lock it in an angled cup, and he would wake, working nervous fingers up and down a wrapper, the pain locking his thumb to wrist, elbow to scapula.

In the new factory on East Pratt, Baron and Company, he would need to have Kraus watch sharply. The workers should rotate tasks: mornings, palms up; afternoons, palms down. Kraus would have to see to it that the "Germans" gave the colored men their turns at rolling while they trimmed or bunched.

Not that any of the men, except for the few yeshiva bred, minded the dark girls trimming for them. It was sharing the bench with the men that raised hackles. Baron had often seen younger Bohemians "teaching" the girls how to roll, their gartered sleeves wrapping the thin backs. This was another matter Kraus would need to manage.

He had, of course, let himself in for more of it last night. Boarding the train back from the Wilson auction—his shipment paid for and due at Locust Point by month's end—he had hoisted his satchel into the Negro car. Amid the crumbs and greasy paper of Negro families, he slept fitfully, drifting in and out over the rattle and the bickering of three boys whose parents were too exhausted to scold. At dawn he had hired the whole family—mother, father, and boys—to work for him.

Experience told him that the mother would be easiest to put in the line, for her fingers were slender and long. But she would soon see a better opportunity, putting herself out to service on Lombard Street.

But her man, half her size, needed the indoor job more. Too slight for dock work and unlikely, with that short curing-house cough, to adapt to the wind and slush of the oyster sheds, he would, with luck, prove to have a good eye for examining tobacco. Someone needed to look out for badly cured lots or too much cheap burley. Baron liked the idea of this man, with his quick looks and air of caution, becoming a silent adjutant to Kraus. He added an offer to slip the two older boys in with the St. Mary's lads. They could learn the trade and also have some schooling. The little one would have to stay with some alley-house woman.

In Baltimore in the early 1880s Baron had begun work on the machine that would carry him and others to London.

After the boys of St. Mary's finished sweeping up and Heinebach left, Baron stayed in the factory, tools scattered around his workbench—wrenches, tiny screwdrivers, and baskets of standardized parts, the kind that came in kits obtainable through *Inventors* magazine.

Big manufacturers were crying out for an automatic cigarette rolling machine. Prototypes had been built; the Bonsack, winner of Allen and Ginter's contest, was the first. But none so far could run continuously, and so Baron used his many lonely evenings to stay at the factory, working on his own version of the automatic cigarette machine.

He was often alone in these years. Within three or four years of arriving in New York he had acquired a wife, which meant a wife and parents, who were in-laws of the tidy, fussy, German Jewish kind. Moving them all to Baltimore in the late 1870s had been harder than he'd expected. His son Louis, a softhearted, loving boy, showed an aptitude for the business, even accompanying him to the factory and to St. Mary's, though his wife expressed her worries about Louis be-friending the boys there. The girls, however, longed for their cousins back in New York. They found Baltimore hot, alarming with its rov-ing Negroes, and too full of steep hills.

So more and more he sent his wife and the girls on the train to New York, which was why he spent so many nights at the factory, sometimes falling asleep, as so often in the past, with the smell of to-bacco, the siftings of tobacco under his head.

In 1881 or 1882, with business thriving and the newspapers re-porting a clear downturn for Jews all over the Russian empire (even in Riga there were incidents), he hit upon the idea of finally bringing his two sisters to join him.

He knew in his heart that he could have done this long before and that the idea now was for selfish reasons. He had concluded that more family—girls in particular—might help his daughters acclimate to their new city, might provide more of that atmosphere of giggles, bows, and furbelows they craved. His sister Deborah was a dowager with children. Her girls—Amelia, Lena, Lilly—were more or less his girls' age and hardly a comedown, hailing as they did from Riga, as elegantly "German" as one could desire.

Moreover, Sarah, eight years younger than her dour sister and still unmarried, might act as older sister, taking some burden off his wife, who was not robust. He was under no illusions that the whole plan would be cheap. Deborah would be, if he knew her, disinclined to be-stir herself from where she was, being suspicious of America and miffed to be summoned after so long. She would need a house big enough for her crowd of petticoats, and her husband Moses Elfant—Morris, they could call him—would need some sort of employment, something to write on the line in the city directory next to the address. Oh well. He would not be the only skinny pious apple of his family's eye to find himself in America assisting his stout, bossy wife at the counter.

Best perhaps he would bring the younger sister, Sarah—round, sweet, curly haired Sarah—first. She had a beau, a boy at polytechnic studying agronomy and one who'd already changed his name from Perel or Pinchas to Paul and whom Deborah and Morris suspected of "radicalism."

So much the better!

Perhaps an agronomist with progressive tendencies might be just the help he needed—showing talent at choosing leaf, an expert in worms or acidity of soil. He had a need for competent, educated people at Baron and Company, and he could use a capable brother-in-law. Or two. If the boy Paul was serious about Sarah, he'd bring him over and his younger brother Jacob also.

This was how it happened that in 1881, when Jacob visited Paul in Riga, where he'd met his brother's beloved Sarah, he might first have heard from Paul about the notion of going to America. Bernhard had written more than once to say that Baron and Company was now on solid footing, and why shouldn't Sarah come to Baltimore. If she and Paul were serious about each other, she could bring Paul along as well as his brother Jacob. As soon as they said the word he would send steamship tickets—Bremen to Baltimore.

SEVEN

Beautiful Machines

Down the hall to Aunt Myrtle's apartment I went, walking slowly, a week after her funeral in 1995, to see the things still left unclaimed and to choose what I'd like to be mine. It was the first time I had ever walked that hall without finding Aunt Myrtle there to greet me.

Aunt Myrtle and Aunt Fanny lived, for the first ten years of my life, in two garden apartments in the same sprawling brick complex in Philadelphia. In the mid-1970s, when their father's business—begun in 1900 in his Baltimore basement, its name now changed from Levy's International Shrinking Company to Synthetics Finishing and its clients now worldwide—was thriving, my aunts' sons Fred and Dan moved both of them to elegantly appointed condominiums so that they could enjoy their last years in style.

A visit to either sister went like this.

After parking in the spot marked "Visitor," the visiting family informed the doorman that they were here to call on Mrs. Rosenstein or Mrs. Goldman, depending on which of the two had decided to serve today's guests. Either way, the doorman would nod politely, smiling with his eyes as he glanced us up and down, noticing the spit and polish of children dressed on a Wednesday afternoon as for a holiday.

When I visited my aunts I was literally dressed for a holiday, having been decked out in a frock my mother had bought with checks from the aunts. My own birthday checks—fifteen dollars from Fanny, ten from Myrtle, five from Jean (in exact reverse order of their means)—were for me to spend on anything I wanted, but in years when my young parents were pinched, in the same mail as my three birthday cards my mother would receive checks for new clothes for the Jewish High Holidays.

There were various important reasons that the doorman should duly announce our arrival. For propriety's sake, of course, but also because his intercom connected to the system of flashing lights rigged up to accommodate the growing deafness of the aunts, though Aunt Myrtle got her flashing lights a full five years after Fanny. Indeed, among the many meaningless but funny competitions these devoted sisters engaged in, Aunt Myrtle prided herself in being not nearly as deaf as Fanny, her younger sister.

While we rose in the elevator Aunt Myrtle, having been alerted by the doorman, would post herself at her doorway, standing on the threshold so that one saw the tips of her little shoes and the forward poof of the hairdo she had done the day before in preparation for us. Not five feet tall, she did her best to stand at attention, to square her shoulders against the osteoporosis that was curling her. At the end of the hall she smiled, the sconces in the hall giving her thick glasses a merry glint and her arms opening to draw a child in with, "There's my little girl!"

I think Aunt Myrtle adopted this rather formal greeting because she knew she could never replace the welcome she'd offered children in her old garden apartment. The new greeting at the end of the hall, though warm, was a makeshift adaptation of her former famous and more intimate ritual of welcome, one impossible in a doorman building. Our letdown feeling in the elevator was unavoidable, but on see-

ing her down the hall, we were consoled to realize she'd devised this
second ritual for us, for all the children young and old who might
miss her old "helll-*eeoo*-whoo-hoo." In earlier times, Aunt Myrtle's
apartment had been up a flight of steps behind a garden level outer
door. Halfway up, this door had a hinged flap for the mailman. Before
the stairs became too much for her, Aunt Myrtle would descend to
the vestibule and fit her fingers through this mail slot. By the time we
knocked, she would be calling from behind the glass with her trilling,
multisyllabled "Helll-*eeoo*-whoo-hoo," the red ovals of her manicure
waggling toward us and the Baltimore vowels waggling too.

Now Aunt Myrtle was gone, and there was, it turned out, much too
much in her apartment for me to choose from.

With Aunt Jean so recently gone and Aunt Fanny ailing too, assorted women of the family had already carted away silver trays and
sundry vegetable dishes. The younger of us, granddaughters and
great-nieces, tended to have jobs that brought us home at seven
o'clock to untidy houses piled with red plastic toys. It was hard to
find occasions to use the Limoges and Lladro, Baccarat and Wedge-
wood, the stemware, flatware, the napery we'd been given at various
showers and engagement fetes.

Even more than Fanny's, Aunt Myrtle's apartment was an altar to
the decorative arts, celebrating that abundantly tufted epoch after
Victorian but before art nouveau whose style I think of as the Age of
B: vaguely belle epoque, faintly beaux arts, and certainly a bit Baroque. My aunts, who were born in its heyday and raised in a Baltimore townhouse with two pianos and parlors both upstairs and down,
had tastes that belonged to an exuberantly feminine age, when every
object not curved could be dispatched to a room for gentlemen only.
Femininity was given free rein, so that the objects seemed not merely
material and talismanic but intimate and resonant: emanations of

Woman, and of style itself as a female faculty. This feminine claim on a whole age, a whole culture, was unmistakable.

But in pacing Aunt Myrtle's rooms, I saw that was not all.

It was not just the female expressed by the naiads and vines twining cups in the breakfront, by the curve of the chair legs, by the silver in its velvet-lined drawer, not even just the female expressed in several sets of dessert dishes, and not even just a vision of *comme il faut.*

No, Aunt Myrtle's things were also an avowal, a celebration even, of things that were *made,* evidence of ingenuity's triumph over randomness, of skill's transcendence over brute force.

Even before I found in Aunt Myrtle's closet (behind the automatic card shuffler, the box of crayons and other toys, and under her Persian lamb coat) the one precious item, my own most beautiful machine, I had begun to understand the particular satisfaction my aunts took in being the children of manufacturers, the strong correlation between complexities of production and refinements of civilization. The home into which they were born and the men who superintended their growth were joined in a common view of what industry could do to improve the world. For these men, not only progress but civilization itself would be made by machine, and the prosperity of the world would be in the hands of inventors.

It was a giddying vision.

> Could a man of the last century—A Franklin or a Priestley— have seen . . . the forest tree transformed into finished lumber— into doors, sashes, blinds, boxes or barrels, with scarcely the touch of a human hand . . . steam hammers shaping mighty shafts and mighty anchors, and delicate machinery making tiny watches . . . his heart would have leaped and his nerves would have thrilled.

Henry George's words above capture some of the excitement felt by young men in the late-nineteenth-century booming industrial city of Baltimore, a city of smokestacks and rails whose steel possessed, as one historian put it, a feverish and lifelike energy.

Baltimore had always prospered from innovation, since the abundance of the American continent was sent abroad through its port. Tobacco was the first important article of trade. Its delicacy had presented numerous technical challenges, including challenges of preservation that were applicable to keeping other goods—flour, spice, oysters—free from spoilage. It had a long-established infrastructure for manufacturing, plus far-flung networks of commerce with close ties to Germany, whose industrial juggernaut was transforming Europe.

A person arriving in Baltimore in 1881 or 1882, perhaps following Paul Levy from the railway station, could observe in moments the transformation wrought by machines. On little platforms over the water were canneries, oysteries, and stripping sheds for tobacco. On the docks themselves and in the streets just inland from the port, workers engaged in the ruder trades. But now among the butchers, the carpenters, and draymen appeared small workshops, and every day newspaper advertisements solicited skilled machinists, molders, box makers, photographers, and sponger/shrinkers. Alongside the classified columns were advertisements for a plethora of goods whose salient claim was the newness that can only be possessed by machine-made goods.

Machines are attractive! The city directory for Baltimore in 1888 shows an increasing number of persons willing to pay extra so they could offer the "latest improvements" as well as the most "up-to-date" and "up-to-the minute" characteristics of their goods. This new form of business, which preserved what had once been wasted—space, money, and labor—needed to project itself beyond the local into a world of yet uncalculated need. Every manufacturer marketing the new had to offer not only craftsmanship or personal service but the capacity to ship to "any city," to cover "all businesses and professions." To make it in Baltimore was to make it in other port cities, by mass-producing uniqueness, patenting the inimitable, and saving labor.

Adding to the industrial exuberance of this city, the 1880s saw the arrival of the world's most impassioned theorists of modern industrial life—the émigrés establishing a German beachhead at the Johns Hopkins University. By day, they taught the first American graduate seminar, with an emphasis on social thought. After hours, retiring to the handsome new German blocks of Eutaw Place, they gathered at one another's houses, smoking the good local cigars and discussing matters of political economy which they then applied to Baltimore's dynamic scene. For them, Baltimore became the outpost of European labor theory on the application of machines to any city's labor community.

Political economists found Baltimore to be an ideal laboratory for their studies of labor and the machine and social advancement. The American born but German-trained Richard Ely, endeavoring at the newly endowed Johns Hopkins to put economics on a modern— German—footing, was as convincing as George that the age of craft was passing and that of machines was nigh. Lecturing at Mechanics Hall, teaching night courses and serving on the tax and relief commissions, Ely expressed an unmistakable sympathy for collective versus individual well being. By the time Ely published his *Political Economy* in 1889 as a primer in the Chautauqua self-improvement series, he had tested its chapters in Baltimore workmen's halls, speaking for industrial training as well as labor organizations with their heated discussions, political life with universal suffrage, and "labor-saving inventions."

Jacob Levy, arriving in Baltimore in 1884, would have been delivered into the very workshop of progress, and, what's more, into companionship more congenial and intellectual ferment more exciting and free than was ever imagined in Shavli. Moreover, if work for a man with mechanical skills was plentiful, he'd have found in his brother Paul's little shop some space and materials to begin his own projects. In his first year Jacob told the city directory people his profession was locksmith, but he soon learned skills with gears that entitled him to call himself a machinist.

It was not what he wanted ultimately, but "machinist" described his interests and gave him a bit of independence from his brother Paul's new brother-in-law, Bernhard Baron, whose kindness to Paul and Sarah and now to himself could not be denied. With Paul's own pants shop installed in the annex of Bernhard's tobacco factory, and he, Jacob, at least for now, installed there too, it was impossible not to see that Bernhard had need of more help. And he must have recognized what someone in Shavli or Riga could have told him in a second— Paul's unsuitability for industry.

It was flattering to Jacob that his brother's brother-in-law, by far the most energetic, imaginative man he'd ever known, had his eye on him, was already thinking about making Jacob foreman or steward. Perhaps as Bernhard saw his quickness, he would let him into the work he was doing with a cigarette rolling machine. But Jacob had his own plans and would probably resist entreaties.

Still it was wonderful of an evening, the sky above the shops growing humid pink, to sit on a box with Bernhard, tiny wrench in hand, pencil stub in the pocket, to fiddle with making things—inventing. They made many things together, some small and useful, some more ambitious, just the two of them working together on problems of continuous motion. Every invention spawned others, and every good idea could be applied to different problems.

What Jacob found irresistible about Bernhard was that it was still the problems that interested him, not the success. Already a businessman in Baltimore, his brands of cigars selling well across the South and his reputation always growing, Bernhard could, if he wanted, employ double the "hands" he now had, adding to the hundreds at their benches more hundreds of colored orphan boys and Lithuanians. He spent his time out of Baltimore as other cigar makers did, making the city rounds to place his product.

Newspaper stands and corner stores—not to mention taprooms, the anterooms of eating establishments, hotel lobbies, college refectories, and the various venues for American sport—were more likely to display a box of Barons Seal or Perfectos if they received a visit from the nicely dressed, German-accented person whose prime cigars were "hand made in the traditional way by rollers specially brought from Europe." Making these rounds had become the manufacturer's job, but it was not the activity that Bernhard preferred.

What he liked better was sitting at the bench with Jacob, discoursing in German or Russian while they threaded tiny pins through oblong beads of polished metal or hammered scrap rubber to dowels, stretching it between them. Sometimes when they needed an extra hand they called Paul, and he would do as they instructed, a third set of cuffs now in the picture as they worked on a new invention.

～ッ～

In recent years I have come across two artifacts that evoke the deep friendship between these men.

Of course, I wouldn't need an artifact to infer from their later activities and highly emotional forms of expression what they'd have loved about each other. One can imagine the impression Baron made on young Jacob in 1884. About the same age as Jacob's older brother Max, with a temperament marrying a strong drive to high idealism, Bernhard's warm face and bristly moustache marked him as the older man but, I think, the needier one. Seventeen-year-old Jacob, not forced to leave Lithuania—indeed, with two brothers ready to look out for him—could have had the upper hand over Baron, for the older man would later crave not only business associates but the large family that was denied him.

Yet the artifact brought much of these men's lives into focus, convincing me the scene I described above is not far from what actually occurred during many evenings passed at 63 or 65 East Pratt in the late 1880s and early 1990s, before Bernhard Baron left Baltimore.

This particular artifact was a sheet of printed letterhead that I found on one of my visits to the Jewish Museum of Maryland, along

Office of

Paul S. Levy & Co.

Makers of

Fine Pants,

405 W. Baltimore Street.

THE ONLY WAY
TO GET OUR
BUTTONS OFF.

"The Only Way to Get Our Buttons Off " patent pending, on Paul Levy's letterhead, 1905. Courtesy of the Jewish Museum of Maryland.

with Paul's grange buttons and ribbons and tintypes of his beloved Sarah. The letterhead announced "Patent Pending." Right next to it was an artist's drawing.

Three men's hands—all three, I notice, emerging from proper shirt cuffs—hold three axes. One up, one down, one raised and ready to fall, and all aimed at the shank of a button engraved "Paul S Levy trade mark," A caption underneath boasts, "The only way to get our buttons off."

The advertisement on the letterhead is exuberant if also silly, in the manner of the period, for it speaks to an era mad for improvements of any kind, and convinced that labor saving devices elevate life in every way. The labor of resewing buttons—ladies' work—has now been eliminated by a button so strong it would take two grown men with three axes to remove it. Still, the men are emancipated enough to sport cuff links.

I naturally imagine the hands with the axes as those of Jacob Levy and his comrade and friend Bernhard Baron, and I see the trademark as an artifact of the period when, late in the 1880s before Bernhard's sister Deborah and her daughters were installed on Hanover Street, Jacob, Bernhard, and Paul and his Sarah were inseparable.

During that period Bernhard did not mention his secret thought that perhaps Jacob might be attracted to one of sister Deborah's girls and make a marriage that would tie the two families even closer together. Nor did he yet admit to his wife—or perhaps even to himself—that he was subject to a growing anxiety. He feared that what he was building—Baron and Company—would never be Baron and Sons, and then how would he manage?

His one son, Louis, a kindly child, was a natural with the younger boys at the St. Mary School, always generous and genteel. He adored his father and was even willing—when asked—to stand at Bernard's elbow, handing over a wrench or length of India rubber or even buffing the roughness off a pipe end, but he had no aptitude for the machines. At twelve or thirteen, Louis had been so cosseted by his mother that he was still a child. Any time he might spend at Baron and Company was a pleasant excursion but nothing more.

On the other hand, Bernhard thought, there was Jacob, only three or four years older than Louis. Argumentative, hotheaded, hanging about the workmen's halls to listen to the speakers, carrying various dictionaries on his person (already his English was better than any of theirs), he was also a marvel with a wrench. Since setting himself up as locksmith and then machinist, he was in demand by various jobbers—working in winter for the canvas concerns that, when schooners were replaced by steamships, began making awnings, tarpaulins, industrial coverage. Later he worked in the more delicate "sponging" trades, which converted woven to wearable fabrics by removing scratchiness or unevenness of weave. Unlike Louis, who treated a tool like a toy, Jacob was a demon with technical activities, attacking the problems that dogged Bernhard, the small technical snags that kept him up at night as he worked on the Baron continuous cigarette rolling machine.

A continuous rolling machine had to solve two problems, whether the material being rolled was a ream of cigarette paper or a bolt of cloth. It had to have a uniform tautness but not stiffness. Too taut and the cloth or paper becomes stiff, without drape (fabric) or without that nearly gossamer mouth feel a smoker wants (cigarette paper). Thus the problem was getting these great lengths to roll at uniform speeds and at just the right tension—which was to say with sufficient slack—to manage small irregularities, slubs in a bolt of cotton, twig in a line of tobacco. For Bernhard the problems all applied to his designs for the continuous cigarette rolling machine, which he shared with Jacob as he tried to interest him, so likely a young man, in his operations.

For Jacob, though, the applications were all to the business which was so big in Baltimore that Jacob planned to enter it himself. That business was *shrinking*.

❧

Members of my family, Jacob's great- and great-great grandchildren, still own and operate factories in Philadelphia and North Carolina, and Jacob's original inventions, machines for cold and hot water shrinking patented in 1895, are still in operation. If a manufacturer wants say, 5,000 yards of military khaki fabric to remain supple and sized despite soakings by sweat and changes of temperature, the best method of pretreatment is good old-fashioned shrinking. In Jacob's day, shrinking allowed Baltimore to build on its industrial and ship-building past to become a center for producing the various protective textiles—all the varieties of canvas and duck, straw and silk, that keep humans from getting drenched or fried—from tarpaulins to umbrellas, from straw hats banded with jaunty ribbon to the awning over your mother's porch. This does not mean that when I first began to hear from my proud aunts that their father had been a *shrinker*, though he had started out as a mere *sponger*, I didn't have more or less the reaction anyone would—bafflement at either industry, mixed with amusement that shrinking was a step up from sponging.

Shrinking turns out to be the solution to an ancient besetting problem of civilization: the fact that almost all cloth materials, when first subjected to a hot or cold liquid, contract and become smaller. *They shrink*. Once I began to understand that shrinking can be both bad and good, I learned that shrinking is an ancient trade, first developed to help sailing ships stay afloat. Imagine what would happen if the

sails, great flapping, snapping yards of cloth, that were carrying you
from the port of Riga to Germany, had not been shrunk. What if the
fibers of the sails on which your life depended absorbed, rather than
repelled water? What if they decided when to shrink and expand on
their own, going slack when expanded, stiff when shrunken? Good
luck getting across the gulf.

After my aunts explained to me the importance of shrinking, I went
through a period when I began to see its glories everywhere, and to
this day I peer curiously at the garments I wear to determine whether
they have been shrunk and if so, also sponged.

Why did Jacob go into the shrinking business, and how did he succeed so rapidly in it that he could buy two large houses on West Lombard for his family in the late 1890s (only ten years after arriving) and
go on, despite setbacks, to "expand from shrinking" (his business
motto), managing a company that still flourishes today and is run by
his great-grandchildren?

My theory is that problems of shrinking were not new to him, that
patents he filed just a few years after arriving (at twenty-five and
twenty-six years old) bore parallels to the Baltic leather trade, which
offers all the challenges of cloth shrinking and more. Growing up in
the backyard of the Frankel Leatherworks, his own brother sent to
Germany to learn the most modern methods, Jacob had been exposed
to the most advanced technology being developed. The rendering processes would have been quite familiar, since the problems in curing
leather are even more challenging than those with any large textile.

Thus it happened that in the waterproofing capital of the world
between 1885 and 1900 my great-grandfather experimented with variations in shrinking and lofting, and with extracts such as Frankel was
using at the same time. In the first years he learned his trade as a
shrinker or sponger working out of his brother's pants store, but eventually his own business offered "shrinking, sponging, and inspecting
of cloth." The great bolts of material arrived at Lombard Street early
in the morning to be dunked in cold or hot baths, depending on use,
and then hung on rods suspended from the ceiling. By 1900 he had

opened a factory comprising three floors of workshop and drying space in a house adjoining his own. Yet he did not hesitate to call his business Levy's International Shrinking Company. The "international" had, I'm sure, many meanings, quietly proclaiming his "internationalist" sensibilities. But it was also, perhaps, a subtle way of showing himself the equal of the prodigy Bernhard Baron. Coming from more modest antecedents than Jacob, Baron already outpaced him as an inventor, a socialist, and an internationalist.

の業業

A while back in these pages I mentioned that two artifacts symbolize for me the era when beautiful machines were beginning to populate the world. The first artifact was Paul's letterhead. The second is a truly beautiful machine, if a small one, and it is now my own. I found it in a leather case in Aunt Myrtle's closet.

Since I was the only young person in our family who didn't possess what we called a "breakfront" for the display of collectibles, I had already been promised the great rosewood china cabinet, along with random salt cellars, some bits of chinoiserie, and various floral sprigged dessert dishes. Though they were items I'd never have chosen for myself, I knew I'd love them since they'd been hers.

Now, on my last tour of Aunt Myrtle's apartment, I peeked into the closet that had once held the children's toys, and I noticed a compact black case, leather bound.

Flipping open its square lid and lifting off a roomy compartment still containing an ancient instruction booklet, I looked down at what seemed to me the most beautiful of all Aunt Myrtle's possessions. Still brilliant in black lacquer, glints of its gold detailing winking in the light, the writing on its side a proud flourish that said "Featherweight," what I discovered in the closet was Aunt Myrtle's own precious pride and joy, her beautiful Singer sewing machine.

During my mother's teenage years, this square black-gold thing had been the tidy, lovely factory from which mother's splendid wardrobe

Joan New (the author's mother, with Ronald New, the author's father) in 1955, dressed for a dance. Joan's frock was made by Myrtle Levy Rosenstein on the author's own Featherweight Singer sewing machine.

issued, and of which I still had a few samples: a beaded ball gown stiffened with bone, a pale blue cashmere sweater with sheer white muslin appliqués, a camel's hair coat, silk lined. Later my mother purchased her own machine during my parents' impecunious era and made some beautiful things, dressing me in them on visits to the aunts. Eventually I learned to sew on it too. But my mother's machine was a big sedan of a thing, gunmetal gray, with an ungainly flywheel and a way of finding every unevenness in a fabric's weave.

Aunt Myrtle's beautiful machine was different. It represented the high point of Singer technology. On its debut in the 1940s it was advertised as the machine a woman could pass on to her daughters and granddaughters. This delicate thing, about the size of a toaster or percolator and powered by an electric foot pedal, enameled as glossy black as a tea tray and detailed in gold, was not a tool but an instrument.

I held my breath as I asked Aunt Myrtle's son Fred, so full of grief it was a bother to him to answer, if I could have Aunt Myrtle's Featherweight. "Of course," he replied, and I cradled the case carefully as I carried it to the car.

The week after I took it home, I found a place that refurbished old sewing machines. I had been afraid to turn it on lest it seize up in my hands. The man in the store reminded me of Aunt Myrtle's doorman—grizzled, middle-aged, black. He lifted the machine out of its box and shot me a significant look. Drawing a piece of fabric under the foot, he reached around to drop the little lever, flicked the light on, and then set sail across a scrap of material.

"Man!" he said. "That is one . . . [and he drew out the sound, just as my Aunt Fanny would have done] *beooooteeeful* machine."

Such beautiful machines remind me of the various construction projects detailed in the Old Testament of the Bible—the building of the ark, the tabernacle, and then the temple, and of a timeless love of *making things* as an intimation of godliness. My machine, on the other hand, seems made for the operator and preserved out of some era with a different respect for machinery. My machine is not only a handsomely made thing in itself, but its use instantly summons up in me a delicacy, refinement, and artistry we accord the finest mechanical constructions such as an exquisite, tiny watch.

In my life today there are periods—after classes end, or when my children are away at school—when I spend a meditative hour with Aunt Myrtle's beautiful machine, eager to be worthy in my craft of its fineness. Turning and reading the pages of the booklet she kept so snugly in its little compartment makes me more careful than I would usually be in using a machine.

Rather than turn down edges of a hem hurriedly, I measure; rather than improvise the color of thread, rationalizing that no one really looks that closely, even at topstitching, I trim small swatches of cloth and carry them with me to the fabric store. There I marvel at the industry that brought so many colors and weaves so far, at the machines that wind the yardage on the bolts, and at the hundreds of colors of thread, facing, seam binding, hem binding, elastic, cording, and then all the fabrics, their names lushly sprouting from every letter of the alphabet, as if to mark, somehow, the marvels of technology that give each fabric its own stiffness or drape, its own intensity or delicacy of hue, its own particular set of appropriate uses—a merino and not a muslin, the moiré or the *mousseline de soie*. I get lost in these places, buy sets of scissors, pins with pearl heads, packages of pin cushions. Though my life requires me to sew little more than pillow covers or the occasional hallway drapery panel, I long to make truly worthy items on my beautiful machine.

To me, using such a machine is to experience the true wonder of the industrial age, not in its dirtiness or cruelty but in its power to improve human wellbeing.

I run a seam on my beautiful machine whenever I want to experience what my great-grandfather and my great-great-uncle Baron may have meant when they used the word so important to them: *civilization*.

EIGHT

What She Wears, What He Wears

There was a feature in the Baltimore *Jewish Comment* that ran from the late 1880s and into the first decades of the twentieth century. Called "What She Wears, What He Wears," the full-page feature offered the latest in fashion developments of interest to the consumers and producers of Jewish Baltimore. Like all Jewish weeklies (including those issued to this day), the *Comment* arrived on Friday afternoon in time for Sabbath day reading, and it addressed itself to women as tastemakers and purchasers. But unlike today's fashion columns, "What She Wears, What He Wears" gave its readers weekly proof of their own leading role in making and keeping their city current. The column made clear that whatever Baltimore had been in the past, it was now, courtesy of its newest citizens, a fashion town.

In Baltimore, buckboard serviceable was out and city style was in! Out with canvas, calico, and denim and in with notions, beads, and haberdashery! Antebellum Baltimore had been a place where new Americans outfitted themselves for rural life. Postbellum Baltimore was a destination in itself, and, what's more, a city that advanced America's culture, placing it on a par with leading cities of Europe.

From the Baltimore *Jewish Comment*. Collection of the Jewish Museum of
Maryland.

News in the *Comment* was substantive and copious, its coverage
heavily tilted toward the doings in European capitals; the paper's Jewish, liberal readers gave close attention to such events as the first
Zionist Congress, the Second International, the Dreyfus trial, and
the fascinating activities of the rising industrialists and financiers.
This cosmopolitan flavor carried over to the fashion pages. Written in
English (not a Hebrew, Russian, or Yiddish word to be found), the
Comment put Baltimore at the center of the world's marketplace, encouraging its readers to shop the international emporium. After all,
now they could afford it.

"What She Wears, What He Wears" was a weekly witness to advances in precision, speed, saved labor, and variety that brought manifold objects of refinement within reach of many. Once, only the most fortunate could afford complex stitchery or garments constructed out of ten, twelve, or fifteen separate materials. Now any woman might have a garment in which the whole history of fashion was compressed, and, at the season's end, she might have another.

In lieu of buying such a garment, there was always imagining, poring over a page rendered in the finest detail. Lavishly produced, each week's feature showing the work of several commercial artists, the text descriptions in "What She Wears, What He Wears" offered readers something no longer available except in museum exhibitions or fabric stores: a fully dimensional, imaginative experience of dress, with every detail of adornment assigned a particular name and function. The language of this fin de siècle fashion is pitched at a level of technical understanding lost to modern fashionistas. For who is now versed, as readers of the *Comment* were, in the differences between *glace*, *guipure*, *surrah*? Who today would not goggle at a sentence describing a "capote" of "black spangles embroidered with black chenille with a torsade of white mechline tulle placed at the right side"? Who today has the visual and cognitive patience to appreciate, in an artist's drawing, the bonnet whose "black and white ostrich plume springs from a bow of peau de soie of an ibis pink shade."

No one I know, woman or man, can recognize peau de soie.

But the young girl who became my great-grandmother Amelia (daughter of Deborah, Bernhard Baron's sister, and later the wife of Jacob Levy), plus her sisters Fanny, Lily, and Lena did.

Amelia and Fanny were experts in the stuffs, the tricks and nomenclatures, of the art of dress. Their mother, dark browed, shapeless even in her best black silk, stood hours behind the counter in her fabric shop, measuring guipure or moiré, counting pearly buttons, and measuring out feet of narrow ribbon and embroidery floss along her arm. The brilliant narrowest edged ribbon—sea green, pale lavender, tulip pink, shell pink, cream—was priced at ten cents a yard, but of course the girls who bought it wanted no more than a couple of inches, suitable to trim a hat. Five cents a foot, their mother Deborah glowers at the girls, unwilling to sell less and not unaware that her arm measures only ten inches.

Say it is nine o'clock on a bright September morning. The young Amelia pours a morning drink from the kettle set on the dented sheet of tin (lukewarm, she fumes, like the poorest Jews from Zagare drink; and tea not coffee, as one gets in town). She takes two thick slices of challah, butters them, and plucks the *Comment* from the hallway carpet, holding her cup of tea, and gently lifts the kitchen latch that connects to her mother's store.

Opening the paper to "What She Wears, What He Wears," Amelia turns and faces the wall of laces, grosgrains, linens, and removes from her pocket another slip of paper, headed "Novel Effects in Decoration." It will be a mere ten minutes work with her mother's machine but it will have to be done quietly, aided by just a small scissors and a basting needle.

First, remove the turquoise-blue grosgrain (suitable for May but not late September) in the moiré bell skirt. She could rethread through the slashes at the skirt's bottom something more handsome and heavier, more appropriate to the season.

Her hat? Long since secured. The hat, in fact, was her inspiration for this morning's whole venture into the closed-up shop. Upstairs in her reticule was the *cleverest* chocolate straw—with a russet plume and a tartan ribbon of gray, wine, and brown.

When the little clerk turned her back at Hutzler's, it was nothing for Amelia to crook her wrist and quickly slide her hand inside her poplin cloak—then out with the crowd into the thunderstorm. She found that shopping late afternoons in August—many crowding the stores to be off the sultry streets, but everyone then exiting in a rush when the skies opened—allowed her the coverage she needed. And now with her dress retrimmed, her new hat, plus a flower plucked from the neighbor's garden, she would not look less put together than her sister Fanny. Fanny always looked just so.

For all I know, my great-grandmother Amelia Elfant Levy may already have been showing signs of illness when she married my great-grandfather Jacob in 1891; twelve years later she was sent to what my own Aunt Fanny, her daughter, called the inst-*ee*-tution.

It was easy to see, even when I was just a little girl, that the subject brought shame to my aunts Jean, Fanny, and Myrtle. And so the details about how and why their mother—and then their mother's last child, their brother Emil—lived out their lives in a mental institution not far from Uncle Paul's farm, was a topic each handled in her own way.

By 1913, when her mother was hospitalized, Jean (born in 1894) was married to her first husband, Percy Adler; already she was becoming her father Jacob's trusted right hand at the factory. As the eldest daughter, Jean exploited the freedom her mother's absence provided and enjoyed the esteem that went with being elevated to the position of her father's confidante and partner. In her later years Jean was the sister with the greatest narrative sense and the one most invested in communicating how "fine" her family was. She always stressed her mother's elegance. A "real society lady" Jean called mad Amelia, raising her voice to emphasize that her version brooked no contradictions.

Far be it for my Aunt Myrtle to contradict indomitable Jean. Still, I remember distinctly the look she had once when she mentioned how it had been hard for her father, and for them all, when her mother was "taken sick." Remember—she looked at me keenly—there were three little boys in Amelia and Jacob's house: Emil, 6, Theo, no more than 8, and Paul, 10. Who would take care of them while their father was at the plant? While they all lived in Balt-ee-mewer, Amelia's three sisters had helped with the boys. But then Jacob opened the second Levy's Shrinking plant and moved his family to Philadelphia, and things became more difficult.

In later years, brother Theo—Aunt Myrtle made sure that I understood this—took *good* care of Emil, sending money for his care from England. But one mustn't forget that Theo too had been just a boy when his mother left, and took most of his badness out on little

Emil, who seemed to suffer most because of their mother's illness. Think of it. One day he was a little boy pampered, petted, taken everywhere with her—on shopping expeditions and to his aunt's fine new house where the fountains twirled, and where sometimes a boy might watch the bigger fellows guide horses down the Gentleman's Riding Trail. Next day, his mother was gone. The pathos of it, the children's lonely bewilderment—Myrtle made this clear.

I would not have expected the information to come from Aunt Fanny, but it was she who once let something slip that gave me my only glimpse into what life might really have been like for Amelia's children. At a certain point (no one knew quite when) it became clear that Amelia had developed a habit of shopping—without money. On pronouncing this very odd fact, Fanny had looked at Myrtle, guiltily perhaps but not to be silenced, for then she turned to me and burst out that she was the one who *knew,* for she had been the one who was sent when they called from the *dee*-partment store to go and fetch her mother home.

I have since discovered that certain psychiatric diagnoses, schizophrenia among them, emerge coincident in the literature with the rise of the department store. New patterns of aberrant female behavior (not the lingering in darkened rooms, the "sick headache" of the previous century) but an alarming flare-up of drives, desires, hungers began to present themselves in women of the "modern" era, women hungry for experiences their mothers never tasted. Amelia was a duskily sexual looking woman who has a distracted yet rapt look in her photos, her gaze turned away from the camera. I shall never know what was really wrong with her or what her children suffered, or her husband thought.

But I cannot think of Amelia, Jacob's wife, without thinking of the child's poem: Ladybug ladybug, Fly away home, Your house is on fire, Your children alone.

I would like to think that when Jacob married Amelia in 1891, three years after she arrived from Riga (he now 24, she 21), she was not already far gone. Evidence points both ways. By the time they married, they had been acquainted a long time, a fact that argues either for youthful affection nursed into love or, perhaps, for Jacob's own uncertainties, which someone—Bernhard Baron—may have persuaded him to put aside. If so, he'd have had reason to wonder whether Bernhard hadn't cooked up his Rumpelstiltskin plan very early, scheming to marry Levy boys to Baron girls for his own purposes.

Still, I can imagine that after a day's work in the back of Paul's shop, followed by more hours hammering and talking with Bernhard, Jacob would have found it more than pleasant to end up with Bernhard at his sister Deborah Elfant's house on Hanover Street. Often he could glimpse the daughters in their mother's fabric shop, working on fine sewing projects by gaslight.

Jacob would have happily succumbed to the atmosphere created by these lovely girls, all luxuriant of hair, full bosomed, with features more large than delicate, but womanly. The kitchen, smelling of meals more elaborate than anything cooked in Paul's flat, drew him in. Arriving just as the streets darkened on a winter night, he felt the warmth, glimpsed the girls at their work in the shop through a crack in the swinging doors. Sometimes, against the festive wall of ribbons and bows, he might see a bare-shouldered girl perched on a dressmaker stool while her sister pinned up the hem of her new dress.

On the wide counter, along with the ribbons, the *Comment* was open to "What She Wears" to aid in the all-important trimming decisions. For while every girl looked forward to a garment's completion, who among them did not enjoy the process of composing it, putting a whole ensemble together with the aid of sisters, cousins, schoolmates, friends. Little stores with their walls of ribbons and bows sometimes remained open late, and the voices of the girls grew giddy and sometimes raucous as this sister dispensed her wisdom; that, her tastes. Keeping *les modistes* and shop girls on their feet was nothing out of the ordinary in fin de siècle Baltimore, where fashions changed season by season, and every Saturday night brought another opportunity for a girl to stroll the streets and stop at parlors of fine photography to have a picture taken with her swain.

The photographs I keep tell me that Jacob and Paul were among those swains. Whatever time they arrived for family dinner and the proposed stroll, they'd have to kill at least an hour conversing with Deborah's husband Morris until, primping and giggling, the girls descended the stairs looking *just so*. The girls were in no hurry, for the great photographic parlors remained open all night. No wonder there are so many photos of my great-grandmother Amelia and her sisters for me to pore over, more than a century after they strolled the streets of Baltimore.

❧

To read the numbers of "What She Wears, What He Wears" during the years before Amelia and Jacob married is to see a new epoch in Jewish life now under way. My great-grandparents' generation—and especially the female members of it—felt keenly that emancipation of a new and giddying kind was theirs, and they were able to document it in pictures.

I imagine a fall Saturday evening in, say, 1890 as Seebold, Photographer (Studio Open Day and Night!) prepares for an evening's commerce. Seebold views the street; the weather is excellent for portraiture. The day's long rain abates, and a rim of acid horizon brightens over the last drizzle. It will be a good night for him and for all Baltimore's photographers, with the Jewish New Year coming up and the city's fashionable young out in force. Members of the new, unchaperoned generation—the married, betrothed, or just keeping company—will soon be strolling out of Sabbath houses and Sabbath-breaking houses.

The water sluicing down the cobbles toward Fells Point brings up such an ammonia stink of brine and urine that the mud of Thames Street steams, but few of Seebold's customers come from that direction. Rather, his clientele ambles downhill from the western streets or even farther, the carriage circles and limestone facades of the new Eutaw Place *arrondissement*.

The women would be lifting their hems now over the rain-glazed cobbles, enjoying the breezier blocks of East Baltimore and Gay. Seebold's ungraded frontage is still puddled. But the Negro, paid jointly by Seebold, Whitehurst, and the half dozen other photographic artists of the 200 block, has gotten the planking in place, and Seebold has posted his own son at the downstairs door to broom puddles away for the passage of slippers.

The extra Saturday effort pays Seebold handsomely. In the hope of a second location out on the Park Heights streetcar line, or maybe a week in a boardwalk hotel, the photographer puts in the hours to catch the fashionable night trade; photos will be paid for by squires who would not dream of haggling. Heaven bless his new address, two full blocks closer to the new fashionable crescents. Bentleys at 806, Shulman's at 824, Hebbel's at East Golden 921, Udelowitz at 1224 had to settle these days for the second wave. They would get the muddier skirts, the greenhorn gabble, and the volume business coming up from the east.

Seven o'clock. Out of the shifting canopy of hats and umbrellas, Seebold's first customers step onto his sodden rug: the Levy brothers with their female companions. The men idle outside, struggling to close the umbrellas. The ladies duck through the doorway with expert swivels of their heads—trying not to move the great heaped saucers of hats off their pins. Seebold knows he owes tonight's visit to Friday's installment of "What She Wears, What He Wears," page 2 of the *Comment*. The Jewish weekly, its eye on European fashion, often predicts his weekend business. As he might have known, the millinery in the *Comment* has the girls out in the Sabbath rain to beat Monday's milliners. It is a kind of game. Perhaps the girls ran up the *mousseline de soie*, pompom, and taffeta in yardage from their mother's stock.

Now they dispose their razor-nicked, wry escorts in straight chairs.

Amelia stands behind Jacob Levy. Swiveling her chin, throwing her shoulders back and her bodice forward, Amelia cues Seebold to make the most of her Bertha frill. Seebold catches her full front, allowing the light to play on her soft chin, aware, proudly, that a portraitist less progressive, less modern, might already be compacting Amelia in a dowager's chair, setting her formally at her intended's right hand. Seebold prides himself on his intuitions as well as his tact.

Next, Fanny, enjoying what her mother would think, swivels her body. Then she indicates by a quick, practiced movement of index and thumb that Seebold should upend his lens. Laying one light finger on Charlie's shoulder, Fanny extends a slippered foot behind, and, winking at Sarah, drops her head back. The portrait will capture the full spill of ruching down the back of her great skirt. The skirt, as the *Comment* justly notes, is "a pretty style, but one not adapted to easy walking or unpleasant weather."

As ever, Sarah misses the wink. When her turn comes, she stands artless, swaying slightly with her big bosom encased in limp stripes, while Fanny and Amelia just raise their eyebrows. With her brother Bernhard off to New York, now manufacturing machines as well as smokes, Sarah runs on her own. She stays out all hours, teaching sewing, English, how to wipe a baby's bottom. She sits through lectures wearing any old thing.

Her hat lies disregarded in the picture's far corner like a great collapsed meringue. Still, Paul follows her with his eyes. His relatives had thought he would never marry, but there he is, helpless with love.

Would Jacob ever find the kind of love that had come to his brother Paul with a woman who, unbeautiful to everyone else, was a goddess in his eyes? Would Amelia ever be to him what Sarah was to Paul?

In their engagement pictures Jacob and Amelia make a handsome couple—he, dark, intelligent looking with his direct gaze and sensitive hands; she, attractive in a slightly exotic, Slavic way with her wide-spaced eyes, broad hips, and the fashionable frizzle of hair on her forehead.

Before Jacob met Amelia, he admired, perhaps even loved, the qualities of her uncle, Bernhard Baron, who had introduced them. An enlightened man, though one born to meaner circumstances than his own, Bernhard became not just Jacob's sponsor but his mentor, guide, and, despite the age difference, friend.

I wonder if Jacob felt crushed when Bernhard left Baltimore for New York and then, a few years later, moved on to London. Jacob likely understood that his older friend's departure was not abandonment of him or, heaven forbid, part of some nefarious plan to leave the Levy brothers, Jacob and Paul, in Baltimore to care for Bernhard's sisters and nieces while he went abroad, awaiting such time as the fertile unions of Levys and Barons produced a crop of sons.

Whatever Jacob thought later, at the time he probably understood. Attuned to progress as he was, Jacob would have sumpathized with Baron's reasons for moving on.

Chief among them: the day of tobacco's ascendance in Baltimore was clearly past. Baron and Company was a case in point. The firm had grown to be as big as Baltimore would let it be. The company was constantly expanding to keep up with demand, shipping nationally, and Baron trying his best to obtain capital from various partners and backers. But enough credit to shift production from cigars to cigarettes was simply not forthcoming. The nuns of St. Mary's, keen to see their poor colored boys employed, were the only ones sad to see Bernhard Baron go. The old German tobacco burghers with reputations built on tradition might have felt threatened by the speed of production he was achieving with his machine. Their comfortable businesses did not grow. Each one, supporting its thirty or forty rollers, had a steady output of so many hundreds of cigars per month, fully adequate to satisfy their buyers.

Nothing had changed and nothing would change in the tobacco business in Baltimore.

Change was coming in other fields, though. Soon the only thing the workers in Baltimore would do by hand was roll cigars. Everything else—everything—would be done by machine.

꙳꙳

At this juncture my great-great Uncle Baron was gone from Baltimore, off to become a legend in the family and a genuine notable in London.

By the time Jacob and Amelia's children—coming one every eighteen months through the 1890s—were born, Bernhard's patents—emerging at about the same rate in 1893, 1894, 1895, and so on—had carried him briefly to New York and then, with the opening of the Baron Automatic Cigarette Rolling Company, to England, there to stay.

Histories of the great British and American cigarette war of the late 1890s all tell the same story, describing how the unstoppable James Buchanan Duke was stopped by one Bernhard Baron, who came out of nowhere and showed up in New York with a cigarette rolling machine. And just in time! For Duke was then preparing to take over the world tobacco market, his power derived from owning the only fully functional cigarette rolling machine, the Bonsack. Developed in response to a call from the Richmond tobacconists Allen and Ginter, the Bonsack was flawed in its first several designs. But by the mid 1890s, Duke had bought the rights from the disgusted Richmonders, got the machine working, absorbed all of his American competitors into a trust, and put the world on notice he was moving across the Atlantic. Swaggering, redheaded, drawling, Duke sponsored demonstrations of the power of the Bonsack against the human hand. At a competition held at Tobacco Trades Exhibition of London, the reigning roller, Miss Lily Lavender of Islington, failed to come close to the production of the Bonsack of Virginia. While Miss Lily could roll 162 cigarettes in thirty minutes, the Bonsack did the same in ten seconds.

It was a tense moment for British tobacco that brought back the humiliation of the 1790s when George Washington, with exquisite spite, ended England's tobacco reign by bestowing the lion's share of American tobacco trade on German ports.

But at the very moment it looked like British tobacco might be foiled again by a drawling rebel, along came a sandy-haired Jew, Bernhard Baron out of Baltimore, holding forty or fifty of his own patents on cigarette machines and ready to deal. Slower but more reliable than the Bonsack, Baron's machine turned out hundreds of cigarettes a minute, and he had other innovations to sell as well—devices in development for carton manufacture, ink stamping, and more. By 1898 Baron was leasing his machine to the manufacturers of Players cigarettes, and this gave British tobacco the wherewithal to repel Duke.

"Rule Britannia! Britannia Rules the Waves" ran the advertising of a new amalgamation, the Imperial Tobacco Company: "Britons to Yankee Trusts will ne'er be slaves." Beseeching British smokers to "call the Yankee bluff/To support John Bull with every puff," the various companies of the Imperial set the monopolist Yanks a good example by commencing to compete furiously against each other, now free to concentrate more on marketing than on speed of production, using pretty girls, sports figures, national icons, and other images to put the now plentiful supply of cigarettes in every bloke and gentleman's pocket—and for a price hitherto undreamed of. Now the Brits had the technology to remain competitive with the aggressive Yanks. Producing his machines in New York but also in Aldgate, Baron shipped to manufacturers all over England. The little Jew from Baltimore had restored to England her original and most profitable colonial product—tobacco.

Had Uncle Baron been satisfied to remain in machines, he would have done handsomely, and he certainly would have left a more open field to European manufacturers. But he had been a tobacco man since arriving in New York in the early 1870s—rising from pushcart cigar

seller, to East Side roller, to Yale College tobacconist, to Baltimore tobacco foreman, to purchaser at Danville and Port Tobacco, then Baltimore manufacturer, owner, exporter, and inventor. Not a year had
passed since the 1870s that he hadn't ranged Maryland, Virginia, and
the Carolinas to lift the great hands of gold leaf and press them to his
nose before bidding. Thus in 1903, when William Johnson Yapp
sought his investment in one of London's choicest and most alluring
pipe tobaccos, a Virginia blend, Uncle Baron not only put up capital
but set to manufacturing the blend himself. Although the mixture was
once available to gentlemen only, Baron began to roll it into a handy,
cheap, and readily accessible cigarette.

It was not just any blend. It happened that the blend Baron purchased and then set his machines to rolling at record speed came with
a bit of literary pedigree.

Since 1851 fashionable gentleman had been making their way to a
Leicester Square shop where a black cat snoozing in the window told
them they had reached the premises of the Spanish tobacconist, Jose
Carreras. Here London's smokers purchased the secret blend of Virginia and Turkish tobacco known as Craven A, named for that loyal
tobacco aficionado, Lord Queensbury, the Earl of Craven. Here too
they came to purchase the milder tobacco blend named for the mas-
cot in the window: Black Cat. If the atmosphere of this shop—snug,
Spanish, adorably fragrant and clearly exclusive—drew only a select
clientele, among its regulars was a London personality and crowd
pleaser, the playwright and novelist J. M. Barrie. In 1890 Barrie had
published a book entitled *My Lady Nicotine*, a divertingly disposable
sheaf of chapters on smoking and bachelor life that had been serial-
ized in the *Pall Mall Gazette*. Its subject was Craven A.

What's more, in 1902, the year before Baron purchased the Carreras line, Barrie burst back on the scene to disclose that the blend he
had called the Arcadia mixture, the discerning smoker's only choice,
was none other than Craven A. As his narrator rhapsodized in *My
Lady Nicotine*:

One need only put his head in at my door to realize that tobaccos are of two kinds, the Arcadia and others. No one who
smokes the Arcadia would ever attempt to describe its de-
lights, for his pipe would be certain to go out.

Now manufacturing and distributing a premium luxury article in
mass quantities, Uncle Baron caught the first great wave of modern
advertising. Craven A and Black Cat spread all over England and
then beyond. Bernhard Baron had hit the big time.

❧

Back across the ocean in Baltimore, Jacob would have been too busy
through the late 1890s to notice Baron's departure, let alone brood on
it. He may have been pleased at his mentor's successes and enjoyed
hearing about Baron's rise to prominence in England. Except for his
son Louis, Bernhard was alone in London, his wife having died and his
three daughters remaining in New York, where their father's growing wealth secured them entry to the better German Jewish circles.
Poor Bernhard, Jacob may have thought, is almost alone, while he
could claim both a growing family and a thriving business.

After marrying Amelia in 1891, Jacob probably found it tough going
through the first years when he and Amelia and their first three children, Edward, Robert, and Jeannette, lived in his in-laws' house on
Hanover Street. However, by the time the national census caught up
with the Levys in 1900, Jacob's family had swelled to five children. Jean
was followed by Myrtle in 1896 and Fanny in 1897. All of them were installed in two handsome houses on West Lombard, walkable to those
grand new emporia, the department stores, and also to the Loft District,
where Jacob was making his name among major manufacturers.

As opposed to the filthy, cramped sweatshops around the curve of
the harbor, Baltimore's Loft District in the year 1900 boasted the
largest and some of the handsomest manufacturing spaces of any

American city. Baltimore's accessible location was serving it well, as it had in the past. The same geographic situation that once made Baltimore a tobacco hub—the gateway city to the South and the West, the oldest and most established deepwater port for international cargo—now gave it access to markets north, south, west, and east.

Moreover, as innovations in sailmaking, canning, and sugar refining had long been adapted by the city's clever mechanics to other applications, Baltimore continued to attract skilled workers in generous proportion to its unskilled labor force, including the overflow from Europe's busiest industrial centers. Finally, thanks to an established German bourgeoisie ever mindful of its progress toward civilization, Baltimore's manufacturing elites were, above all, modern. Fifty years of growth had allowed the city's German Jewish dry goods purveyors to open multistory department stores, more glittering than even those of Philadelphia, and now the city boasted the most up-to-date garment manufacturers too. The spacious, ventilated factories of Greif and Sonneborn offered only the best in ready-to-wear, while the advertising flowing out of these concerns instructed consumers to equate quality with machine-made goods.

This was the period when hand labor, traditionally associated with quality, was increasingly stigmatized and made synonymous with exploitation and filth. "Sweated" goods, the modern manufacturers argued, goods produced by "exploited hands," were inferior to those produced through "scientific methods" under "strict standards" of production and cleanliness. By attending to brand-names and trademarks, consumers might rest assured that the products they purchased, while made in quantity, were no less reliable. Mass-produced goods achieved standards of perfection, Greif and Sonneborn insisted, that no sweatshop could approach. "Replacing," as the industry trade journals put it, "dozens of mongrel, unknown, unacknowledged makes of fabric . . . with a standard trademarked brand, backed by a national advertising campaign," large companies committed to modern methods achieved a "guarantee of worth" to the public that now led to the consumers' and retailers' golden age, the age of the "American standard of living."

Of all garments, it was the men's suit—as fashion historians explain—that in this period came to stand for the elevation and freedom that was equally shared by consumers and producers of modern goods. Men had worn suits for centuries, with farmers and clerks wearing cheaper versions of the elegant garments worn by the better-off. The difference—and it was huge—was often in how these suits "wore." Even after sizing was standardized, the male sophisticate knew that a suit might pass inspection on the rack but not wear well. That is, unless the "goods" of which this suit was made were truly good, or had been made good by passing through certain intermediate stages of finishing.

Unless the suit fabric has been inspected for flaws—irregular weave or uneven color—the suit will begin to bag or pill, stiffen with sweat or bleed dye. And with a first washing, it will shrink. But fabrics—woolens especially—that have undergone careful inspection, pre-shrinking, and sponging remain crisp and keep their tailoring. Pre-shrinking, in steam or in hot or cold water, shortens fibers, reduces "give," and helps a cheap garment retain a crease and keep its gloss.

Consumers were not the only ones, the manufacturers argued, to see their standard of living elevated by modernization. Henry Sonneborn, one of two or three manufacturers whose astounding growth from 1905 to 1914 kept my great-grandfather Jacob's business growing, made clear in a fortnightly company newsletter how much the success of his "Styleplus" suit ($17 nationwide) improved the lives of workers by allowing employers to consider their "comfort and well being," by supplying "sufficient sanitary toilet facilities for the men and women actively engaged . . . to proper facilities for eating their lunch, and for rest and recreation during lunch hour . . . and taking care of their clothes during working hours."

If Bernhard vaulted from success to greater success in the 1890s and the early twentieth century, Jacob didn't need to feel small by contrast. He was now an established finisher, holding contracts with the most modern manufacturers in the city, using machines of his own design, patents pending or on record. From the factory space in an adjacent house, he expanded to Lexington Street and then to Redwood, where the largest menswear manufacturers in the nation were located and where he, whose processes guaranteed the quality of their goods, was located too.

On his occasional visits to Baltimore in 1905 and 1906, Bernhard Baron found good reason to admire his young protégée. While Paul Levy drifted farther away from commerce, Jacob, twenty years after arriving as a penniless boy, prospered. His family was established in an imposing double house. Not a word of any language but English was spoken there. Two pianos were displayed on two separate floors, and Amelia had a girl to help with the cleaning, the cooking, and the seven children. After Edward, the first, there was Bob, quieter, ever at his father's right hand. And then, in addition to the three little girls, two more boys—Paul, scampish and strong, and then the one named Roosevelt Theodore. With Amelia now pregnant for the eighth time, Jacob soon would have five boys to carry on the family name, while Bernhard had only one.

Imagining the situation today, one wonders whether Jacob might have told Bernhard of his growing worries about Amelia. Was it possible for an infrequent visitor to notice that Amelia acted strangely, smiling oddly, sometimes talking in a way no one could follow? Other than his brother Paul and Sarah, did Jacob have confidantes?

Probably not. Jacob probably did not confide in his old friend and mentor about the many times he came home to the Lombard Street house and found the children romping unsupervised. He wouldn't have wanted to admit that if he idled over the machinery until 6:00 PM or remained over his ledgers until 7:00, he might still walk in to find no wife, the table laid and ready for dinner, the cook confessing Miz Levy not yet arrived, the baby squalling in her arms.

How to explain the irregularities that would seize Amelia, the mumblings on the avenue, the affectation of a flower in her hair, the constant fretting about what she wore. He may not have talked about these things with Bernhard because Louis, Bernhard's son, often would be present. Louis's presence gave Jacob a pretext not to speak. He and Bernhard would pass an hour discussing the machines, soliciting advice on patents, or talking about Bernhard's doings in London. As the conversation flagged, Jacob would turn to Louis and suggest he go fetch the boys.

Some of this is mere guesswork, of course, based on stories I remember my aunts telling, plus what I have been able to gather about the hopeful prospects of Baltimoreans in the city's most dynamic decades, and some photos of my great-grandfather Jacob, posing stiffly beside a wife, a child in her lap, she looking not quite there. Sometimes when I gaze at these pictures I think I see on Jacob's face a look of tension, of impatience chronically repressed, even a martyred mien at the tiresome ritual of the photograph. But then, in other lights, the photographs show me none of this, show merely a man on the younger side of adulthood, his smooth shaven face set off by his glossy moustache and a dazzling white shirt front. Around him in some of these photos gather the children, nicely attired in their sailor suits and lace collars—well dressed examples of rising industrial prosperity, of modernity, of success.

Did Amelia's illness blight Jacob's happiness? Or did Jacob find his own means of consolation, forms of happiness pursued from within, but at a distance from, his family? Something I found some years ago has convinced me of the latter, convinced me Jacob found, despite the events that embittered him, much satisfaction, even happiness.

What I found were twenty-six patents granted to Jacob M. Levy by the United States Patent Office. I love these patents, these artifacts of hope, technique, and sublimated passion, for what they say about Jacob's life of invention and how they place me in a history of invention: Jacob's own.

Eloquent genre, the patent, with its own moral beauty. So sharp, so revelatory the light a patent sheds on the maker's temperament! With the patents in hand, I could see that the more official documents of

158

B. BARON.
CONTINUOUS CIGARETTE MACHINE.

No. 543,839.

Patented Aug. 6, 1895.

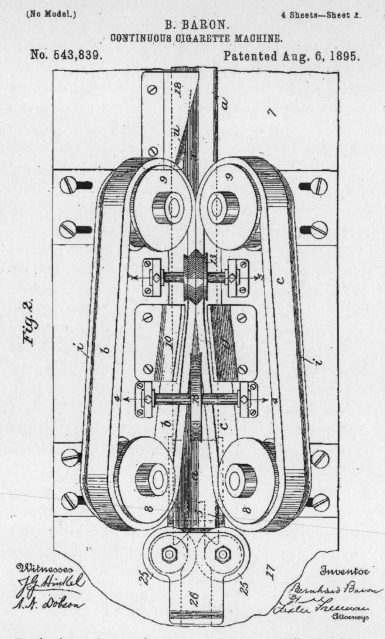

Bernhard Baron's patent for a Continuous Cigarette Rolling Machine.
Patent #543-830.

naturalization, filed a decade before, represented the attitude of a person still a boy and still an alien.

Who cared about who he was or what he said? One Jewish immigrant, whether "German" or "Russian," was more or less like another. Any differences between Jews of Prague or Berlin, of Moscow or Moldova, of Latvia or Austria, were lost on the functionaries who wrote down what they heard or misheard, inventing as they went.

Some clerk had renamed Jacob's in-laws the Elephant family (for Elfant) and thus they remained until Jacob insisted Amelia go and correct the matter. Thus he had made himself on that day long ago into a character of his own choosing, a dandified Austrian, brave enough to renounce all loyalty to the emperor.

But by 1903, when he began to file his patents, he had become by life and deed a citizen of the United States of America. As Jacob M. Levy, neither of "Russia" or "Germany" but of Maryland, husband and father of seven children, manufacturer, inventor, and owner of his own business, Levy's International Shrinking Company, he offered his talents to a public he trusted could use them.

What joy in sharing with the world a new device to better satisfy consumers and ease the labor of producers and workers, and so contribute to social good! Behind Jacob M. Levy's "device for holding cloth while spreading or piling" (Patent no. 760,133) and "machine for drying fabrics" (733,224), as behind B. Baron's "cigarette machine" and "continuous cigarette machines" of 1895, 1896, and 1897, are all the frustrations and risks of a less sophisticated industry—the pinched fingers and scalded palms, the cramped forearms or phlegmy lungs, the back strain, neck strain, and mental strain, the headache and heartache, lost time, lost wages caused by error, wastage, and inefficiency.

This is what Jacob's patents have come to mean to me, these most intimate, most revealing documents of my great-grandfather's creative years. Into these patents he put the best of himself.

Despite bad luck in marriage and disappointment in his sons, Jacob's patents convince me that he may have been happier than he let on. If unlucky in aspects of domestic life, he was blessed to be born at a moment in the history of the world most suitable to him; he was lucky to be a progressive, a utopian, a dreamer, a reformer living in uplifting times. How appropriate, for such a man, to have a third son just as the great progressive Theodore Roosevelt makes his strenuous grip on the nation. Knowing the boy will go by Ted or Theo, what luck to be a father in the great age when a son named Roosevelt Theodore may put his own shoulder to the wheel of progress.

It's obvious that Jacob got satisfaction from announcing his broad social views in the name of his company: Levy's International! "We finish your goods to perfection!" he vaunts on heavy stock cards, printed in blue, which he hands to his daughters, Fanny and Myrtle. It's their job to slip the card underneath the twine tying up finished goods. The card offered:

Cloth Examining, Shrinking, Refinishing,
and X-L Finishing Work
In addition to Canvas, Hair Cloth and Tape
Quickly, Promptly and to

BETTER SATISFACTION

than you had before.

There is pleasure in his letterhead, in the signage and the advertising, which changes all the time. Sometimes he lists himself as "inventor" or "Mnfgr" or "Manager," sometimes as "Proprietor and President." He is proud of his cutting-edge technology, his constant plant improvement and expansion, his announcements of moves to larger spaces and then of expansion to a new plant in Philadelphia. He is proud of the care and solicitude he gives to his workers and of the high quality he boasts about on his delivery wagons: *"Levy's fast finish makes fabrics fine"*—the "fine" not exclusive property of the rich but the right of all. He writes to clients:

The landlord has generously doubled the rent and promised
further boosting. Wages for all kinds of labor have increased
enormously, and as the high cost of living is rising skyward,
wages will again have to be increased to enable workers to live
the American Standard of Living.

No, despite a wife losing her mind, despite the rigors of train travel back and forth from Philadelphia to Paul's farm, where he stays to be close to Amelia, he is not as unhappy as he lets on.

When not at the plant or on the train, he reads and reads in German and English, losing himself in the great literature of progress. He fills shelves with books and more books. They are often bought in sets, handsomely bound, nicer than most Jews have ever owned.

In the evenings, he leaves his house on West Lombard Street, sometimes before Amelia returns, and goes off to hear the community lectures by professors of the Johns Hopkins University or to attend meetings of the Socialist Party, growing stronger every year, its leadership ranks swelling with enlightened Jews. Morris Hillquit from Riga and Sidney Hillman from Zagare are the rising stars. Late at night or early in the morning, he sits at his desk absorbed in his current invention.

What he shows the world more and more is a mask—distractedness, preoccupation, a jaded, resigned mien. His in-laws, Deborah and Morris Elfant, complain of rudeness and hauteur. Amelia mopes, is querulous, and then leaves without a word—to return at some unknown time. The children too leave him alone.

Some nights, putting off leaving the plant, idling over the machinery, then walking over to the workmen's hall to hear a speaker, he would arrive at home to hear nothing but the large clock ticking, the girls having put their little brothers to sleep and then themselves. For just such occasions, he would think not without some relief, God created books.

NINE

The Social-*eest*

What had possessed my great-grandfather in 1914 to commit his time and energy to a run for Congress he surely knew would be unsuccessful? Like the questions surrounding Jacob's birthplace, Amelia's illness, Uncle Baron's character, and Jean's decision to send her sons to England, my aunts didn't agree on an answer. Why should their father have chosen so quixotic a way to spend the spring, summer, and fall as the Socialist Party candidate to represent Baltimore in the Congress of the United States? And why, after this venture failed, did he continue to defend socialist ideas in spite of his business success and his family's bourgeois aspirations?

Aunt Myrtle and Aunt Jean each had her own way of explaining what it meant that their father—a captain of industry, as they represented him—could be a Red and a foe of unions simultaneously.

From a certain slight tightness around the mouth and the faintest wrinkling of her nose, Aunt Myrtle showed that to her socialism mostly meant domestic inconvenience. Myrtle was the person who took care of her father in his later years after his wife was institutionalized and after Jean had moved on to her second of three husbands.

Living with Jacob and keeping him in breakfasts and dinners, in clean shirts and pocket squares, in stamps and envelopes and typewriter ribbons, Myrtle had the experience to prove that political commitments are hell on the housekeeping. With the whole top floor of her house given over to her father's comforts, every entrance through his bedroom door was a rich tutorial in the slovenliness of the intellectual.

Cheap weeklies dropped by the armchair, books piled in teetering heaps, ashtrays overflowing, cigarettes loose, coffee dried to syrup or Scotch whisky left in a cup—such were the habits of international socialism.

For Aunt Myrtle, her father's socialism made him late to dinner, distracted with his children, tedious in company, and intolerant of what others thought "nice." She, who could set her boys' rooms to rights in fifteen minutes, came to know well the graceless habits of a sardonic socialist. Or at least she knew the tastes of one without a wife to keep him in line. His daughters did their best to cope.

My Aunt Jean's version of her father's socialism was quite different. Perhaps because as an adult she did not live with but only worked with him, perhaps because he had freed her to act more like a son than a daughter, Jacob's intellectual and political life seemed to set him above the grind of merely working for a living, above the mere operatives and other small-time manufacturers Jean feared he'd be confused with.

Thus her favorite anecdote concerned a financial crisis—I date it at 1907—followed by an industrial depression that threw vast numbers of urban proletarians out of work. Consequently, in Jean's account, well established industrial figures like her father would stand for hours at a time on wooden boxes, handing out loaves of bread to the poor and hungry. Jean, eleven years old, may even have joined her short but intense father, walking with him to the dingier streets where he worked the bread line and then back to their comfortable house on Lombard. The image of Jacob handing out bread would have appealed to my Aunt Jean for its dramatic immediacy but also,

I think, for putting Jacob's activism in the flattering light of noblesse oblige, thus allowing Jean to remember her father as reformer and grandee; not just an international socialist but also a philanthropist. As friend to the downtrodden, as a man of ideas blessed with an abundant heart, Jean's father Jacob leavened the politics she could not deny with an upmarket profile like her own.

Understanding Levy's International Shrinking Company as a model of international progress could easily be reconciled with her own managerial style and creed of the ne plus ultra. His municipal zeal was a natural forerunner to her turned-out city smartness. His pugnacity—expressed in a quixotic candidacy, in a collection of subversive books, and in manifold suspect subscriptions—set the stage for her own contempt of government intervention. A hardheaded woman, Aunt Jean never tried to hide her father's leftist political leanings. It was her genius, in a few crisp phrases, to show her father's redistributive zeal as the early, cruder version of her own beneficence. As he had handed out bread to the poor—she drew the parallel—she herself provided bread and cold cuts for the factory workers, giving Levy's whole workforce a daily lunch.

One has to wonder, though, whether Jean's fond memories of her father handing out bread on street corners were not in part a feint, a screen. A diversionary narrative, colorful and innocent and focused on Jacob's generosity, would have been of help to a girl desperate to retain innocent memories of childhood. Such a talismanic memory would distract attention from the period of Jacob's intense political activity, a period when Jean's own world, along with her father's, was turned upside down.

This was the period, with World War I raging in Europe, when she was married and widowed so quickly that her first son, Earle, could not remember the father who was off to France before Earle turned two. Her second, Jerry, was born while his father was dying of influenza in camp. And so she began her service as helpmeet and partner, secretary, aide de camp, hostess, and comrade to a distracted, irritable congressional candidate, while at the same time, in the years before she shunted such work off to Myrtle, functioning as cook, nursemaid, comfort, and scold to her five younger brothers and sisters. By 1913 her mother became too much for anyone to handle and Jacob committed Amelia to an asylum in Baltimore. Then he saw his first son off to London (ostensibly to pursue a musical education) and, with three boys and two more girls still at home, took the giant step of leasing a factory in Philadelphia. All this was in addition to launching a campaign to represent Baltimore's Third Ward, its industrial heart, in Congress. It was quite a year, 1914.

With the steady wartime demand for shrunk woolens, it made sense for Jacob to take a business risk by opening a second facility in a second city. The move entailed long-term possibilities.

But the run for Congress?

That was harder to square with the responsibilities this forty-five-year-old man had: the institutionalized wife; the unmarried daughters; the rowdy, restless sons; the boiler to light, workers to placate, orders to get out, trucks to keep in repair; the first son abroad; the second son assuming decision-making powers beyond his years; the worries of the in-laws, of his wife's sister, of his brother Paul; his own constant worries. Perhaps he ran to get away from it all.

He must have felt sheer terror when he realized what was happening to his family. Perhaps he developed a desperate resolve to fill his days and thoughts with distractions. A new business! A new city! Escape from the heart's cares. Thus do men of a certain active, intellectual sort climb aboard bullet trains.

Jacob's lucky break was in finding a train that seemed bound for glory. He climbed aboard the express train of the Socialist Party of America, a party that had gained so much strength and influence that in 1912 its candidate for president, Eugene Debs, garnered a million votes.

Debs's spectacular showing, the remarkable respect and influence wielded by Socialist Party members in Congress, especially Morris Hillquit, gave the party a level of momentum and visibility inspiring to many. The party's remarkably successful campaign to marginalize

Bill Haywood's Wobblies as radical extremists of the Wild West, and then Hillquit's besting of Samuel Gompers in a debate, made the Socialist Party seem to be, in 1913 and 1914, defining the terms of national debate.

A visitor dropping into a Socialist club in any major city might mistake the speechifying, leafleting, canvassing, and such for the signs of nonstop campaigning. The party's embrace of journalism as a dynamic tool in the spread of socialist thought gave persons of ideas immediate political relevancy. Despising the merely material gains sought by Wobblies and unionists, the 1912 platform of the SPA decried organization by industry or craft in favor of solidarity by class, and it encouraged its members toward more universal gains than the shorter work day or a union wage. Appealing to new unity among all those "forced to work for a living, by hand or brain," the party's first objective came to be constitutional reform, gradual but sure, toward the "cooperative commonwealth."

To get where they were going, the Wobblies wanted pageants of worker unity, nonviolent or violent as the case required. The unionists wanted to be at the table with management. The Socialist Party wanted candidates for Congress, and my great-grandfather Jacob answered the call.

To bring socialism and the party and its ideas into the mainstream, the SPA needed candidates for national, state, and local offices. With the party's need for candidates coinciding with his own need to find a distracting occupation, no wonder Jacob ran.

Had Jacob not had Jean at home, could he have done it without her? Without Jean, smart, capable, and ready to spring into the vacuum Amelia left, would he have run for Congress?

Probably not. The fact that her father depended on her was probably one reason Aunt Jean in later years romanticized his socialism, even as she avoided discussing the time of his greatest activity. While Jacob canvassed the Third Ward, singing the praises of Debs, mouthing the slogans of Hillquit and some of his own, it was Jean, the eldest daughter, who kept the family on track.

Pictures of the period show how imperious, how imposing she looked, even as a girl of seventeen. Hair swept into a chignon, her forehead smooth, her wide belt cinched over her hips, and her coat's flared hem brushing her tapered heels, Jean presents a smoother version of the ninety-year-old woman before whom we children trembled, slipping with our Coke and ice cubes past the brocade chair.

It was Jean, I surmise, who traveled from Baltimore to Philadelphia and back in one day, acting as her father's emissary to bankers and landlords, to trade journals, and to the printer with orders for the company stationery. It would have been Jean proceeding to rental agents and around the unfamiliar city to find a house for all of them. It would have been Jean who, back on the train and then home to her brothers and sisters, sulked at what they were now, so far from what she expected them to be. Jean would have reminded them of the duties the family now required of them, since the newly hired maid was not good for much at all. Jean would have told her sisters that, since Amelia's care ate up precious funds, their father would need more effort from them and, perhaps, a move away from Baltimore.

Of course Jean did all this in the same year she became pregnant with her first child and married Percy Adler. And in that order.

Although her sisters, nieces, and nephews always had pungent words to say about Jean's typical brazenness, in particular how she began an affair with her third husband, the brother of her second husband who was dying of Parkinson's, no one ever breathed a word about her hurry-up first marriage. I learned about it from Jean's English niece, Paula, who had it from Jean's first son Earle, conceived before his mother and father wed. The marriage occurred just before Percy went off to war and proved useful to Jean, for it got her out of Baltimore, away from the burden of brothers and sisters and, for a few years, to the relative freedom of the family's Philadelphia outpost. As Jacob's scout and on-site manager, the size of her belly kept safely beyond the calculations of the Elfant in-laws, Jean's residence in Philadelphia gave her a reprieve from endless supervision of her brothers and sisters. As for Jacob, living in Philadelphia gave him some breathing space away from his glowering mother-in-law Deborah and the insufferable Morris Elfant. Even before Amelia's illness and Jacob's decision to put her in the home near Paul's farm, the Elfants had blamed every untoward event on him, showering disapproval on the pair of Levy brothers to whom Bernhard Baron had paired their girls.

No, the Elfants did not like Paul or Jacob. Paul, the dreamer, the crazy farmer, had dragged Sarah off to the goyish wilderness to share his foolishness. But Jacob the "social-*eest*," as Deborah called him, had been a disaster.

In the beginning he'd looked like a more than suitable son-in-law. He spoke perfect German as well as Russian and Yiddish, and wrote English without error. He had excellent taste in haberdashery, a habit of wide reading, and the conversation of an educated man. Fifteen years after arriving in America, he'd transported himself and his family out of East Baltimore to a tonier section of the city, West Lombard Street. Deborah and Morris deemed it unreasonable that no Yiddish was spoken in the household, and that the children were forbidden the happy casual running about the streets allowed to the neighbor's children while, shockingly, they were permitted milk with meat, Sabbath breaking, and all manner of loose behavior.

But the warning signs were there. The Elfants might have guessed that something was off when, after some economic success, Jacob did not move out of the city like other Jews, but stayed close to the wharf on the other side of the bay from the industrial center. All the clothiers to whose back docks he delivered the woolens made their homes in the apartments whose broad lobbies glowed golden with tawny marbles and low sofas. Contributing handsomely to the Hebrew charities and attending proper religious services, such Jews comported themselves with decorum and seriousness.

Not Jacob.

Although he might have lived among Baltimore's elite, he maintained a house near the Loft District on Lombard, within smelling

distance of the bay. As for his politics, as Baltimore Jewry raised its
tone, he let his sink. Not for him the pat pat pat of hands, the sedate
supper served before the lecture, the swish of gloves and gowns as
the leading citizens entered the Lyric Theatre to hear their honored
speaker, Supreme Court Justice Brandeis, expand on the glories of
citizenship. Brandeis compared his fellow Hebrews to the early American pilgrims. The lights of the theater silvering his handsome head,
Brandeis—Harvard trained, modern but Jewish—epitomized that
progress, that refinement to which the decent Jews of Baltimore as-
pired. Was Jacob even there on the breathless night when, unified by
patriotism, "Representatives of every Jewish class and group were
present. . . . throughout the house could be seen workingmen and
women, and not infrequently a patriarchal beard and even a *shaidl*."

Probably not. From the genteel and tidy rim of his residential street,
its narrow townhouses brightened with white marble steps and its rises
flanked with ironwork, Jacob plunged—inexplicably—back into the
sink of the city with its strikes and crowds and agitations. Dangerous.
Dirty. Embarrassing. Not *nice*. Not proper. Not respectable.

Given the level of alienation existing between the Levy and Elfant
families, I assume that Jacob returned his in-laws' disgust, not hiding
his scorn for those who considered "social-*eest*" a term of oppro-
brium. Why should he associate with people who did not understand
that he was not nearly as radical as he might have been, that his party
was, far from rowdy or unlawful, in love with the law? His own run
for office was part of the party's nationwide effort to put Socialists
inside the tent, to elevate American citizenship and not, as the Elfants
claimed, to threaten it.

He left no diary of the period when he plunged into politics, but
hints of what he read and where he went, of the company he kept,
suggest the Elfants were mistaken about him.

To be a candidate for the Socialist Party meant he was no radical,
no rabble rouser, but rather a respectable member of the optimistic
ranks, hopeful that ideas hatched in Europe might—at long last—be

applied in America. Big Bill Haywood thought the Socialists' leader, his own Hillquit, a milksop. Haywood mocked the "pink teas" where Hillquit was a popular speaker, suavely assuring the ladies that "socialism didn't care how many dresses they had." Both from the right and the left, Socialists were criticized for being out of touch with the workingman and in love with theory.

Hillquit, from Jacob's native region in Lithuania, used just those terms to draw Jacob to his party. Hillquit did not seek to tear down civilization but to build it up. Courtly and eloquent, Hillquit smoothed the way for the socialist advance by assuring ladies at their pink teas and workingmen in the halls that it was "ever improving methods of wealth production, ever growing keenness and profundity of the human mind . . . and so [an] ever rising level of human morality" that guaranteed the survival of civilization. Haywood and Gompers might mock Hillquit's popularity among the better educated, but Jacob thought that Hillquit's socialism was the enlightened creed, not just politics but a philosophy and an intellectual practice.

Why should Jacob be bound by these petit bourgeois Elfants, these ghetto Jews with their worship of Eutaw Place and not even two thoughts in their heads?

For their part they called him *Luftmensch*—someone who lived on air, neglecting his family and lacking decent feelings or opinions. They said that Mr. Jacob M. Levy was a disgrace, a man who'd choose a workmen's lecture series over a *shabbes* dinner. What to do with a man who preferred a book to human contact, who sat in company with his face behind the daily newspaper, nothing but his plume of cigarette smoke drifting above? One could not, after all, live in books.

❧

One of my greatest regrets is that at some point in the 1970s, when I was already an avid reader myself, I didn't visit and perhaps take a few souvenirs from my great-grandfather's library.

It makes me wince and also, I admit, brings out my own intolerance, my snobbishness, that in contrast to all the goblets and ramekins saved for me and others, no thought was given to saving Jacob's books. Would I not trade, I've said to myself, the set of six flowered dessert dishes or the pink vegetable bowl, the green painted scene of a Chinese girl bending under a willow tree, or the nut or pickle forks (still wrapped in plastic) for just a few of the moldy books? Salt cellars, parfait dishes, cake servers I have in quantity, but not one book from my great-grandfather's fabled library, books floor to ceiling, which even my mother, age four when he died, remembers.

Of the large collection he amassed over forty or fifty years all I've seen are his Morocco-bound Bible, in which he kept the notice of his firstborn son Edward's name change, and one other book—an illustrated *Don Quixote*—now possessed by Aunt Myrtle's granddaughter Carol. And that is all. A picture of him holding a copy of *The Call*, the organ of Morris Hillquit's Socialist Party of America; copies of the election results of November 1914, Jacob Levy, Socialist candidate for the Third Ward; and certain pungent letters on the rights of landlords and workers are all I have to tell me what he read, to give me a picture of the ideas he entertained.

It vexes me, frustrates me, and makes me blame myself for not catching on sooner, for not getting myself to the factory annex where, from 1939 till 1979, my great-grandfather's books remained unread and unloved, until they were carted away to a dubious destination after the Philadelphia plant was closed in favor of new ones in the suburbs and in North Carolina. I feel not only frustrated but angry that I failed to realize the value of that library in time, that I've had to go to some lengths to retrieve my great-grandfather's personal catalog by other means.

At a certain stage of my quest I thought I might get help from librarians at some of the branches where he'd gone to quiet his nerves with a day of reading. But my inquiries won me only a rebuke; the librarian I spoke with was unwilling even to entertain the idea of sharing a borrower's reading record. What was a public library, she

reminded me, but a bulwark of intellectual freedom and privacy?
Would I want someone seeing what I'd checked out?

This failing, I've spent more than one afternoon lost in various historical collections, my interest not just in the ideas of Chernechevski,
Lasalle, Sorge, and Hillquit, but in the imprints of 1899 and 1903,
whose bindings I've fingered lovingly, thus creating on the floor the
virtual library he would have read. I've thumbed and leafed through
all manner of paper-bound tomes and pamphlets, glorying in the distribution networks, the marvelous freedom in the democratic country, imperfect but yet free, that allowed a Jew from Siauliai, Lithuania,
to purchase, unchallenged and unmolested, a whole library of subversive classics such as the *Intercollegiate Socialistic* or the *National
Ripsaw*; to read, if he chose, *The Call*—sedate, thoughtful, cautious,
patriotic—or perhaps the naughty *Masses* ad that waggishly reassured: "Anarchists! O Dear No! Law and Order is our Middle Name!
THE MASSES should be on every library table. It will entertain the
babies, upset Ma and give Pa a jolt regularly once a month. WE
GUARANTEE TO ANNOY. Have you a little dynamite in your
home?"

Which of these books did Jacob own—all of them, none, more
radical or less? I could easily have learned what he accumulated in
his library had I gone to see it. But I have only the memories of certain afternoons with Jacob's grandsons and nephews, who loved to
recall their grandfather's trove of red journalism; his enthusiasm for
Marx and Engels and Stalin's five year plan; his zeal for the American
communist Earl Browder, for the Spanish Republic and the Jewish
homeland in Birobidzhan. Looking at each other, leaning back in their
chairs and laughing, they would describe his collection as "a whole library of subversive literature!"

"If they'd ever raided grandpop's annex next to the plant, can you
imagine what would have happened?"

The answer, of course—the amazing, fantastic, inspiring answer—is that Jacob might, in 1914, have trumpeted from street corners, in circulars, and from speaker's platforms anything he wanted to

say. *Nothing* would have happened. The Socialist platform's first political demand was "absolute freedom of press, speech, and assemblage," and Jacob was its Baltimore standard bearer.

In America he could have any ideas he wanted, no matter how incendiary, and express them without fear of retribution. Whether in the library, where his right to read as he chose was safe in the hands of the ladies in shirtwaists, or in the offices of the city clerk, where he filed his intention to run, or the fact that the name the clerk printed on the ballot (Candidate: Socialist, Jacob M. Levy) was Jewish, did not matter any more than the name his brother registered as owner of his acres in Glyndon.

His children and his in-laws might not comprehend why he and his brother did such things, might call him, and his brother Paul too, *Luftmenschen*, purveyors of dreams and notions, crazy filers of writs and plats, in love with sashes, buttons, and any kind of regalia. Crazy!

Jacob and Paul did not care. They loved to declare intentions, take positions, forward motions, outline objections, weigh in. They loved putting themselves on the record and seeing their names in the paper. They loved the accoutrements and ceremonies attached to office of any kind. If they ever lost their tolerance of democracy's rudeness, its motley population, its smelly public halls, they might think about their older brother Max, still in Raseinai—Max, whose prominence helped him not a jot.

A worthy, notable man of education and means who sent his children to university and had the most elegantly appointed offices in town—what was Max doing now?

Max, who sent stately New Year's cards and appeared each year in the annals of Kaunas Guberniya as esteemed member of the Board of Jewish Electors, the Fire Prevention League, and even the Russian Sejm. Max, with his sinecures and emoluments, his leadership in the Society for the Spread of Enlightenment, his standing as member of the diploma intelligentsia, his desirable credentials. Where was he now?

Standing in a tightening noose, that's where he was.

Every day in Raseinai, the *Jewish Current* reported more outrages committed against the Jews of the western Pale, rich and poor. Economic security meant nothing without political security.

Max and his liberal friends, the Jews trained at Kovno, Riga, and Tartu, had pierced the law all over with loopholes, and for a few decades Jews had slipped through. The laws that forbade Jews from living outside the Pale of Settlement, from doing business, from traveling as they liked were punctured in manifold invisible places by exceptions through which ambitious Jews rushed.

But in this year, 1914, Jewish privileges were being revoked, as reported in the Jewish press. Readers of the *Jewish Year Book* of 1914 could see that the loopholes Jewish *sechel* had opened were now being cinched shut. A whole world of exceptions and privileges was being eliminated.

At Vladivostok, only those Jews might remain who possessed certificates that they had rabies and required attention at the local Pasteur Institute. At Vilnius, authorities forbade the performance of a song in Esperanto, because the inventor of the language was a Jew. Esperanto was condemned as a Jewish language. Jews adopting Islam were forbidden to live outside the Pale, as were Jews working as printers, millers, builders, photographers, gardeners, cabmen, or menders of musical instruments. At Tsaritsyn, Jews were forbidden to appear on the streets during church services. In Raseinai and in Shavli, a Jew's accomplishments mattered only if they could be put to use. Jews filled the market stalls and university quotas, but nothing they did left its mark, nothing stuck on the record.

This is why Paul and Jacob never tired of spelling out the advantages of democracy to each other. In America, what mattered was not privileges but rights, free and public access to the rights guaranteed by the Bill of Rights: freedom from search and seizure; freedom of movement; the right to a fair trial; freedom to associate; freedom to rid oneself of national, ethnic, and tribal affinities. Here, one might say unpopular things in one's own name, in one's Jewish name, and still go home to supper.

One of the things I puzzled about before I began to study my great-grandfather's socialism (the socialism of the period from 1900 to 1915, before the Russian Revolution) was how he could have been an international socialist, a progressive of some conviction, while strongly opposing unions.

Aunt Jean made no bones about showing her contempt for unions, the brutes who had, in 1923, forced her father to sign their contract or close his doors.

Unions! The very word made her sniff and, if pressed, snort her contempt. She never tired of repeating how her father had "handed out bread on the streets of Baltimore," nor did she ever let anyone forget that in the years before she became a CEO she'd run the factory herself, not above taking her turn, along with Myrtle and Fanny, inspecting yard goods and even lighting the boiler.

What she reviled was the way the union contract her father had been made to sign in 1923 forced the end of what she saw as his liberal, genteel, and Jewish conduct of his business, and the beginning of capitulation to the thugs and brutes who would plunge them all into misery. Did they really think these union riffraff, these "organizers," knew better than her father how to run a business? These gentiles, coming to work wearing anything they liked—even *dungarees!*—and telling Mr. Levy that the union manager, and not one of the boss's own children, must be employed to supervise the shop floor; that (and this the most galling and painful to her father) only union machinists be employed to maintain and repair her father's inventions.

It was an insult, that's what it was! And not at all what her father had stood for. Not at all.

Of course she was right, though what he had stood for, I later came to understand, was the dissemination of his own European, internationalist, highly learned socialism in America.

It would, I think, have been in 1912, that bellwether year in American politics, when Jacob first decided to run for office in the next election on the Socialist ticket. So far, only New York and Wisconsin had sent Jewish socialists to Washington as congressmen, but 1904 found a Jew, if not a Socialist, from Maryland in the U.S. Senate.

No one could beat the Americans in the pageant of democracy. Men of all parties and stripes had pronounced 1912 a spectacular year for politics. Though the Socialist candidate for president, Eugene Debs, failed to win a state, he had stirred the passions of men from the eastern immigrant enclaves to the railroading West. He had captured nearly a million votes out of 15 million cast—and this with progressive reform high on the agenda of the major party candidates as well. Moreover, for sheer democratic spectacle, the election was unmatched.

Who could forget how, at what seemed the last minute, Theodore Roosevelt had returned from shooting big game in Africa to "throw his hat in the ring." Amply justifying his self-description as Bull Moose, TR lowered his own horns and charged the floundering, dumbfounded incumbent, William Howard Taft, by becoming the candidate of the new Progressive Party. This alone was gripping. But thinking men could also look on as the stately Democratic candidate, Woodrow Wilson, coolly snatched Roosevelt's own bully pulpit. While Roosevelt showed as much animal intelligence as ever, Wilson's speeches introduced a new subtlety of mind into the political mix. With such men as Roosevelt and Wilson—orators both, public men both—talking themselves hoarse at every whistle-stop, vying with Debs for a mandate to bust the money interests, who could resist throwing his own hat in the ring?

Jacob Levy had not yet got his own men to understand what workers all over the world understood—that the enemy was not the industrial entrepreneur, a producer, but the landowner, the holder of leases, the collector of rents, and a government in sympathy with those who held property rather than those who worked with their hands.

It was for them, these workers, that Jacob hit the streets of the Third Ward to spread the socialist word by going to outdoor meetings, visiting immigrant hovels, and collecting signatures. Progress was not parochial or local. Socialism was an idea, not a matter of buttons and work hours.

Nothing made Jacob's blood boil more than a pious pronunciation of the word "local." Local was to labor as, in his view, Ostjude was to Jew: narrow, parochial, and without regard. What could be of less political moment than a geographically limited organization of people engaged in the same puny trade?

Could any politics be smaller potatoes than the Amalgamated's cyclical defense of the buttonholer asking for more money per hole, or any symbol more frail than the shrewd Baltimore girl flattering the matrons of Bolton Hill into the campaign for cleaner toilets?

The politics of Samuel Gompers and his Federation of Labor was, as far as Jacob was concerned, socialism for those without enlightenment, without ideas, unlettered, lumpen. Did not the word itself, the word the unionists used to shut out the larger world of ideas, sum it up? Did not the smallness of the word "local" say it all?

Such is the tone and temper of the literature issued and recommended by the Socialist Party of America, of which my great-grandfather Jacob was not only a proud member but—as a candidate—their man on the barricades.

The prodigious literature of international socialism's golden era reminds me that in 1914 Jacob would have made his run still hopeful, still innocent. His candidacy would have given purpose to his life: the satisfaction of living for progressive ideas, struggling for an international cause.

The city directories of Baltimore and Philadelphia show that Jacob added the word "International" to his company name in about 1911 and kept it until his death in 1939—despite the excesses of Lenin and Stalin and despite the victory, bitter to Jacob, of the unions in his own shop. The election coverage of fall 1914 shows that Jacob's run for Congress was not successful but not unrewarding either, since the candidate for the Third Ward received one-quarter of the votes tallied. Jacob M. Levy demonstrated to himself and all Baltimore that a man named Levy—whom unenlightened cultures might exclude from holding office or owning land or tuning instruments or practicing law or medicine—could, in America, put his name on the ballot. Win or lose, succeed or fail, he could speak out.

Until Jacob entered the campaign, he had not realized the power of the public record. To run as a Socialist in Baltimore was to have no expectation of actually going to Congress. Although Socialists were on the ballot in every eastern city and in scattered Debs strongholds, only one Socialist, Victor Berger of Wisconsin, was predicted to keep the seat he had won in 1912. Moreover, with Woodrow Wilson's presidency still in its exhilarating first stage, it was not credible that Democratic Baltimore would send anyone but a Democrat to the House.

' But the point, as Morris Hillquit urged and Jacob told any who listened, was not the win but the run, the demonstration, as against the syndicalists on the one hand and the unionists on the other, of participatory democracy, which was not just an office but a rostrum, a lecture hall.

Jacob ran as an actual candidate for the Congress of the United States. Public office in a representative democracy was a large, slow, and abstract thing. But candidacy was something else; candidacy was as fast as the races at Pimlico.

Jacob was careful, more careful than most Socialists, to learn every filing procedure with impeccable reliability, and he was not disappointed to find that the Socialist candidate from the Third District was plagued by manifold obligations to functionaries at city hall. The campaign itself, of course, had been no idle act but a long slog of fourteen-hour days, every day's genuine or strained optimism ending in sour breath and sore feet. The Third District was, though certainly not winnable, watchable.

Through the Indian summer after the primaries, Jacob spent long days away from his shrinking company, mounting the stoops of countless brick walkup buildings, climbing splintered stairs to workshops and sweatshops littered with vest cuttings; then descending toward the bay to pitch whatever he had left.

In the years that followed, Jacob would be glad to have his memories of this time. He had of course lost, but only to Republicans and Democrats. He had beaten the Progressive, Labor, and Prohibition candidates. When the results came in, he could feel satisfaction that the Third District led the Socialist vote in the city. For years after, he could look back at having lost the immediate battle but written his small chapter in Baltimore Socialist history.

Jacob's 1914 report of campaign expenses, featured in the *Baltimore Sun*, showed more than a little moxie. The *Sun*'s account, "Socialist Candidate Declares Campaign Expenses," reports that Jacob Levy, "candidate for the Third District," declares campaign expenses of "53 cents and Thanks." Condescending, yes, but he could count it a sign of the city's elevated blood pressure, its jittery recognition of Debs's party, that he, like Debs himself, had made them stoop to condescend.

My own hunch in regard to the unions was that the worst effect they had on my family, aside from wounding its pride, was to trivialize a set of ideas about labor my great-grandfather lived for and believed in. To be beaten by the Baltimore local in the name of labor equity was, for Jacob, not only to see his own German-accented strain of highbrow internationalism squashed. It was also to lose the high ideals of enlightened industry and modern civilization in a set of small concessions on a document.

Consequently I am sad for Jacob. Even before he came to America, met Bernhard Baron, and lost his sons, it was inevitable that he would lose his vision—the family's vision—of not only betterment but happiness.

❧❦

My aunt Jean kept the *Sun* clipping in a white vinyl album, gold tooled, the kind with ribbed sticky pages under plastic sheets. Using one curved, burgundy-lacquered fingernail to pry the corner plastic up, and then a thumbnail to lift the clipping's edge off its sticky matting, she had once passed it to me over the cookies and the cold coffee and had grinned at her father's insouciance and chutzpah, the obvious delight he took in declaring his probity on the public record. Socialist candidate Jacob Levy: hands out of the public till. After Jean died, I lost track of this album. But after I began to dream about Jacob's cane and started writing this account of his civilization, I asked around and found that the album was safe in the hands of Jean's nephews, Fred and Dan, who had kept the clipping along with other artifacts from the early days of Levy's Shrinking. Indeed they held these treasures closely, protectively, as my cousins who now possessed the cane guarded it.

Never having seen Jacob's library, attended a rally with him, or stood in the cold waving to Debs's train, I am a latecomer, maybe a usurper. My writing about the cane and these clippings, putting my own stamp on them, is a way of trying to possess the family history I cannot own, to snatch for my own children a history not really mine to give.

I have brought Yael into it.

I have made the child I took to the Baltics on the eve of her bat mitzvah, now in her twenties, my ally in this theft of Jacob and his cane for our purposes. As I regret the loss of Jacob's books, and as I observe my mature self created out of that regret, I encourage Yael's self-fashioning along the same lines. Inheritance going the way it does, my own disdain for bourgeois niceties and artifacts, my preference for materials recondite and uninviting, is something I have passed on. I love it when Yael shakes her head, looks amazed, and asks, How could they? How is it possible they simply threw away all those books?

A lover of old covers, cracked bindings, Yael is now a collector herself.

Yael has her own growing library, shelf on shelf to the ceiling. Reference first, then modern languages, the avant-garde, film, history, poetry, and the literatures of Europe, from east to west, with books in Russian, her subject, given pride of place. How proud I am of her collection, how much I pardon her for her habits (wrinkling my nose as I look in at the tumbled bedclothes, piles of pants, shirts, underwear, carpet strewn with books, the window open to release the telltale tobacco odor mixed with her perfume), rationalizing as I pass that she is, after all, as much *like him* as I am like him.

Even as I invent us out of him, as I cast a fond and indulgent eye on Yael's room with its smell of smoke and its *books books books,* I realize that I made him out of us.

Yael's tumbled books I cherish as if they were his. His episodes of manic composition, his flight into ideas, are all mine.

Uppity and unbowed, living for and in ideas, I claim him, the patriarch I need, my forebear on the barricades.

❧ TEN ❧

Mother Earth

During the summer of 1917, while war raged in Europe, weekend mornings found my great-grandfather Jacob on the porch of his brother Paul's farm in Glyndon, an hour's train ride from Baltimore.

Down the long slope of lawn near the chicken coops, Jacob's thirteen-year-old son Theodore idled with seven-year-old Emil in view of Paul and Jacob, who kept an eye on them. Theo's punishment for shoving his older but shorter brother, young Paul, off a pier was to spend the whole summer at Glyndon with his Uncle Paul and Aunt Sarah. To the weekly roster of Theo's tasks—which included picking corn, feeding chickens, and mucking out the barn—Jacob added tender weekend attention to Emil. The dusty, stony hollow where the chickens clucked inside their low-windowed houses got the only shade on the lawn, and so there, on two stools, sat Theo and Emil, with a chessboard on their laps, while their father discoursed with his brother in German and, inside the house, their sisters Fanny and Myrtle helped Aunt Sarah with her work.

As in other summers, Fanny and Myrtle helped their aunt by sweeping floors, wiping dead bugs off the window sills, changing linens, and

running Theodore's shirts and trousers through the wringer, while in
the sweltering kitchen fat Aunt Sarah stood over steaming pots of
beans and beets, her cheeks flushed with the heat. Canning was Sarah's
delight, a job she saved for summer weekends when girls could come
help at the farm. These vegetables and jams that she "put up," using
the phrase the Negro girl who helped her used, would be on sale, along
with churned butter, come Monday at the booth of the Reisterstown
Grange, her Paul's own cooperative enterprise.

This summer of 1917 was about the last time Jacob and Paul were
able to discuss the possible comeback of the Socialist Party. In fact,
1914 was the beginning of the end for socialism in the United States.
The three years since had undermined the relevance of their specu-
lations as to what might have happened if the United States had not
joined the war, if Russia were not now plunged in revolution, and if
their party's presidential candidate, Eugene Debs, had not been arrested. The international, outward-looking socialism that had riveted
Jacob's intellect and distracted him from his wife Amelia's troubles
was considered more and more dubious. Still, discussing the future
chances of the SPA versus the SDP, the WWW, and the AFL helped
Paul keep Jacob from brooding on the hard facts he lived with.

He lost the companionship of his wife when he moved her to a mental institution, the best he could afford, a few miles down the road,
where her sisters could visit; he also traveled every week from Philadelphia to see her, taking two or three of the children each time, never all
at once. What marriage he had left was limited to Sunday afternoons.

In order to pay for her care and support his children, he abandoned
the city where he'd lived for thirty years, closed up the stately house,
now let to others, and gave the keys to the Baltimore plant of Levy's
International Shrinking Company to Bob, his second son. He would
legally deed the whole works to Bob just as soon as the Philadelphia
plant could support the rest of the family.

That he'd lost his firstborn son, Edward, to another man was the
worst thing. That Edward had been invited by Jacob's onetime friend,

Bernhard Baron, to "complete his musical education" in London, but was by 1914 Louis Baron's adjutant at the Carreras tobacco company and by 1915 had "completely and utterly renounced the name of Levy" made Jacob ill.

Often Paul would endeavor to distract his brother from the greater losses by engaging his attentions on the topic of the lesser. Seeing Jacob's face settled in its scowl, Paul would remind Jacob that neither of them had ever really believed he'd win a seat in Congress. And even if he had, he was not rich enough to drop everything for politics. Even with Bob running the Baltimore plant, Levy's Shrinking in Philadelphia still needed Jacob. When up to the game of mutual support, Jacob played along, gently chaffing his brother on his new cooperative venture, reminding him that the small transactions of the agricultural collective, the Grange, made scarcely a dent in Reisterstown commerce, since the Negroes of Bond Avenue did a brisker trade at their church sales than the Grangers did with their day-old butter.

Sometimes Paul succeeded in leading Jacob along other paths, reminding him of the excellent job Bob was doing with the Baltimore works, how well suited he was, with his steady ways, to taking over the business. Neither brother was blind to the fact that Bob's success was helped by war contracts. Demand was strong for shrunk woolens to be turned into coats and puttees that could withstand the sleet and mud of Belgium, of Verdun. Bob was running the Baltimore plant as well or better than Jacob might have done and was contributing to the family's support as Jacob tried to get things off the ground in Philadelphia.

Jacob hoped to build the Philadelphia business slowly until he could buy houses of some elegance for all his young American offspring. He told them about this, helping them get used to the Philadelphia move by letting them spend summers in Baltimore. They could, if they chose, stay in town with their grandmother Elfant or even with Bob. They could spend their weeks as they pleased as long as they unfailingly showed up in Glyndon on Friday at suppertime.

Pictures of that summer, gray and grainy and fused to the crumbling vellum on which Aunt Fanny mounted them years ago, suggest that Jacob's saddest summer was—for his teenage children, my aunts, at least—a rather free and golden time.

A number of pictures capture the farm. Various photos of Jacob show him at ease, squinting into the sunlight but looking relaxed, coat off. There are several views of the chicken coops and at least one that shows corn grown to twice a small child's height, while on a facing page young Fanny, dressed in knee pants, hair under rustic straw, is labeled "Fanny the Farmer." Jean appears in only one photo, already with a baby on her hip; she is chic in a summer suit. Her sisters must have sympathized with her, for she had a husband at the European war front plus a squalling infant, their father, and their brother Emil to care for in Philadelphia, while they were still in the last summer of their freedom. There are five or six sets of photos capturing the sisters at various pleasure spots.

There are photos of them at Emory Grove, the old Negro camp meeting ground converted to a pleasure park for the Glyndon young. Or on the Severn River, Myrtle and Fanny being rowed by Fanny's beau. But most photos show the famed Tolchester Beach, a favorite resort in those days, an Eastern Shore area reached by pleasure steamer directly from Locust Point in downtown Baltimore.

Tolchester, twenty-seven miles across the bay from Baltimore, was apparently my aunts' destination on many days that summer. There are photos of them in front of the great Tolchester bathhouse with various friends. One shot shows Fanny and Myrtle and three other girls from the knees down, their shapely legs in wet bathing stockings, and another shows a group of girls in which Myrtle, slim and demure, has let her hair go wild like Lillian Gish's. Their beaux, dark, thin boys, grinning, pile in pyramids and drape their arms around the girls' shoulders.

Taking the midmorning steamer, carrying picnics and money for cool drinks, during Tolchester's best summers young people did not return till late, when the steamer, lit up like a lantern and swaying alluringly on strains of singing and laughter, pulled into the Lloyd Street dock about 9:00 PM. Off the boat, new couples strolled arm and arm. Swinging bags with damp sandy bathing costumes in them, the girls let the boys walk them home and bestowed kisses on them. Day after day that summer, apparently, the Levy girls amused themselves, only on Friday making their way to Paul's farm to meet their father and younger brothers who, after jouncing in the cars from Philadelphia, transferred at Baltimore and napped during the last leg of the trip to the depot at St. Georges. At the farm, Jacob would walk up the hill, using his hands against his weary knees to make the grade. He would muster a smile for

Brother Paul Levy, Pomona Grange.

those he loved, for Paul, waiting on the porch, and Sarah, coming from inside, wet hands brushing her apron, and for the girls, Myrtle and Fanny, whose affection he knew he could trust. Emil would be with them, but as Jacob noticed the screen door shut behind Myrtle, there was nothing but quiet behind her. And where is my son Paul? he would ask, trying to keep his voice level, the anger and the hurt contending.

What could Uncle Paul and Aunt Sarah say? Jacob surely knew in advance that his third son, a teenager, handsome, easygoing, popular with cronies, would not be there. His grandparents would not have insisted he leave their fold and would, as all knew, be coddling him at Hanover Street. Smiling brightly, Jacob's brother Paul took his bag. Just smell that country air, Jacob, Paul might say. Does it not do a body good to be close to Mother Earth?

꙳꙳꙳

As the local train out of Baltimore chugged toward Glyndon, Jacob had time to reflect on the funny place Paul had chosen for his utopia. The townsmen who followed Baltimore's health commissioner out to Glyndon in the 1890s came from the Baltimore burgher class. Leaving Baltimore's summer stink seven hundred feet below, the town of Glyndon was a cool summer retreat for the families of well-to-do professionals and industrialists.

They loved the jitney that picked them up at the station and the large clapboard houses on deep rolling lawns where the jitney stopped. Those escaping the city's heat stepped off the train to church picnics, fresh milk, lawn sports, musicals, and the easy availability of servants. Down in the valley the Worthingtons had once owned, descendants of Worthington slaves supplied ample domestic help, chauffeuring and hauling the summer staples of ice, local corn and tomatoes, fresh chickens, and bay crabs to the summering families. The grounds of the former Negro camp meeting, Emory Grove, were now converted to a pleasant place for strolling, courting white couples. Snatches of hearty singing from the Bond Street Church were heard ringing over the valley on Sunday mornings.

After arriving in Baltimore in 1881 or 1882, Paul had seemed likely to become a captain of industry. He had taken out patents—one for unremovable buttons, one for individually wrapped shirts—and he had joined the hordes in East Baltimore making pants for the big menswear merchants. Ingenious and descended from a family skilled in metal devices, Paul had set up his own shop in Baltimore, establishing a clientele large enough to accommodate his brother Jacob too, when he came. Bernhard Baron used to visit every evening, and they hammered and welded together. But Paul eventually came to hate pants and hate the closeness of rooms full of snipping and loud machinery, the darkness and stink of the toilets, the noise of the city. At first he thought he'd be satisfied with just a bit of green.

So he hied himself and his beloved Sarah north, first to the edge of Bolton Hill and then, a few years later, to the new section where Johns Hopkins intellectuals and the German Jewish manufacturing elite were settling; they called it Eutaw Place.

Round the edge of green Druid Hill Park, where great oaks bent down their canopies, the richest German Jews had built a grand *arrondissement*—a Ringstrasse or Tiergartenstrasse.

Towering townhouses, narrow but deep and richly furnished, were set behind serpentine lawns, tasteful sculptures, and glittering fountains, their musical plash mingling with the sound of the streetcar that braked gently to let off commuters and shoppers with their bundles. Returning home, the professionals and their smart-looking wives would hail the children, who might, at twilight, be exiting the new synagogue schools, raucous after extra hours cooped up in school. The synagogues, which towered over the street, had fancy facades complicated with stonework and lettering. Lofty Moorish-looking houses of prayer, modeled on the great *shuls* of Frankfurt and Berlin, these were not places of piety, strictly speaking, but guarantors of the worthy values, philanthropic openness, and solid citizenship of those who lived in the townhouses with their sumptuous lobbies, gold elevators, and in-house restaurants. It was all in the best middle European style: sociable but not crowded, civilized but not dour. The soaring lines of the synagogues elevated the spirit. As in Prague and Riga, so in Baltimore, one could stop into a synagogue and drift out easily, stroll up the great green hills of the park before the Sabbath meal, read the paper on a bench.

Eutaw Place was no mere ghetto of nouveau riche, but an incubator that cultivated enlightenment. Recruited from German universities, the new faculty of Johns Hopkins University naturally made themselves at home in this quarter out of Heine's Frankfurt. If the Jews who filled the townhouses of Eutaw Place had some of their German *Kultur* rubbed off them in the jostle or forgot some of their erstwhile civilization, the new faculty members at Hopkins provided examples.

The faculty members of a university deliberately shaping its curriculum to European models were not hostile to commercial people or the issues of municipal and transatlantic commerce that concerned them. Economists and sociologists, they made their way from Eutaw Place to their seminars, where they addressed themselves to problems of taxation, labor, and mechanization that were of vital interest to their Jewish manufacturing neighbors. The intellectual fields they were to develop at Hopkins had emerged in Germany precisely as the growth of cities seemed to necessitate a more organized mode of looking at exchange. Serving with their neighbors on the taxation commissions, charity societies, and public health commissions, the intellectuals of Eutaw Place invigorated the air with their practical but also idealistic commitment to the city's progress.

〜〜〜

It was a milieu not unlike what Paul had seen in Riga, an environment that might have gladdened him, had he not so missed the smell of cows and grass.

Week after week, he took the train farther and farther out into the country, picking up Reisterstown Road above the lake and following it out to Reisterstown itself. There were no Jews there, mostly Methodists, and this was land where tobacco had been picked by slaves, the children of whom still lived in little cottages on Bond Avenue. Many of the Negroes, working year after year in the kitchens and jitneys of Glyndon, had been there since slave days.

In this area Paul bought land that once was part of the large holdings that Noah Worthington had held on to until the claims to his "stolen" slaves were refused and he had to retreat down into the valley. Nevertheless, Negro neighbors farther down Bond Avenue could remember the Worthingtons, and others could relate that the street where they lived had, three generations back, taken its name from bondsmen who had been held there in pens.

It was a fitting refuge for a former Jew of the Pale, where his people were not allowed to own land and were restricted to growing small kitchen gardens.

The plat showing Paul's holdings from 1911 to his death reveals he was one of the largest landowners in greater Reisterstown, and thus a man who had realized his fondest dreams. The idea of remaking Jews into men of the soil, as well as the discovery of Jewish community and fraternity based on laboring with the hands, was in the ascendant in Europe in the years before Paul left for America. Every kindergarten had its garden plot, where the little ones were let loose with watering cans and spades. As they got older, some were sent to agricultural schools to gain knowledge of agronomy, farm management, and machine tools to ready themselves for the next stage in Jewish history.

In the mid-1870s in Shavli, with his father recently dead and his older brother Max dispatched to Tartu and then Riga to capture such exemptions from the general rule as a Jew might secure, Paul had been free to cultivate his own interests. Now in Glyndon Paul still had an old photograph, a souvenir of weekends when he had gone to agricultural camps where Jewish socialists, Bundists (labor advocates), and Zionists devoted their adolescent energies to agricultural progress; they sought the renewal of Jewish spirit through contact with the land.

Paul's hopes, though, would have been snuffed out utterly by the Czar's May Laws of 1882, which began, "As a temporary measure, and until a general revision is made of their legal status, it is declared that Jews be forbidden to settle anew outside of towns and boroughs exceptions being admitted only in the case of existing agricultural communities." For a "temporary" period, such hopeful youths as Paul would have read: "Forbidden are the issuing of mortgage and other deeds to Jews, as well as the registration of Jews as lessees of real property situated outside towns and boroughs." The edicts of May 3, 1882, contributed, as the authors of the *Jewish Encyclopaedia* of

1901 dryly put it, only "indirectly to the Agricultural Colonies of Russia."

After buying his own large house with nine rich acres in Glyndon in 1911, Paul, the only Jew in town, proceeded to live out the dream of agricultural self-sufficiency and cooperative community he had absorbed so long ago in Riga.

By 1914 Paul had organized some of his neighbors to establish a branch of the National Grange of the Patrons of Husbandry, a service organization for farmers that promoted translating the beauty and goodness of rural life into social betterment. Paul eventually held every office of his local Grange; he journeyed to the state Grange meetings and once to the national meeting in California, proud as anything of his badge. But he started modestly as treasurer, master, speaker, and parliamentarian.

"Down with monopolies and up with cooperation!" This was the rallying cry of those early farm organizers on whose ideas the Pomona Grange relied. The farmer, as Paul knew, was an agent of progress and civilization, steward of the most valuable commodity there is—land—and on whom all industry depended. The farmer the Grangers organized was a worthy citizen, a man whose hard work in the clean air instilled a natural cultivation.

"Human happiness," read the heady credo of the Maryland Grange, "is the acme of earthly ambition. Individual happiness depends upon general prosperity." Paul was glad to explain this to any who expressed interest. His bible was a volume by Solon Justice Buck, *The Granger Movement, 1870–1880*, which, published in 1913, came out just in time to assist Paul in establishing the organization and ritual of his local Grange.

I have the minutes of Paul's active years. They show that Paul was the most disinterested and particular of the Grangers. Other members might underestimate the value to civilization of the short dairy course offered at the University of Maryland, or of serving on the local fertilizer committee, or might let their minds wander during the report of the Mid-Atlantic state lecturers conference. Not Paul. He gave his passion for Mother Earth free rein, even sometimes exhibiting pugnacity ill befitting a Granger, growing hot in insisting that the Grange stood for a "square deal for everyone."

Brother Levy insisted that voting for officers be carried out by written ballot, that minority reports on the qualifications of candidates be given the same attention as majority reports, and that the minutes of all Grange meetings be faithfully typewritten and entered in the Grange annals and then approved by all members.

It was naturally Brother Levy who raised his voice for farmers as the Consolidated Gas and Electric strung wires and laid pipe up Reisterstown Road, and he agitated successfully for the same rates for country as city service. It was Paul Levy who urged more research on rural mail delivery, it was he who went to the state Grange meetings at Salisbury, and it was he who took the train all the way to California for the national meeting.

Brother Levy's mind never wandered. He never indulged in low resentment, and when any office needed filling, he was there. As president, he installed new officers "with all due ritual and . . . without once [as the minutes of the meeting marveled] using the Grange manual during the entire installation."

Uncle Paul, as Jacob sometimes reminded his children, was not to be made a laughing stock. But admittedly mouths twitched in town, and Jacob's children sometimes laughed aloud at Paul's letters urging that "when school closes you ought to come here with the boys. It will do you good to be close to mother earth; besides, boys should get an idea how to make a living direct from mother earth when conditions require."

Was it his unworldliness or an absurd recklessness that explained the story everyone in town knew: Mr. Levy had lost a diamond cuff link while plowing. The children in town called it buried treasure.

If his family and neighbors found him kooky, Paul seemed not to notice. Photos show a knob-kneed, big-eared, pointy-shouldered man sitting next to Sarah's solid fat, as much in love with her after twenty years as ever. He offered his half-furnished rambling old hall, late a boarding house, as a family dacha. Boys could be sent there to work off misdemeanors, girls to learn the value of housework. Daughters like Jean suspected of overly long walks might be spirited off for weeks of diary writing under the close supervision of her mother's sisters. Had Jean been so supervised, these sisters let Jacob know, perhaps she would have waited for her swain to return from the war and married him properly, instead of (and no one said this) marrying him in a hurry before little Earle started to show. And she would not now be pregnant and alone in Philadelphia had she been looked to. All these, and Jacob too, Paul urged to use the farm for rejuvenation.

For Jacob, though, the family put a cheerful face on Friday evenings. The tenderhearted Paul and Sarah had nothing but the deepest pity, but they did not know what to do for him. After they heard his tread going up the stairs to the small loft bedroom where Jacob slept with Emil, they would discuss his troubles. Amelia, they agreed, had become a burden Jacob's family could not handle. On the other hand, it was hard to know what to say about Eddie, whose desertion to join Uncle Baron in London clearly hurt Jacob more than he could express.

How had it happened, Paul and Sarah wondered, that this dark-browed boy with the sweet smile, the boy who had, just a few summers before, gone like any Baltimore swain to meet girls at Tolchester and Emory Grove, was now sporting British aristocratic manners and sending his little brother, Emil, souvenirs the boy would not leave alone? The pretext of Eddie's going to England to complete his musical education was quickly swept away as Louis drew Eddie into the Baron family firm, asking him to help out and then offering him a position, and then, amazingly enough, a new name. The *carte postales* Eddie sent his brothers showed him in a series of foppish get-ups. He sent Emil tags from country hounds, tickets from clubs and outings, a silver cigarette case the boy carried about, feigning smoking. Moreover, Paul and Sarah worried, could it be long until Jacob lost his son Paul as well?

Young Paul showed no interest in machines nor in his father's internationalist vision, nor did he seem to care that his swagger and audacity offended the factory hands, Czechs and Lithuanians, who were already showing signs of restiveness against Levy's odd work rules. For now, young Paul was happy to drive the truck for his brother Bob, but his restlessness was obvious. As tidings came across the ocean, along with the clippings, the full-page advertisements, the records in the *Times* of the Carreras tobacco company growing growing growing . . . scarcely meeting wartime demand, young Paul distanced himself from his father and sisters, as if preparing for the moment he would leave.

It was not fair, Paul and Sarah agreed, that they should be so happy and Jacob so sad, that they should have so much in the way of love and Jacob so little.

And so brother Paul desperately tried to divert Jacob from worrying about his son Paul with conversations about their brothers Max and Isaac, back home in Lithuania and Latvia, where the European war was pressuring them as the Germans advanced from the west and the Russians from the east. They reassured themselves that Max, the solid citizen, had escaped from the battle zone, for they had received a letter from him, telling a strange story.

～🙣～

One second he was Mr. Lawyer Levy, the next, a Jew on the road with his rucksack. Putting three hundred rubles in the bank on January 1, 1914, and directing his wife to deposit the same amount the following day, he was off for Lianna. Max, who had such princely sums to deposit, was sent packing like any refugee. Later Max wrote from a town in Russia, sending a picture of a picnic, as if all was well. Paul reminded Jacob that things in their homeland were ever the same for the Jews.

Official communiqués from the German and Russian commands were brief. On April 15:

> From Headquarters of the High Command. To the north of the Neman (River) enemy advance units, passing through Rossieny, approached on the morning of 15 April the line of the Dubysa River.

Suvoikin, the military correspondent of the newspaper *Rech*, relying on stories of refugees, gave further details:

> The strongest German column attacked along the banks of the Neman from Jurburg (Jurbarkas). Reaching Borki (Baraiciai), the Germans reached deep into Rossieny (Raseiniai) district and began to make their way through the forests. Passing through Girtakoli (Girkalnis) and the Gruzishki property, they began to reach the rear of Rossieny (Raseiniai). A second German column also attacked from Jurburg (Jurbarkas), but along a different route: through Erzhvilki (Erzvilkis), Nemokshty (Nemeksciai), Tsaritsyno (Sarapinai), and on to Siauliai. This column was weaker, but acted more forcefully. The path along which the enemy attacked was all in flames.

On April 17:

> High Command (Oberste Heeresleitung). The battle of Siauliai has been successful for us. Suffering great losses, the Russians burned the city and fled toward Jelgava (Jelgava). Pursuit continues.

Unofficial publications are more detailed:

> In Siauliai. According to eyewitness accounts, before 8 A.M. on 17 April peasants had rushed in and announced that strong

German reconnaissance units were moving toward Siauliai, at a distance of a few versts from the city. There arose a terrible panic among the residents, the more so when barely half an hour after the warning by peasants German shells began to fall on the city. A panicked flight began on the only free road out, to Ianishki (Joniskis). On the road, not far from the Etulery station, residents were able to observe the capture of our communications unit by German cavalry. But, suddenly, there appeared from the direction of Gruzda (Gargzdai) a strong German reconnaissance force, which opened fire on the fleeing residents.

A chemist, Dr. F., who was working in the Frankel leather factory and escaped just as the Germans captured it, stated: "The German units at first did not prevent the exit of residents, but when the last of them were already 5 or 6 versts from the city, in the direction of Ianishki, opened fierce artillery fire. In general, residential buildings suffered little. Some residents were captured by the Germans. Goods were taken from warehouses. Locked shops were smashed in, windows broken.

Gradually further details became clear:

Siauliai under German rule. Germans spent in Siauliai . . . 11 days. Already on the 15th of April concern grew, because refugees from Rossieny (Raseiniai) had appeared, but there was no panic. It was hoped that residents would manage to leave Siauliai in complete safety. However, on the 16th one could begin to hear strong cannonades, and the flight of the population began . . . The city burned from artillery shells, and since there was no one to put out the fires, they spread and continued until the evening of April 18th.

According to the words of those who have arrived from Siauliai, the German unit had hardly entered the city when indiscriminate looting began. Warehouses, depots, private apartments were all looted. The looting was accompanied by arson in which rabble from the suburb of Shimshi (Sancai) took an active part. These dregs of society served as guides for the "valiant soldiers" and together they carried out "requisitions."

With the Germans stalled in Lithuania, locals blamed their advance on the Jews.

In Headquarters there is the conviction that the Jewish population in the war theater is a focus of espionage and complicity with the enemy. Thus arose the idea of the necessity of cleansing the strip of the front of Jews. Application of this measure began in Galicia. Authorities in the rear have begun to send thousands and tens of thousands of Austrian Jews into Russian gubernias in the interior. The mass of evacuees included the sick, the crippled and even pregnant women.

Far from the scenes of desperation that their brothers endured in Europe, Jacob and Paul were preoccupied with the ordinary problems of family life in peaceful Glyndon. Photos show that this summer marked a turning point in the life of young Theo. His long weeks with Mother Earth had not convinced Theo of the value of the simple life, or drawn him nearer to his father's and Uncle Paul's way of seeing things.

Sweating out the summer eating vinegared cucumbers and the stringy chickens from the coop, working all week with no one to talk to, by the weekends he was in a sputtering rage. While he tossed quoits with Emil on the flattened grass or dragged a stick along the railroad ties, he fumed and stormed, casting dark looks at the two men on the porch—his father with his eternal newspaper and foolish

Trotskyism, anarchism; cooperation, electrification.

Bored, stealthy, cutting into the
backdoor of the house on Saturday
after lunch, Theo would lead Emil
out of the heat. In the cellar, amid
the jars of Aunt Sarah's inter-
minable canning, they spread
Eddie's *carte postales* on the cool
basement floor. While they eked
out what pleasures could be had in
the sweltering Baltimore of mal-
contents, their brother lived the
larger life of a tobacco baron in
London, the life of those who had
no truck with social-*eests*.

Dressed to the nines and mentioned frequently in the *Times* reports of shareholder meetings,
Eddie led a different, a better life.
He had shown the way, Theo ex-

Jacob Levy on Paul Levy's porch,
sometime in the 1920s.

plained, the way young Paul would take when he turned eighteen
next year and he, Theo, would take in turn. And then, Emil, you too.
You too will come to England, will become a bigwig and a Baron, a
rich and lucky man.

Which is how—more or less—things actually worked out, though
not for my grandfather Emil who never, until he died in an institution
just as his mother had, forgot that he'd missed his own chance to be
a bigwig and a Baron. For the few years of his young manhood, when
his oddities were mistaken for those of a boy in his right mind, he
was, my mother tells me, a man about town, reckless, generous, flashing his cigarette case, behaving very much like the heir apparent—
though heir to what his family were never quite sure. It seems

reasonable to suppose that had he not "taken sick" sometime during the trip to Europe with his father in 1928, perhaps he too would have broken away, remained in London, and would now lie, like his brothers, in Bernhard Baron's large and handsome family tomb in North London, the name Emil Baron inscribed alongside those of his brothers, Edward Baron, Paul Baron, Theodore Baron, instead of next to his sisters Jean, Myrtle, and Fanny in a cemetery in Philadelphia.

If he in fact lies near his sisters Jean, Myrtle, and Fanny, this bed too was made before 1917, when Jean, pregnant without benefit of nuptials, was sent to find her family a place to live, a place where Percy, home on leave, might marry her and where she might keep house for her father and her brother Emil.

For by the time Jean had her second child, Jerry, conceived in 1917 on one of Percy's leaves, Jacob and his eldest daughter had forged the partnership of mutual benefit that would succor both of them through the years to come. Fortunately Jacob had Jean, with whom he discussed his idea of adding a second plant to Levy's International, this one in Philadelphia. And it was Jean, two babies in tow, who helped him establish a second household. Into the early 1920s, she was apparently content to act as family duenna and listen to her father's business plans and schemes. Until her sisters were safely married, who else was there to keep house for the whole clan as they moved to West Philadelphia, who else to temper their father's sometimes erratic judgments with practical sense? It was she who surmised the unsuitableness for children of the West Philadelphia neighborhood their father had chosen—no place for Jewish girls to meet husbands—then found the proper house and also the two smaller adjoining dwellings on George's Lane, not nearly so grand as Eutaw Place but with shade trees on culs-de-sac and a handy route into town to the plant by taking the Girard Avenue streetcar.

In the 1920s as business picked up and Myrtle and Fanny acquired husbands and babies and moved their husbands and babies into George's Lane, Jean began to show the determination she had always exhibited as a girl. She was liked and clearly needed at the plant, where her father's preoccupation with the machines and his prickly management style, together with the workers' endless union demands, left her to keep deliveries on schedule, customers happy, suppliers in line. She was not afraid to raise her voice when occasion required, and she was not afraid to get off the streetcar at Front and Oxford, the industrial district. She began to find it more and more convenient to spend the evening in town or a Saturday in town, ringing her sisters by phone to ask them to keep an eye on the boys.

Housekeeping and nose wiping—not to mention the ironing, dishes, and managing their father's books and newspapers—she left to her sisters. They would mutter among themselves that they worked at the plant too, but it was she who took responsibility in her father's weak areas. And she did payroll, dispensing cash to her father and sisters, and paying herself as well.

Their aunts would complain that Jerry and Earle saw of their mother less than was good for them. She was at the plant when they went to school, and on Fridays their grandfather took them with him to the farm, along with their Uncle Emil. She came overdressed to the farm when she came, but more often she did not come. She was in town. She was at the plant. The boys boarded the train with their grandfather and Emil.

Thus she pretended not to see their mouths tighten on some mornings when she had come home late the night before, as she passed her sisters in their quilted housecoats, pulled on her coat, a fur smelling of perfume, pinned her chignon at the hall mirror. And was gone.

ELEVEN

The Arcadia Works

When Earle and Jerry, age twelve and ten, said good-bye to their mother in the spring of 1928, walking up the gangplank of the ship with their Uncle Bob, they did not wonder why they were being sent on so lavish a holiday in March.

That their trip during the spring holiday would not bring them back to school with their classmates seemed odd, but it was far more fun to enjoy the sail on an ocean liner. Snapshots show them squinting into the sun, resting their heads, newly barbered, against the striped deck chairs. Earle even hopped into the lifeboat for a picture, not bothering to sit up straight and letting his legs in their stout socks sprawl a bit.

Jean did not countenance such casual poses, so it must have come as a relief to them to be bound for England with no one but kind Uncle Bob to watch them, plus the prospect of visiting their uncles, Eddie, Paul, and Theo, in London. Their uncles' version of "gentlemanly" seemed to be one they would like.

The pictures and postcards their uncles had been sending them made clear that gentlemanly life was high life indeed. The pictures

showed rolling lawns with little camp chairs. There was Uncle
Eddie's "town house" in Belgrave Square, tall, white, and imposing,
and rumors of a country house as well, with stables.

What they did not realize—until after Uncle Bob went back to the
United States and Uncle Eddie tried to explain as well as he could—
was that their mother, encouraged by her brothers, had decided it
would be best for them to go to school in England, as English boys, and
one day help run their great-uncle Baron's Carreras tobacco business.
They would be raised by Uncle Eddie and Aunt Bertha, eventually to
become, as Eddie and Bertha had, one of Bernhard Baron's perfect
blends. Whenever it was they understood or were finally informed by
their tiny but potent aunt Bertha, they couldn't have guessed how
much thought and planning had gone into the moment, and how completely their grandfather Jacob had been outmaneuvered.

When Aunt Bertha explained the "wonderful provisions made for
their future," she also declared herself "so pleased" that their grandfather Jacob, along with Uncle Emil, would be present in London for
the grand opening of the new Carreras tobacco factory.

Hints, and then a formal invitation to the opening of the great factory, mostly from his son Paul, had been coming to Jacob since 1927.
Careful to downplay what a great day it would be, what a triumph
for the "Guv'ner," and to emphasize the strides in social progress
they had all made, Paul would be casual, dropping hints that Jacob
might want to see what they'd done in the way of ventilation, what
notions they'd had—similar to his own—about the drying of paper
and such. Maintaining the offhand tone that he and his brothers used
to ward off flare-ups, he'd outline the schemes they'd been able to
put in place for the comfort and security of the workers, and if, Paul
allowed, Jacob might not "have time" for the factory, he might want
to look in at the Settlement House whose new building, thanks to
Baron's gift, was to be called the Bernhard Baron St. George's Jewish Settlement. A place for East End youth—Russian Jews of the kind
they had known in Baltimore—the settlement aimed to assimilate

young Jews into their adopted nation by providing vocational training, brotherhood, and fun.

Earle and Jerry's grandfather had responded to the letters by dropping them on the porch at Glyndon for his brother Paul to pick up and file.

Now, to hear from Aunt Bertha's mouth that their grandfather would be coming in the summer, missing the factory's opening but staying with them several weeks, was dumbfounding to the two young boys. Nearly as dumbfounding was the news that before coming to London their grandfather would first be taking Uncle Emil to visit relatives in Europe, with visas already obtained not only to England and Germany but to places much further east. Jacob and Emil would be sailing to Germany and then boarding a train bound for Latvia and Lithuania. They would visit three cities, two of which had unpronounceable names. Riga was the first. The second two were Siauliai and Raseinai.

There was much Jerry and Earle did not yet understand in that spring of 1928. How their mother could bear to part with them permanently, why their grandfather and Uncle Emil were going to Latvia and Lithuania, and why their grandfather would be coming to visit them in London. But one thing was clear: Nothing they had ever seen in Philadelphia or Baltimore prepared them for the grandeur that greeted them in England. The large fortune and high position that Bernhard Baron had achieved with the help of a machine invented in Baltimore exceeded anything the boys could have imagined.

By the time their Uncle Eddie arrived in London in 1913, the story of his great-uncle Bernhard Baron's ascent from Baltimore tobacco foreman to London's preeminent cigarette magnate had already claimed its own colorful chapter in the history of American trust busting. And by the time that Eddie's nephews Jerry and Earle arrived in London in 1928, Bernhard Baron had secured a place as an admired figure of enlightened industry in Europe.

Also one of the richest.

❧

Uncle Baron's spectacular early success owed a lot to his clever machine that turned loose tobacco into cigarettes at a previously unheard of rate and price, as well to another infant industry—advertising. Uncle Eddie specialized in refining the advertising machinery of brands, packs, niches, and market shares at a moment when the cigarette faced an uncertain future. Pipes and cigars—imported, expensive, hand rolled—had been the nineteenth century's talisman of the ruling male classes, giving a particular image of class security and bourgeois solidity. If a machine-made cigarette could put a cheap smoke in the hands of everyone, the British understood something the Americans did not: Smokers wanted something cheap that smelled and tasted expensive. If the apparently limitless market that mass production of an affordable cigarette put within reach of all was ready for the plucking, the trick was to give social cachet to a product available for just a penny.

J. M. Barrie's *Lady Nicotine* might well have passed into the fin de siècle, a relic of an earlier era. But as Barrie, darling playwright of the London stage, prospered, so prospered the brand—Craven A—he called the Arcadia mixture.

The boost that Barrie gave Baron's upstart firm was invaluable, setting the course for half a century of marketing the Carreras brands as the only choice for the boldly metropolitan, socially independent, and exuberantly modern smoker. Barrie helped the blend's new purchasers expand their market from gentlemen to, say, the gentlemanly, making their cigarette the talisman of the self-possessed young fellow on the way up.

The Craven A and Black Cat blends brought with them a high reputation for smokeability and the reassuring bona fides of the Carreras shop, a tony gentleman's haunt. To this combination J. M. Barrie added a dash of reckless urbanity and fugitive youthfulness that would make him, by 1907, not only patron of the bon vivant in the London hit, *When a Man Is Single,* and sponsor of the Grub Street

Advertising vehicle promoting Black Cat cigarettes introduced in 1904. From the collection of Stephen Croad.

chain-smoker featured in *My Lady Nicotine*, but liberator of every boy who, like Peter in Kensington Gardens, wanted out of his pram.

It was at roughly Barrie's own pace that Carreras ventured to coax girls out from under the parental wing and persuade men to tolerate their smoking. In his book *My Lady Nicotine*, Barrie had the Arcadia blend perfume a duel of the sexes not yet Shavian—not a sexy contest of young equals but a tug of war between Victoria's rule and manly prerogative. The book's title hinted at what the first chapter, "Matrimony and Smoking Compared," made clear, namely, a modern chap's need to walk around the block for a smoke, to maintain the poise a gentleman owed his darling. Her sentiments were well-known: "The smell of tobacco is abominable, for one cannot get it out of the curtains, and there is little pleasure in existence unless the curtains are all right. As for a cigar after dinner, it only makes you dull and sleepy and disinclined for lady's society."

Making forbearance to ladies a gentlemanly trait, Barrie admitted all those who suffered such scenes with noble grace into the exclusive club of the twentieth century, the club of boys plotting escape from fans, pianos, mothers, and also long work days and the usual paternal pieties: family, empire, England. Carreras tobacco followed his lead, offering tantalizing images of the urban, especially London, scene and eschewing the more parochial markers of social class and status—titled aristocracy, imperial possession, the fetishes of service—on which most other companies depended.

Which is to say the Craven A smoker left it to his more gauche brother to light up a Prince Charming, a Belted Earle, an Iron Duke, a Windsor, a Crown Jewels, a British Standard, a Three Castles, a Palace, a Park Drive, a Country Club, a White Rolls, a Pall Mall, a Raleigh, a Waverly, a Chesterfield, or—touchingly—a Gentleman.

Such passé appeals to pedigree were not for the Carreras smoker, who breathed in the bracing air of metropolitan venues—the theater, Whitehall, Epsom Downs racecourse, St. James Place. He smoked a Craven A. Or he touched his match to a Passing Show, a Piccadilly, a Club, a Consulate, or a Turf, or, with a wink at English regalia as he passed the Palace Walk, a Guards. But it was another image, one transferred from the window of a Wardour Street shop to his cigarette case, and eventually to the massive Carreras factory facade, that appeared when he lit up Carreras's signature brand—the urbane, luxurious, lucky, sloe-eyed, and increasingly androgynous Black Cat.

The Carreras Black Cat had many lives. Sometime around the 1920s the cat's art nouveau roundness in early advertisements gave way to a deco appearance, the well-fed look stylized, the cat's rounded haunches drawn up into points to approximate more closely the black cat god of the Nile. And then in the next two decades he fattened again. But in all its guises the Black Cat on the Carreras pack boasted city suavity and modern sangfroid. Its expressions included urbane and bemused, careless and sportive, decadent, content, and even frivolous, but always the cat was knowing, wise, unsurprised; this cat knew more than he let on. The Black Cat answered to various aliases, including some in other languages (black cat number nine; Three Cats; Schwartz Katz), and though he was many things, he was never earnest, preachy, timid, parochial, or stuffily

English, never old-fashioned, prudish, or—what summed up the rest—bourgeois.

Sized for hands extra large, large, medium, or small, Black Cat cigarettes brought a whiff of pheromones with them, a gamy, intelligent, adult air that seemed to whisk Wendy and Peter out of Mr. and Mrs. Darling's parlor and into the street in a single feline bound. The cat's sleekness and look of exotic mystery, which turned Barrie's man about town into a bona fide *flaneur*, increasingly appealed to young women weary of piano duets on fusty themes, who were not about to withdraw from the table while the gentleman trimmed their cigars for a long night of port and the Corn Exchange. Secure in its modernity, Black Cat offered women the chance to throw off encumbrances, to be surprising—donning sequins one night and a "smoking" the next, trading the dressmaker's notions for that marcelled, edgy look that could change as fast as the shutter blinked: Call it style.

Highly stylized, the black cat on the cigarette packs went from cartoonish to sleekly abstract. The campaign to launch Chick, a "gentleman's smoke," for instance, featured an image of a befeathered and bosomy bird singing an aria while standing atop the mock gallant cat's head, a circle of black face with two footlights for eyes. Look again, though, and this same bird appears to have emerged full grown from between this same cat's fuzzy black ears.

As abstract as the best poster art and sustained for longer and across a wider range of media was the ad based on the color red used by another new brand, a woman's smoke, Cerise. Born out of the discontinued Sweet Kiss, itself the lipstick red of the Black Cat's neck ribbon, Cerise's brilliant red hue was the same as the one that drew the eye up over the Hampton Road in the spring of 1928. Workers on scaffolds were applying the last coat of thick hand-ground pigment to the burned crimson slash spelling out C-A-R-R-E-R-A-S on the huge new factory building. Along with two massive Egyptian-looking cats guarding either side of the doorway, the Carreras letters represented the last touches on the great factory that Jerry and Earle arrived in time to see completed in the spring of 1928 and which, in their home-sickness, they dreamed of showing to their Uncle Emil and grand-father as soon as they arrived.

To help counter their homesickness, Uncle Eddie took the boys to Asprey's and there, among the heaviness of sterling and wood, al-lowed them to choose as a gift a beautiful cigarette case with E-L on the corner, which Eddie planned to present to his brother Emil when he came to London. The brushed silver of its beveled lid, fine but with a crosshatch like linen, the tiny invisible catch at the front lip (one can imagine Eddie showing them, the gift in his own palm, the lid springing up with a bounce of his thumb) made this gift exactly the thing for a man to produce from a pocket, starched cuffs slipping back on a manly wrist.

"Cigarette?" Uncle Eddie would have teased the boys, extending the case, then putting it on his Asprey's tab and into his own pocket.

Fourteen years gone from Baltimore and long out of his father's good graces, Eddie must have considered it a lucky break that his fa-ther was coming to see his young nephews in London just as Eddie was entering his glory. The boys' eagerness to welcome their uncle and grandfather and show off their new lifestyle would give Eddie op-portunities to reveal, with all modesty, how very nicely he had done at embracing chances that didn't come around for every Baltimore boy.

It hadn't taken much to entice him into the tobacco business. The "musical education" that the papers routinely cited as his reason for coming to London quickly fell by the wayside, and his early resis-tance to Uncle Baron's entreaties that he try the cigarette business were about what one could expect of a twenty-one-year-old boy with a taste for the good life. But Eddie did try the cigarette business and soon discovered he had a knack for the advertising side of things.

By Eddie's twenty-fifth birthday he had begun to contribute to the steady growth of Carreras, supporting its transition from a national to an international brand that eventually necessitated the building of Arcadia Works' brand-new factory. By the time the great "temple of

Tobacco" was built, Eddie at thirty-five was poised and managerial. He was looking forward to telling his father that in the settlement house going up at the same time, the Barons would not only teach boys and girls the trade of making cigarettes, but in their factory they would implement the most progressive set of worker benefits ever attempted in the tobacco industry. They would also fund the most liberal social welfare program for Jewish youth in the United Kingdom—and all without a whit more, but also not a whit less, noblesse oblige than the case required.

His father would be sure to notice, and he hoped be reassured, that Eddie did not disguise his origins. He still—and would always—pronounce Tuesday, Toos-dee, as those from Baltimore did. But he'd also mastered attributes one couldn't learn in Baltimore: magnanimity without patronage; self-deprecating modesty; the jaunty, boyish, affectionate yet respectful note one could draw out of the appellation "Guv'ner."

꠸ꕸ

No one watching the Arcadia Works factory on Hampton Road come out from under its scaffolds and drop cloths would accuse it of subtlety. No one, certainly not the architectural critics who weighed in as soon as the building, built by a tobacco merchant of "Hebrew extraction," was finished, thought its architectural statement possible to ignore.

It was without a hint of rabble rousing or grandstanding that the Barons, with young Paul in charge of this phase, had hired thousands of North London workmen at twice the going rate, and moved thousands of laborers along the Regents canal to find new flats closer to the factory. Without casting aspersions on the nondescript, respectable but run-down Englishness of Camden neighborhood, they had hired the architect of the Firestone factory and the builder Sir Robert McAlpine and simply leveled the Victorian garden terrace.

The black cats in front of the Carreras Cigarette Factory at Mornington Crescent. One original and one replica cat guard the building's entrance to this day.

Their builders were under instructions to give the Barons a building as au courant, daring, metropolitan, and giddily youthful as any in the metropolis, a landmark not only of iconic but also entertaining appeal.

Though the company letterhead always called the factory the Arcadia Works, and though its facade proclaimed CARRERAS as the walls rose, appreciative neighbors were already calling it the Black Cat factory.

Whenever I go to London, I visit the former cigarette factory, marveling at its facade as I ascend to the street from the Mornington Crescent underground.

A popular London landmark from its first days, the Black Cat factory seemed to revel in a brazen eclecticism that expressed at least one version—not everyone's—of what modernity should be. The building capitalized on the Egypt craze that swept the world after the discovery of King Tut's tomb by British archaeologists. The *St. Pancras Chronicle*, on hand for the opening ceremonies in 1928, praised the new "Temple of Tobacco" in an article several columns long, admiring the Tutankhamun-inspired facade especially: "Something fresh in London architecture—a Conventionalized Copy of the Temple of Bubastis, the cat headed goddess of ancient Egypt." Local guidebook writers had to hurry out a new edition when in Mornington Crescent (the dingy backstairs entrance to Regents Park, the neighborhood tone set by Gilbey's Gin Works and the Camden Goods Yard), of all places, arose a radiant, parti-colored monument. The writers could not marvel enough at the "magnificent premises of Carreras Ltd," with its huge black cats guarding the entrance, its ground glass colored columns, its "solar disk emblem of Ra, the sun God, mellower of tobacco."

But the architectural establishment was not so sure. London's modernists had kept quiet as Victorian preservationists fought the commercial development of the Crescent, horrified at the Crescent gardens being replaced with a factory. That the gardens were run-

Postcard to the author's grandfather, Emil Levy, in 1928, shortly before the opening of the Arcadia Works, the "Black Cat Factory."

down and the buildings around them broken up into poor bed-sit flats with cookstoves on the landings and privies in the yard did not matter to the newly organized defenders of London's residential integrity.

The modernists, unperturbed as the walls went up, followed with pleasure the rise of the largest reinforced concrete structure in England, an edifice poured out of 80,000 tons of modernism's wonder material. They admired the pale austerity of the factory's interior spaces, with its sloping walls, the skylights angled to admit morning light and block afternoon heat, and the nine acres of floor space covered with palest maple. Yet all the enthusiasm inspired by the bold use of poured concrete trickled away as the facade was applied and this architectural travesty could be seen for what it was, a grossly commercial embrace of ornament, the beauty of its modernist bones traduced in art deco crowd pleasing and King Tut mania.

When finished, the building managed to violate nearly every canon of modernist doctrine: derivative where it was supposed to be the embodiment of its occasion; decorative where it was supposed to be strictly functional; eclectic where it ought to have been indigenous. Next to this "bogus" modern building, "abominable" as architectural purists agreed, the Mornington Crescent Terraces deserved credit as ambitious. Whether the commercial intent, leftist leanings, and mixed Jewish, Russian, and American "extraction" of the building's baronial builder—unfailingly mentioned—were part of the problem the critics were too polite to say. But in the *Architect's Journal* Maxwell Fry led the charge by calling the Carreras factory "Bauhaus with bells." Better gaze at the back side of the building, better study its estimable loading dock and exhaust towers, than waste a minute on the frontage along Hampton Road: "a piece of ponderous scenery secured to a factory for the purpose of advertisement."

As if advertising were not the point! Uncle Eddie, feet up in the Egyptian boardroom, must have been amazed. To the sober view that architectural detail should follow the bare contours of function, his building let out a thin stream of amused smoke: Restrained it was not. For blocks, the warm smell of Virginia and Carolina tobacco drifted round corners and over rooftops. The aroma gusted down the underground vents, filling the Mornington Crescent tube station with the sweet savor of tobacco (cured by the sun god, Ra!). Though Eddie's campaign to rename the Mornington Crescent tube stop "Tooten Camden" (a pun on the factory's Tutankhamun-inspired look and the fact that the two terminals of the Northern Line were Tooting and Camden) did not succeed, his spirits were undampened. He flood-lit and eventually affixed neon lights to the facade, and then a cigarette and neon plume of smoke, so that at dusk, as the guidebooks breathed ecstatically, "the whole frontage was flooded with colored light."

Lit up like a cabaret by night and smelling like one too, the Black Cat factory stretched itself with a great purr along the Hampton Road. Baron's protégé, my uncle Eddie, having raised this pyramid in eighteen months and having transferred thousands of workers from the other factories in a weekend, did some purring too. After the

ceremonies capping the two-day move to the Arcadia Works, he was
reported to have made paper airplanes of hundred-pound notes and
sent them over his blotter, calling "Catch!" to those in the vicinity. Yet
his reasons to purr were not all plutocratic. In 1929, with Bernhard
Baron still alive and his philanthropic reputation now legendary,
Eddie stood to inherit a company that not only did very well but also
did good. The building might look like a pyramid—archetypal image
of civilization's rise on the backs of slaves—but the papers all called
it a temple, and its owners, the Baron family, were called not tycoons
but great Solomonic benefactors. Anyone looking past the facade
could see that this Egyptian pyramid was one of the world's most ambitious experiments in social, or industrial, democracy.

୭୶ଏ

Did Eddie have Bernhard Baron to thank for his father's stop in London? Would Jacob have been interested in the great social progress
the Black Cat factory was making, perhaps curious to see the works
even if he were not anxious to see the man who was responsible for
them? Certainly the works fulfilled all that he and Bernhard had
dreamed of long ago when they'd hammered together in Baltimore,
confident that labor-saving machines would improve civilization.

If Jacob had let Bernhard speak to him, his old friend would surely
have pointed out that, in 1919, blessings on the progress of worker
welfare in the British tobacco industry had been pronounced by the
Fabian Socialist, Sidney Webb. Webb agreed that mechanization had
gone a long way toward remedying conditions in an industry Lloyd
George's inspectors had found unspeakably filthy. But Carreras went
well beyond a clean-up. The Arcadia Works was not only, as the old
man modestly put it to reporters, "a clean and pleasant place to
work," but, among local working people, a place whose name alone
conferred prestige and suggested privilege. Anyone who heard you
worked at Carreras, reported employees, "thought you must be rich."

On the factory's opening day, with film crews, journalists, Roth-schilds, Samuels, Belishas, and other eminent personages in atten-dance, thousands cheered the seventy-year-old Bernhard Baron, who stood modestly on the podium, handing out sterling silver medals to three thousand of his workers.

Such a numismatic hymn to labor ideals probably struck many as odd, but it was Baron's way of signaling the end of tobacco's op-pression of the working man. Carreras, this medal proclaimed, would exceed even Sidney Webb's predictions. It would be a place where a world-class product was manufactured profitably and efficiently in an atmosphere of complete worker satisfaction.

And once the factory was up and running, efficiency, the catch-word of progressives on both sides of the ocean, received nearly as much promotion as the cigarettes themselves, the beauty and humane benefits of efficiency eventually becoming the theme of the popular Black Cat factory tour. Carreras workers wore color-coded buttons indexed to the floor on which they worked, and a corps of time man-agement experts had their own department. Cosmetics, which affected the taste of the tobacco, were strictly forbidden, and any worker com-ing ten minutes late would find the door to the factory from the heated tunnel under the Hampton Road to the tube station locked. Directors were to be addressed as Mr. Eddie, Mr. Paul, Mr. Theo, and Mr. Baron, and a crew of workers was employed simply to keep the ma-chines clean and shiny. Baron ran a tight ship, yes, but he had no doubt that worker happiness was efficiency's best safeguard.

To ensure continuity of production and low worker turnover, he liked to employ whole families, and those transferred from one fac-tory to another received help with moving expenses and resettlement near the factory. Carreras employees got subsidized meals, with spe-cial vouchers issued to supplement the subsidy for those without other well-paid family members in the company ranks. They got medical care, including dental, at an on-site clinic, staffed with a doctor and nurse. Underage workers had work-study release plans that enabled them to finish school and collect their diplomas. Married workers finding it hard to conceive found adoption help; retirees were settled in the country; and long-term workers, of which by 1928 there were hundreds, were given paid holidays for years of service earned. The year was punctuated with various celebrations, as on Christmas when workers received their tins of salmon and maple from the Canadian affiliate, and of course free cigarettes; the party started at noon when the company band began tuning up and it blared on till midnight.

Bernhard Baron might have reflected that if his old friend Jacob would not praise him for any of these accomplishments, perhaps he'd approve of the brilliant match he arranged between Eddie and Baron's granddaughter Bertha.

Years ago Bernhard had provided the funds to send Bertha to Baltimore for a bit of finishing at the St. Agnes Academy for Girls, which was loose enough about weekend visits to allow Bertha to mingle with the Levys and their older son, Eddie. It would have seemed equally prescient to invite Bertha to visit London when, shortly after Eddie arrived, he so needed the support of a confident American girl to keep his chin up. True, Bernhard had his own urgent reasons. His own line was thin. His only son Louis, kindly but not imaginative, lacked his father's business sense and ultimately outlived his father by only two years. The restocking of Baron's managerial ranks would have been the only prudent move for the head of a company that in the 1920s was just tapping into its greatest markets. It was Bernhard's intention that Eddie and Bertha, plucked from humbler settings, would use their privilege to advance the cause of social justice.

Still, the young people had their own way. Bright, hard, and vivacious, they humored him, calling him Old Man and Guv'ner. Bernhard spent his own cash to coin sterling silver medals for his workers, but how many thousands per year his protégé Eddie put on his Asprey's tab he did not want to know. Eddie was energetic all right, tirelessly dreaming up new ad schemes—illustrated cards for the cigarette packs featuring film stars, queens and kings, roadsters and fashion models, and racehorses. And he and Bertha were just as energetic at spending—she on Worth and Balenciaga; he on racehorses, stable fittings, weekends in Monaco.

Bernhard did not live to see the worst of his granddaughter's antics as Mrs. Baron or, after Eddie was knighted during World War II, as Lady Baron. Such as the time Bertha, visiting America, held out her closed hands to Jean, Myrtle, and Fanny, bidding them pick their gift. Looking a bit threadbare, with Levy's Shrinking barely making enough money to keep up their house payments, what could they do but play along? What delight Bertha professed as each sister chose the present selected especially for her—each sister tapping one arm or the other and receiving a magnificent jewel—a diamond for one, a great ruby for the second, an emerald for the third.

The woman who ran the Bernhard Baron boys home, an orphanage, told me about a package that arrived for her on the day that her husband, the home's beloved warden, died. What would a woman want who'd spent her life in East London ministering to the poor? A mink coat, surely! To wear to Basil's funeral.

Bertha would have her portrait painted the way others posed for photographs. Sir Orpen would be called in for a sitting, and she'd pose in a newer gown. If she didn't like the portrait's look—say, how he caught her head but not her gown—well then, off with her head, she'd say whimsically. Put it in an oval frame and do what you like with the rest.

❦

While Baron gave full rein to social welfare programs, Uncle Eddie worked hard to lighten the tone and modernize the Old Man's progressive zeal. In the early years, Baron had pioneered stamp albums for cats and coupon schemes, and had even given his blessing to the *Daily Mail's* National Black Cat Day of 1913, when the nation's smokers were encouraged to walk the streets with their packs, hoping to meet the Black Cat Man with his sack of gold sovereigns. But as the medal with its hygienic sentiments illustrated, the Old Man, as Eddie knew, could grow pious and lugubrious where workers were concerned.

So it was Eddie who cooked up the dottier advertising schemes, and Eddie who established the factory's theater groups (two shows a year, variety and drama; a stage hired out in Bloomsbury for performances), the many sports leagues, and the book club. How to be sure the hum of the machinery found accompaniment in the humming of workers? Music while you work! How to make sure Carreras girls dressed suitably for work: the annual Miss Carreras contest (frocks and corsages; no swim suits, please). How to sell cigarettes? Richly colored collector's cards for everyone—the obligatory kings and queens of England, golf clubs, great houses, great horses, great gardens, but also great escapes of history, the stars of Paramount, the automobiles of 1929. There was the great Black Cat football competition, providing a safe, harmless outlet for a bit of a wager, and discount coupons redeemable for shoes and razors and toasters, with the distribution station right in the factory.

While the Old Man focused on the working family, closeting himself with his lawyer to set aside trust funds for the Bernhard Baron Cottages for retired workers and the Bernhard Baron Fund for obstetric medicine, Eddie made sure the gift to the tennis courts in Regents Park was sufficiently handsome to bear Baron's name, and that there was plenty to drink at the annual picnic at Honeypot. The workers who streamed out of the Tooten Camden underground and into the Carreras tunnel were no longer the Old Man's immigrant Germans in suspenders, mustached intellectuals applying Marx and Engels to cigar molds. They were twenty-one-year-old English girls from St. Pancras and Holborn, some of whom had moved out of mum and dad's house to live together in bed-sits, cooking on coils and obeying rules to stagger the visits of gentlemen. So long as there was time left for the cinema, they were eager to work long hours, for they spent money at a rate that alarmed their parents. They knew their parents felt safe with them at work, especially because the subterranean tunnel took them right from the basement, piled with tobacco, and into the tube. These workers read fashion magazines and bought stockings, and after hours they painted their mouths and their nails and danced in cheap halls.

Eddie allowed that workers in modern industry did not fall dead of heatstroke or cough into a handkerchief. But modern industry did not lecture itself hoarse either.

Modernity said, Ain't we got fun!

TWELVE

Jacob's Cane

Late in the summer of 2007, I was riding a train bound north from Berlin to Sassnitz and the overnight Baltic ferry that would take me once again to Lithuania. As the glitter of Berlin gave way to the deep green of rural towns, I tried to imagine the thoughts of my great-grandfather Jacob Levy in 1928, when he was traveling in a train clicking over these rails, on his way to visit the brothers he had left behind forty-four years ago.

I couldn't be sure of his precise route. The stamps on Jacob's passport—Germany, Lithuania, Latvia, Lithuania, London—revealed that he'd taken an ocean liner from Baltimore to Germany (Bremen or Hamburg) and then a train to one of the Baltic ports. But who knew which one or if it still existed? In 2007, since air travel had long ago replaced the many passenger vessels once departing from a score of western Baltic ports, I'd chosen Sassnitz, making it easy to visit Berlin first. Jacob's train journey, like mine, probably was not long. When he boarded his train for the coast the reckoning he would present to his brothers—the tally of his accomplishments during the years away—drew closer.

I had some of the same feelings. Years had passed since I'd first visited the Baltics with Yael. By tomorrow morning the ship *Vilnius* would have crossed the Baltic and set down in Klaipeda on Lithuania's amber coast. A few hours later, I'd be back in one of the towns on Jacob's cane, ready this time to follow Jacob's route of 1928 and not one dictated by a tour guide or too much reading. I, like Jacob, had some accounting to do, some mental mustering of what I had to show for all my research and journeys. While it was absorbing to imagine Jacob's struggle, I was not thinking only about him but also about myself and the book I'd been writing about him.

People who knew me thought it only natural that I hadn't finished my big book yet, noting all the changes in my life since I'd first set out to understand the inscriptions on Jacob's elegant cane and the Jewish civilization from which he and Bernhard Baron had hailed. Shortly after Yael and I arrived home I had started working on this book in earnest. But in the same year I'd also left the University of Pennsylvania, started teaching at Harvard, and finished most of a book on the literature of New England. I'd gotten divorced, become a single mother of three, and then, just a few months later, met and fallen in love with Harvard's brilliant, funny, bighearted president, Larry Summers, who had also been lately divorced and was also the parent of three. My friends were right that life with Larry meant big changes in my life.

Larry was a larger public figure than I'd ever known, and life with him brought limelight, public attention, and stress, as his controversial struggle to reform the oldest, most complacent institution in America began to win him enemies.

And so, four years after Larry and I met and a few weeks before a faculty uproar forced his resignation, we got married in the dining room of the Harvard president's house. It crossed my mind that wedging a wedding canopy into this bastion of WASP gentility might turn out to be my greatest contribution to Jewish civilization. What with, my relatives and friends assured me, two divorces, six teenagers (all smiling with us under the *huppah*), and the role of helpmeet to Cambridge's most notorious Jew, not to mention my own scholarly accomplishments, I had much to be proud of.

And I was. But I still felt it was high time I finish this book that had me in its grip. There was the aging of the generations in my family. The children of my great-aunts Jean, Myrtle, and Fanny, who had told me so many stories that I wished to preserve, were now the age my great-aunts had been when I'd first started to ask about great-grandfather Jacob. I needed to get their stories into print.

As the train pulled into Sassnitz and then as I stood on the platform waiting for a cab to the ferry terminal, I realized that the awkwardness I felt was linked to my need to explain the writing on Jacob's cane and the life journey of its owner, which had become a crucial part of my life's work and meaning. Without reaching an end to the story of Jacob Levy, Bernhard Baron, and their families—the buried horrors as well as the brilliant successes—I would feel some important work of my own left undone. I had obligated myself to imagining, and so honoring, the lives of my forebears, as well as teaching my children to honor them; writing this story had become for me a discipline and a form of Jewish observance, a strict practice in whose ways I walked and had taught my daughters, each in her way, to walk.

The evidence of this was that I was not, anymore than Jacob had been, traveling alone. Traveling with me, as before, was Yael.

❧❧

A few weeks shy of twenty-one, the same age my grandfather Emil had been when his father, Jacob, took him on the journey of 1928, Yael was again my companion on a trip to the Baltics, the intervening time having delivered her from junior high to college, as well as from naïveté to wisdom beyond her age. Years before, she had stumbled along the route with me, interested but also nonplussed at the strangeness of the places

I took her to, the smoky compartments, the nasty bathrooms, the grim sights to which I'd exposed her so far from her life in Philadelphia. She'd trusted me, as children trust their mothers, to protect her, and I'd tried not only to reassure her we'd be safe but to teach her my traveling philosophy: With a pile of maps, a tank of gas, and a debit card, one could get lost but not in too much trouble.

A few years earlier, Yael had accompanied me on another book-related trip, a journey along the Rhine to see where Aunt Myrtle's son Jack had fought and died in 1945. The three months Jack spent fighting Hitler, first in the frozen, hilly terrain of Belgium and then in Alsace, represented to me the American Levy family's fight against the Nazis. I like to believe that it may have prevented the very last of our European relatives from perishing. As we drove into Belgium and then along the Rhine, Yael's high school French had supplemented my college French. On that trip I had been very much in charge, but now I planned the itinerary to make the trip convenient for her busy life, and I was feeling too the shift in—what, authority?—that comes to parents as their children find their stride.

Since Yael had learned Russian and her historical and literary expertise now outstripped mine, I hadn't hired a translator but would rely on her. I hoped that a second journey with my now grown child would produce something in the way of interesting incident. As we dragged luggage into our cabin on the ferry and she cocked her head, listening to the purser's announcements on the public address system and smiling, I thought that it had been years now since I'd had the memory that allowed her to integrate so much vocabulary into so many grammatical forms.

At that moment she asked me for about the fifteenth time if I'd managed to come up with the list of questions in Russian I'd be wanting her to ask. She'd brought her dictionary and could work on readying the sentences after dinner.

On deck alone, leaning over the rail, I watched the red Baltic sun descend slowly into an expanse of pinkish ripples. For years I'd thought about the actual Baltic, the sea, as I'd flipped through books of maps and traced trade routes across the ocean. I'd developed a passion for maps with trade goods marked, for the little symbols for timber and tar, dried fish and turpentine, and I liked to imagine the different vessels and conditions of passage. It was, I thought, a beautiful journey for those who had eyes for the beauty. Had Jacob? I doubted it. With my daughter napping snugly in our cabin, I was free to lose myself in the seascape, but I thought about how much more anxious Jacob must have been, how apprehensive as he turned over in his mind what he'd made of his life, what he had to show for his years away from Shavli.

Jacob would have the happy story of Levy's International Shrinking Company. The story would begin with how he arrived in Baltimore at sixteen and toiled at making pants with his older brother Paul. How he endured the airless immigrant rooming houses, the anti-Semitism of labor unions that were, he might explain, just as jealous of the Jews' progress in America as they were the world over. How five years after his arrival, he was in a position to start a family and then to buy not one but two houses in a desirable area. By the end of the Great War, he'd established another factory in another city, with his name on the letterhead as inventor, manufacturer, businessman. He would have to explain that he had not won his campaign for a seat in the U.S. Congress, but he had represented his party proudly. This took place while his son Bob—a boy who had the family knack with a wrench—ran the Baltimore plant and his daughter Jean pitched in to help with the children, since his dear wife Amelia was . . . ill. His daughters were his mainstay, as he was their provider.

Now came the place in his narrative where the story began to break down, where he feared his brothers Max and Isaac would lack, if not sympathy, understanding. The problem of course: his sons. The prodigals. Jacob could hardly solicit much compassion from his brothers, since he himself had left them and his loving mother at the age of sixteen. Did he deserve pity because his sons Eddie, Paul, and Theo had abandoned him, joined their uncle Bernard Baron in London, and changed their names from Levy to Baron?

Nor did he want pity from these brothers whose own sons were loyal to them and stayed close by. So much of his trouble was due, Jacob thought, to what had befallen or maybe had always been wrong with Amelia. But how unburden himself of this, how share the slow unraveling of hope and then the boys' peeling off one by one, gone from his life? Better perhaps to try the other tack, brazen it out, chalk the dissolution of his family up to the opportunities now beckoning young men.

Such is the modern world, he would say. Sons set off to make their fortunes! He might explain that the chances young men have in the West are so splendid that even his two young grandsons' departure for London and Bernhard Baron's cigarette business was an example of the wonderful spread of commerce.

The only catch here, he was aware, was that too glowing a report of the departed ones could set his son Emil off. In public, Jacob broadcast the hope that Emil, now twenty-one, would step up to take over the Philadelphia plant of Levy's International, just as Bob had taken over the Baltimore plant.

The truth was, however, that Emil's talk was all about the great Carreras cigarette empire; obviously he expected to be invited to join his brothers in their London life. To indulge Emil's love of grandeur, his extravagance, had been one reason for this trip. In recognition of his coming of age, Jacob bought Emil some new suits, a traveling equipage, and promised to rent a roadster for the tour through their ancestral homeland. But Emil was, Jacob admitted to himself, prone to responses he could less and less successfully predict. The greater risk was that the relatives in four cities now making elaborate preparations to entertain them would see, in short order, what he feared: that Emil was touched, troubled, and maybe afflicted with a terrible disorder like his mother's, and that he would never run Levy's International Shrinking or join his brothers as Barons.

Later, lying in my tidy bunk by the ship's casement—the sky now inky, though pierced with stars over the rippled slate of the Baltic— I looked over at the other bunk, at Yael sleeping there, her Russian dictionary in the covers. What worries had I that compared to the worry my great-grandfather Jacob would have had, traveling with an unwell son and headed, before long, to the scene of his rival's and his prodigals' triumph?

The next morning only increased my sense of roles reversed. The ship we traveled on might be called the *Vilnius*, the fleet's Lithuanian company, Lisco, after the old Polish Lithuanian capital, but the languages over the public address system were—Yael stressed for me— Russian and German: Russian first, then the German. Interesting, she thought. The old Soviet influence was still so strong, despite the ship's German port of debarkation. No Lithuanian at all. But she could tell? I asked.

Tell? Of course she could tell! Lithuanian being an Old Indo-European language, its roots tangled up somewhere with Sanskrt's, while Russian was a Slavic language; everything was different.

Her dictionary? On deck. For simple announcements? For the call to dinner, "Bar's open." "Kind passengers, please to bring your documents to the first deck station?" No, she did not need her dictionary for these.

Indeed, since everyone on the boat was old enough to have lived under the Soviets, and our ferry journeyed from what had been East Germany, she guessed that not one person, not even the truckers whom we'd watched latching their rigs onto the lower deck, failed to understand both languages coming over the PA system, German and Russian, plus their Lithuanian. Except you, Mommy! she laughed, as she counted out the euros into the cashier's hand while I carried our instant coffee to a picnic table on the breezy, now sun-splashed deck. She said it fondly, I noticed, and I understood from her face that she was having fun, enjoying being with me again on the odd sort of adventure I liked and had taught her to like. Out in the middle of God-knows-where just taking it all in.

Our ferry hauled tractors and rail cars along with people, offering dinner and breakfast to those "respected passengers" who did not mind views of stevedores arriving at a destination. She knew I loved such views: great fork lifts arching over the deck, oil derricks and industrial signage crowding the foreground. The night before, certain men leaning on the rail in T-shirts had locked their rigs into the ship's great lower deck and then taken their cigarettes into the little bar and gotten drunk. The German tourists, mostly middle-aged and elderly, had already brought their baggage to the dining room, while the younger ones, some with bikes chained below with the trucks, zipped things in and out of their backpacks. It was not luxury travel, probably even less luxurious than it would have been in 1928.

And so, putting the flimsy ribbed cup with its tepid coffee down, swinging her leg over the picnic table, Yael gave me the look I'd been coming to recognize and was learning to get used to—a look of fondness, of happy tolerance. Yes, she thought she understood and didn't need to review the various questions I wanted answered. The lists of persons and places Jacob and Emil visited and where they went and what they wanted were fine. She'd looked up any phrases she might need and hadn't needed to look up words for purge, extermination, repression, mass grave, and so forth. They'd been the basis—she looked wryly at me—of her second year Russian syllabus.

No, she didn't need to look at the map either. I could amuse myself with maps in the car.

Nor was she especially concerned by the fact that somehow I'd left Berlin with only forty euros, that between us had spent them on dinner and breakfast, and we were now sailing along an industrial spit as prepossessing looking as maybe Galveston or Newfoundland on a good day. She was certain the driver I'd managed to find would be there to greet us.

As it turned out, the ship pulled in early, and the expected car was late, and so—confused and ambivalent—I held my peace while Yael smoked a cigarette. What had seemed necessary to do when she was eighteen—conceal her smoking—seemed stupid, puritanical so far from home. It seemed especially so, as we saw, strolling up the walk as she stubbed out her cigarette, our driver, stubbing out his.

The first time Yael and I had come to the Baltics, our guide had been Chaim, kindly, with a wandering eye and a big belly. Chaim had greeted us with a warm "Shalom" and gave us his best version of the Jewish roots tour. The second time I'd come, I'd hired a tireless, efficient translator, a young, non-Jewish woman named Victorija who showed with her briskness that whatever image I might have of Lithuanian women did not apply. Still, nothing in my past experience of Baltic guides prepared me for Alexejus.

As he presented himself before us on the walk I'm sure both Yael's and my eyes widened slightly. When he wheeled our bags away Yael looked at me sternly, furrowing her brow as she saw I was not to be repressed from speaking my mind about him.

"Oh my God," I said, sounding old and completely ridiculous. "He's *adorable*."

꣓꣓꣓

Siauliai, the town I called Shavli, as its Jews once did, was far hotter than when we'd arrived in town eight years ago. But it was looking considerably sleeker, richer, and more upscale than when I saw it on either of my last visits. Yael and I had the afternoon free. I'd hoped Alexejus would take us to Old Klaipeda to see its old Jewish center and the balcony from which Hitler reclaimed the town in 1939. And Alexejus was clearly disappointed because a mix-up had assigned him to another client after he transferred us to Shavli. All the way to the town I watched him glancing at Yael, taking in her lovely face and natural ways and Russian sentences. He hoped to be back the next day. But it was just as well. From our hotel we strolled to the cafés on Vilnius Street, remembering the place where we'd eaten borsht and fish with Chaim and noting the greater prosperity of the town, happy to see its pedestrian promenade lined with glossy shops, filled with strolling couples, its outdoor restaurants alive with conversation. In the summer light, the facades and bright trim of the buildings glowed and the antic sculptures for which the town was known gave the street great charm. In the refurbished tourist office, tastefully appointed, I learned that Shavli's museums were all open—not only the cultural museum but also those devoted to bicycles, photography, and cats, and what I was most interested in, Chaim Frankel's great art deco palace. Its upper floors, the tourism clerk explained, were now an exhibition space for artifacts of the landowning classes. Its ground floor boasted the furnishings of—what do we call it? she looked at her colleague—ah, yes a "vintage" cinema.

And the factory? I asked.

Oh yes, she answered. Some of it had been destroyed, of course, some carried off. But much of the Frankel Leatherworks stood just as it had before the war. It would take us only a few minutes to walk to it, for the factory and the house had both once been the center of Shavli life.

Like everything else in Shavli, Frankel's palace was getting a facelift, the fresh scaffolding around one wing an augury of the building's eventual restoration as symbol of a history Shavli was not ashamed to claim. Certainly the building was gorgeous. Inside, the carefully hung walls and exhibition cases of the lofty upper floors held artifacts of the Polish-Lithuanian Commonwealth as well as of czarist days (imperial era rubles big as placemats; cloisonné pipes and snuffboxes, and a whole wall of polished sabers, swords, and canes), but downstairs the stylized parquet floors and ceiling ornaments were unalloyed 1920s. This bottom floor included one room devoted to prewar Jewish Shavli (although considerably more wall space was given to the town's leather, sugar, and chocolate factories) and also a complete replica of the Kapitol movie theater, an entertainment palace of neon, and poster art that had been run by Shavli's Jews.

As we left Frankel's palace, crossing the street to get its facade into a picture and looking down the slope to Tilzes Street, I saw in a flash my ancestral town as it might have looked to those preparing to welcome Jacob and Emil, arranging for their comfort in the small but nicely appointed hotel—Solomon having been sent by his father, Isaac, to check on his uncle Jacob and cousin Emil's rooms.

Those engaged in such preparations would have had—I thought, with a little rush of pride—no cause to be ashamed of the town welcoming back its American cousins.

That Isaac was the easier, the more genial of Jacob's two brothers was a conviction I formed early on. The brother remaining in the ancestral town, unperturbed by anyone else's idea about ambition, would, I reasoned, have been the one you'd relax around.

Moshe too had described his father Isaac (esteemed by gentiles as "the Jewish tanner") with pride for a man who managed so few airs; despite his German education, local workmen accepted him. Most convincing to me, though, is the fact that the one 1928 picture in which my grandfather Emil actually appears was taken in May in Shavli, and shows Isaac, his son Solomon with wife and children, and, at Jacob's shoulder, Emil. Since Emil does not appear in the pictures taken in June and July, and since family stories trace his first "episode" to this trip, I surmise that he remained with Isaac while Jacob traveled on. Even after many years away, it was Isaac whom Jacob trusted enough to leave his son with him, Isaac he let persuade him it would be best for him and Emil that the family try to help the boy settle down while Jacob finished his trip.

What would Isaac have said, I wonder, to get Jacob to go? For one thing, perhaps, that it would be no trouble to spend time with the young man. When he retired from his work at Frankel Leatherworks, his son Solomon, a machinist and engineer, had taken his place, and Isaac, his own wife dead, had moved into the modern flat kept on Tilzes. Of course, they still owned the old family house on Smallprison Street, stone and wood and without central heat. Its location, just steps from the Frankel factory though in a poorer section, made it a convenient place for Solomon to think and tinker. His young family lived in more modern style near all the shops, the cafés and cinemas, and the little girl's school. Grandfather would often walk her to class, the baby toddling along, and Emil could join them and then—if he liked—look in on Solomon at Frankel's.

Frankel's. One can imagine that Isaac and Solomon, like all of the thriving managers and "specialists" this cynosure employed, breathed the very name with pride and satisfaction. Most of Shavli had been destroyed during World War I, but Frankel's energetic rebuilding—not only of his factory but of new synagogues and schools, of the town's first fire department, and of new blocks of flats—had lured its citizens back, devastation yielding in just a few years to the return of civilization.

Evicting Shavli's Jews in 1915 did not prevent the near leveling of the town, as Jews ironically observed among themselves. And it was the Jews' return that brought the town back to life, even though they had almost got used to their resettlement in Russia. Solomon and his brother Aaron had both married there, and only when they heard Frankel was back with plans as big as ever did they return and find, within a few years, a prosperity justifying the risk in returning.

The prosperity paid for the lovely clothes that Solomon's Russian wife Fanja wore, and for the indulgent fancy she lavished on her little girls. *Kol kach yaffah*—so beautiful—Moshe and Tanya had said long ago in Israel when we looked at the picture of Fanja, and beautiful too was their little girl, with the outsize bow in her hair and her hand on her little hip. Since Fanja had left her family in the east and would be homesick at times, Isaac saw to it that Solomon indulged her—what harm, after all, in a woman feeling adored? And what harm (whatever his brother Max thought) in children feeling they had lots of room, lots of freedom to be young. Isaac had not fussed or objected when his son Moshe had moved as far away as Palestine. Four of Solomon's younger siblings were now in Riga, and who could blame them? Kalnu Iela was an excellent address, where Solomon's daughter, Zarah, had no task but to supervise—though loosely!—the activities of the younger students and working persons who crowded into her Riga apartment.

Not that, Isaac warned, the Riga digs were always in shape for visitors! The phone rang off the hook, and behind doors was who knows what mayhem. But with a bit of warning the children would always set things to rights.

This was why I think Isaac would have insisted that Jacob should leave the boy and go. Isaac and Solomon would arrange some excursions for Emil. Picnics by the lakes. Strolls. The cinema. Jacob could drive on to Riga, enjoy the city, and not worry too much about his son. On his return Isaac would send Jacob—and he hoped Emil too—on to Raseinai.

At worst, if something happened, Riga was only an hour or so away.

That is also what, the next afternoon, Yael told me, giving me that indulgent scolding look again, after saying that if I didn't mind being alone for dinner, she and Alexejus were going to Riga for the evening.

She explained how they had decided to go there. In Zagare, the signs for the border had piqued her interest and reminded her of Riga, only sixty kilometers away. When she mentioned to Alexejus that she was disappointed not see Riga this time, he asked her if she would like to go.

Alexejus had assured me earlier that what I planned to say about Riga in my book was true. It was, always had been, a great city for night life. Things got going late and went strong, sometimes until morning. It was a late sleeping town, what with so many students and so many bars.

A source of dubious comfort to me when Yael was still not back at 3:00 AM.

❧

The Riga that Jacob explored alone in June 1928 would indeed have been as exuberant as the town to which, worrying a bit, I'd sent Yael and Alexejus. With its northern situation, its young and cosmopolitan population, but also its new role as free capital of independent Latvia,

Riga circa 1928—like Riga today—was into its second decade out from under Russia's yoke. Or Germany's. Both neighbors loomed, and as right-wing governments and factions proliferated on all her borders, Riga noticed. But Riga, as ever, thrived, "flaunting," as one historian puts it, her art nouveau facade and reasserting that "curious blending of St. Petersburg, Hamburg, and Vienna" that had ever molded her character.

In summer, Riga's beauty prompts forgetfulness.

The breezes from the Baltic coast waft sea wind around the graceful buildings. Mornings, as the sun comes over the city's walls, the lindens in the courtyards move, dappling the pavement with patterned sun and shadow. By noon, the open squares blaze with light, the matte gold of the cobbles shimmering with sun pouring down from the impossibly blue sky. Late afternoon, peering into the same courtyards that the morning's press (of lessons, or business, or the list of purchases) left deserted, one sees domestic life—urban style—in its most charming aspect. Two friends sip tea on iron chairs disposed in the little courtyard garden, a low table between them. Mingled voices from the stairwells. A small girl kicks up her hem, her shoe. Laughter.

Evening. Down the street. Into a larger square. Cool now.

What's this? Cellos tuning up. Strains of a rehearsal leak from the Opera House, door propped open. As lights switch on, the older buildings of the city reassert the dated but still impressive majesty of breasted nymphs and chained rosettes looped in curlicue. Today the rage is for curved and linear, the archways low, their shallow polished staircases rising superfluous next to elevators. Yet the old burghers', the old barons' sense of the *comme il faut* remains.

Night falling. The sky not darkening so much as deepening. Returning to the Petersburg Hotel, one finds the lobby full of agitated types (the Sejm, the parliament, just across the street; the president's residence, catty-corner). No matter. The provincials are easy to identify by their officious, harried, overeager mien. Riga's true na-

tive, an émigré, is ever at home and does not imagine that street signage needs to be changed to reflect the times. Hotel Petersburg
(where Jacob stayed) gives the czars' heyday its due. The little café
where you sip morning coffee offers only German newspapers; Latvian was for the countryside. The restaurant where one dines on cut-
let of veal, potatoes, torte, and the other where one eats shocking
pink borscht with sour cream, were the same at night. Both places are
crowded with young men drinking, couples leaning against the wall,
the girls with sweaters on their arms against the northern summer
chill, the boys letting half full glasses rest against their ribcages, their
jerseys dark.

Not even by closing the hotel window tightly could a visitor block
out the sounds of Riga's young as they trailed along the streets, their
voices drifting up into the casements. Not even by pulling the pillow
over the head, sighing at the absurd hours kept by the young, could
one shut out the raucous voices, their accents free and mingled.

What did he think about all this, Isaac might have asked Jacob. Of
course, in Riga the young people carried on, walking in the chill air
in thin jackets, taking the tramcar on a whim so they could loll bare
legged on the dunes of Jurmala till late, eight or nine o'clock, when,
shaking pine needles from their clothes, they crowded in next to others on the roadway crusted with sand and caught the last tram back
to the city center.

He and Jacob, Isaac might have said, knew how to leave well
enough alone, how to give young people breathing room when they
needed it.

I did not overreact when, around 4:00 AM, Yael came back to Shavli
from Riga, her voice, still speaking Russian, floating up from the
street. Taking my cue from my forebears, at least as I imagined them,
I drifted off to sleep, glad to live in the modern world, the moving,
mobile world where a city like Riga played its own emancipating role.
A city like Riga, so civilized, proved—did it not?—humanity's glad
transcendence of the dark past.

Photo of the Levy family, Jacob holding the cane, next to his brother, Max Levy. The only one in this picture, besides Jacob, to survive the Nazis was Rivka Levy, far left with flounced dress and bangs cut across her forehead.

⁓⁓⁓

Jacob Levy's oldest brother, Max, judging from everything I'd heard and learned about him, would not have been so indulgent with a young person.

Driving to Raseinai in the late afternoon with a new, less attractive driver on duty and Yael asleep in the backseat, I remembered some things Moshe had said about Max.

Uncle Max, he told me, had ruled his family with an iron hand. His son Adolph, walking in Max's footsteps, had been subject to certain nervous ailments, but it was hard to say whether his anxieties were his own or simply the result of being Max's son. It was a demanding role. Although Isaac's children were assembled for photos with their Uncle Jacob in, I surmised, haphazard fashion—many absent—no one in Max's family would have even thought of not appearing for the family photograph with the American uncle.

Later, Max had sent the photograph of this occasion to Moshe in Palestine, to brothers Jacob and Paul in America, and, I assume, also to every one of Jacob's children. So many photographs mounted, packed, and sent was a tedious task for anyone to perform, and also costly. But this did not deter Max. No, the brother who had doubtless taken it on himself to make the proper arrangements for Jacob's trip; the brother who'd gone to Sedova to order a presentation cane; who'd made the reservations for Jacob's stay in Riga, deciding on the Petersburg Hotel just across from the new president's palace; the one who made sure to bring a photographer to capture the three brothers at their father's grave, would have gotten every last one of his family to Raseinai for the photo session, refusal impossible. I had seen the photo in four separate albums in the states, Aunt Jean's, Aunt Myrtle's, Aunt Fanny's, and then in Buddy's house a few months after first beholding the cane. And I had seen it at Moshe's, too.

Max also made sure to arrange for the photograph to be taken at home, the better to show the far-flung relatives and even posterity the handsome room with a Turkish carpet, draperies heavy with ball fringe, and Max's family. Everyone had showed up as instructed; the sons and sons-in-law stood behind Max, the daughters-in-law at his side, and all the children gathered around their parents. For Max would not have it be said (though perhaps he knew it was said) that they felt they had no choice.

Max's son Adolph, named after his own uncle Adolph, had no choice but to come into his father's law practice and live next door, taking over the files of the Fire Commission, the Board of Electors, when his father—*Mister* Lawyer Levy—had finished with them. Like his estimable father, Adolph worked in Lithuanian, German, or Russian, mediating relations between farmers and grain merchants, Jews and gentiles, the volatile, wet-behind-the-ears young nationalists of the fledgling Lithuanian government with the stolid burghers of their deceptively tranquil-looking town.

Too much wheat and rye, too much milk and livestock traveled in and out of this town bound for the coast and beyond for the Jews and

their representatives not to remain in *active* (Max emphasized) discussion with all parties. The job that had long been his—legal broker,
pleader, Solomonic dealmaker of the Lithuanian breadbasket and but-
tery—he entrusted to his first son. To help his son make sense of it,
Max left the files.

⁓

Now these files reside at the YIVO archives in New York, where I
turn their pages and imagine Max as he must have been—his feroc-
ity, his overbearing ways.

I imagine Max in order to understand Jacob's pained look in the
photograph Max had carefully arranged. But I also imagine Max in
order not to let him die with nothing to mark his passing but the notice of "prominence" given in the volume of Lithuanian Jewry lost.
I wanted to give him a full measure of life, not only of death, but to
remember and honor the memory of this irascible, demanding, difficult man whom children obeyed but often resented, whom brothers
placated or evaded, mollified or fled from entirely—but *never* forgot.

Not an easy man, Max Levy. Far from it. Impatient, condescending, and brusquely dismissing those less accomplished than himself;
these descriptors are written on the YIVO files in purple carbon. It
would not be an easy man who kept tabs on the numbers of Raseinai
students inoculated, corresponded with every American native of the
town who sent money for the Talmud Torah library, maintained ties
with the Zionists, inspired the young Pioneer Guards, was so persistent in petitioning the government for exempting schoolteachers from
the military service that, in the end, the schoolteachers were exempted. No easy man would be so punctual in getting the letters out
to sundry millionaires concerning vocational training for the poor,
clothing for needy children and old folks. And no easy man would
allow himself to be put upon, not only by Jews but gentiles, and not
only by residents of Raseinai but of smaller towns too, towns to which
he travels to straighten out communal budgets, determining what

funds will go to the kindergarten, the fire wagon, the municipal cleaners of Pig Alley and Cow Alley, plus the joint funds for shopkeepers and the Independence Day parade.

No, to leave so many signatures on so many pages was not a job for anyone, least of all for any Jew so very alive one day, then killed the next.

But it was the job of someone I honor by journeying every year to read the papers of this Max Levy, who is as forceful and vivid as if his typewriter went silent only yesterday.

Such a man would have tolerated no deviations.

As to the matter of the uncle visiting from America and Max's grandchildren appearing for the family photo, the children would come whether they liked it or not. All the sons and all their wives, not excepting those in Riga, would come to Raseinai on the day appointed.

And they did, as the photo shows and gathers them together this one time so that I can see who they were, and how many, and then count those lost. Summoning them all together, Max would ensure that this historical record was achieved—the picture in which the brother from America (the magnificent new cane, token of the family's respect, in hand) sat at his brother's left hand.

Disappointment over Emil's failure to appear on this occasion becomes, after decades, more and more discernable in the faces of the patriarch and his brother. Now, nearly eighty years after Emil failed to appear, sixty-plus years after nearly everyone in the photo died in a Lithuanian ditch (this a year or so after Jacob's death in America), and more than thirty years after my aunts explained to me that their brother Emil "took sick" in Europe, the expression on their faces is finally clear. Jacob, in his sleek creased suit and with his fine shaven chin, poses with his relatives, turning his face slightly sidewise and holding in his tense hand the cane, which had been ordered and purchased by Max and then presented to him. If there had been some look of empathy in Max's eyes as he presented the cane, some look of understanding kindness, Jacob must have missed it. Emil's failure even to ride in the roadster with his father to pay his respects to his many cousins, his odd unsuitable behavior, affronted Max and caused Jacob agony.

To me, this is all preserved on the ebony walking stick with the names of four brothers arrayed next to names of towns.

In the picture taken in Raseinai, the picture taken without a son but with a walking stick, Jacob's look expresses not arrogance but shame. Misery.

Posture erect, temples sleek, he sits there suffering. Of five sons, not one stands by him to project the vision of family achievement and solidarity. Even a former prodigal like Jacob Levy believed it was the task of sons and fathers to present this united front.

❧

A few weeks later, Jacob was in London. This was the hardest part of his trip: greeting the prodigal sons and the little boys, Jerry and Earle, who still wondered what they were doing there. Managing Emil's strange unreasoning insistence that he would stay in London and join his brothers and help run Carreras cigarettes.

When of course he wouldn't. Couldn't. Emil would go back to America with his father, who would make out a will leaving Levy's Shrinking in Baltimore to him; would even encourage Emil's marriage to a lovely girl in hopes that somehow he would get over his strange ramblings and ravings.

Which he did, or seemed to for a time before "taking sick," as his sisters put it. His "taking sick" took the form of dreaming about being a London mogul, a man about town, a bon vivant with a cigarette case (I still keep the cigarette case in a china cabinet that once stood in his sister Myrtle's sitting room). The events of that late summer in 1928 shaped, informed, gave color to a life of mental illness.

I do not know if the Arcadia Works factory tour was yet in place when my great-grandfather Jacob and his son Emil arrived in London

A photocopy of the medals presented to Bernhard Baron's workers on the day of the Carreras Factory opening. Gift to the author from Daniel Goldman.

in August 1928. The tour brochure I keep in my files is not dated, and so I cannot tell if the whole theatrical show was up and running when Emil spent three weeks there with his older brothers. Still, everything indicates that this last year of Bernhard Baron's life, with the grand opening of the Carerras factory as its centerpiece, was about as close to a Metro-Goldwyn-Mayer movie as Jacob's son Eddie (now sur-named Baron) and his wife Bertha could make it. Other events of the year included the wedding of Bernhard Baron's daughter Sarah, on the Riviera. Carlos Gardel, the international tango sensation, was hired to dance the couple across the floor with, photos suggest, Char-lie Chaplin in attendance.

Nor did the distractions connected with the factory's opening keep Eddie's publicity operation from branching out. The Prince of Wales himself was secured to spread his blessings at the groundbreaking of the Bernhard Baron Home for Boys. The year before he died, the Old Man had opened his checkbook and hired the architects of the Arca-dia Works to begin construction of the world's finest Jewish settle-ment house. All his life Bernhard had nourished a tenderness for children, and I believe this expenditure gave him great pleasure. How Eddie and Bertha beamed as the Prince looked on while hundreds of children sang this song:

> *Good Mr. Baron said one afternoon,*
> *What do you want in the way of a boon?*
> *We said, "The Prince said, "he hopes very soon"*
> *Yes, very soon! O, very soon*
> *We shall rebuild in a sumptuous way"*
> *Our only trouble is who is to pay*
> *Good Mr. Baron said*
> *"I, if I may"*
> *Hip Hip Hooray, BB!*

Did Emil, on arriving, hear from his brother Paul the story of how, with a wink and a humorous shout ("Catch!"), Eddie gave Paul the job of getting three thousand employees from the City Road over to the new Arcadia Works without interrupting production? Did he hear of the journeys Theo took by liner in pursuit of the world's best leaf—journeys to Virginia, Maryland, North Carolina, Turkey, and Egypt? Had Eddie perhaps conceived the idea of the Carreras factory tour with the vague, dazzled Emil as his audience, determining the stops on the tour as Emil looked on, trailing him through the great light-washed floors?

Eventually a pamphlet, *The Story of Your Cigarette,* helped guide tourists, schoolchildren, and socialist pilgrims through the processes of stemming and cleaning the baled tobacco in the factory basement and up to the laboratories and inspection desks on the fourth floor. Its message was simple: Industrial progress furthers civilization.

Long ago, tobacco operatives working by the piece in New York's cigar quarter had no way to increase their meager profits but by more speed. In the 1880s, Eddie's pamphlet explained, the falling price of hand-made cigars locked men to rolling benches, their lives narrowed to a blur of painful repetitive motion. This motion multiplied as first wives and then children took their places on the bench. Bernhard Baron himself, Eddie would explain to tourists, had been among those pushing muscles, tendons, and joints into spasm to beat the downward spiral of the cost of a cigar. True, even at Carreras, the "job of stripping leaves from center veins must still be performed by human fingers." But the pace on the Carreras floor was regulated by a team of medical and efficiency experts, and the hand strippers were celebrities. Lucky tour groups might be treated to an old style tournament, the company directors all on hand, as Rocking Orse Minnie, queen roller of the Millionaires Gangway, stripped tobacco till she could strip no more, her handsome bounty a pound sterling for a pound of tobacco. "Her fingers specially trained to work with lightening speed," Rocking Orse Minnie used a rocking chair to keep her rhythm going.

Nor were tourists allowed to miss the fact that Minnie wore a mask. But on the next floor, the rolling floor, no masks were necessary: "Baron's original machine, patented in 1895" had worker protections built right in.

The Baron cigarette rolling machine justified the claim that Carreras was London's "most hygienic factory." Once cigarette workers had suffered the full range of ailments that airborne particles cause. Moreover, the poorer, unregulated cigar shops were petri dishes of the dread tuberculosis, which spread as hurried operatives licked wrappers closed, bit off ends, and nicked fingers while slicing with dull knives.

The Baron machine's slim polished rollers, rotary knives, filtration screens, and quick brushes not only spared wrists and fingers repetitive motion but also helped prevent lethal lung diseases. "A line of tobacco falls evenly on a continuous stream of paper," sifting the tobacco through a "fine screen that collects the dust." The machine then seals the wrapper: "One edge of the paper is turned up, and a small rapidly revolving wheel puts a thin line of specially prepared paste along its edge." And then: "A rotary knife divides this giant cigarette into the correct lengths." But not before those on the tour got a look at a giant cigarette. From one hundred machines, "eighty yards of paper enclosed tobacco in the form of one long rod comes out, every minute."

Two floors away, the tobacco was loosed from the rough twine denting the bale, moist, musky, yellow from the curing barn. By the fourth floor, this product of a Virginia or Turkish summer emerged dressed in sumptuous imagery, new for every season. There was the famous Black Cat cigarette, now soignée, now hugger-mugger; the fetching Chick, coy in feathers or putting her foot down; Turf, with its hint of horse stalls and the adrenalin of the race; the rainy London streetscape of the Passing Show. Here, on the packing floor, the brilliance of the papers and ink, the precision and cleanness of the printing, stamping, creasing, and folding operations all went on under soft illumination coming through the skylights.

To the sound of piped-in music, workers tended the immaculate machines, doing little more with their hands than ensuring the cardboard fed straight into the mechanism that "creased, glued, folded and refolded the boxes into single hulls." They ensured that the brilliant collector cards, emerging from the press "fitted with a roller carrying steel engravings for printing," were as vivid as they ought to be, their colors thick and true, before the cigarettes, swaddled in waxed paper wrapping, were gently pressed into the curled shells, and then the whole folded and the flap sealed in gold.

Inspection—last stop on the tour. The workers of Carreras looked sharp, for they knew that others of keen faculties would "minutely examine" their work, using their eyes to "detect the slightest imperfection," tapping the sealed tins bound for export with "light wooden rods," and only those emitting the "proper high pitched tone" passed muster. Did the process defy any but modern imagination? Thousands of Black Cats, all sealed with gold paper tabs and tumbled into trolleys, were sent in lorries to ships and out to sea and then to shores and cities distant.

Imagery of the last stage of the tour lingered on this theme. Pains were taken to distinguish perfection from standardization, regularity from monotony; the modern factory stood for the ingathering and dissemination of all the world's copious variety, just as a person anywhere smoking a Carreras cigarette—blend of Virginia weed, Turkish sun, Portuguese cork, German ink, Canadian paper—touched the world to his lips, and all for a penny. The last stop on the tour was the laboratory where "atmospheric conditions ranging from the Arctic to the tropics can be reproduced . . . the temperature altered to correspond to the climate."

It was a temperate clime, and a fair one, that Eddie had found. *The Story of Your Cigarette*, written by Eddie Baron, ended with the reminder: "London may be shivering or sweltering, damp or dusty. Inside, every day is a fine day; all weather is fair weather."

THIRTEEN

Blitzkrieg Barbarossa

In green rubber boots reaching above my knees, I followed Dick Shergold, building supervisor of Greater London House—once the Arcadia Works of Carreras cigarettes—though the immense basement of the former Baron family factory.

"The river does come up," Mr. Shergold warned, a bit apologetically. In the supervisor's office near the off-loading dock he'd urged me to put on the boots before we descended to see how the workers of Carreras cigarettes, some thousands of them, survived World War II.

They were essential wartime employees, Dick emphasized, confirming what I'd been told before: Cigarettes were an essential wartime industry. I'd heard stories from my family of the three Levy/Baron brothers' valiant patriotism. The Carreras managers took their turns at fire spotting, the brothers themselves up on the big roof watching over smoking London. And with the tunnel running into its basement from the tube station, Carreras was the biggest shelter in the area. Parents of the young persons working there were happy to send their children to work as many hours as the brothers wanted, on weekends too, for where else but in the underground dormitories of Carreras was there so much safety?

I'd read all this a few years back in the oral history entries collected in the archives of Camdentown. But before I descended with Dick Shergold to the old hogshead storage and wartime shelter, I'd never actually been inside the factory. Three or four times I'd ascended from the Northern Line to Mornington Crescent, making the trip just to see the Egyptian ornaments on the facade expanding across my view as I rose.

In 2000 the return of architectural eclecticism had persuaded certain developers to tear off the sober modernist apron that had been draped over the factory's highly colored King Tut whimsy after our family sold Carreras. By 2003, when I visited, sober modernism was played out. Today full-color brochures hail the original building as one of the great art deco achievements of Europe. With its two huge black cats coming into view as one exits from the Underground, the building camps it up, brazen and retro. It is as fresh and fun and young as ever.

From the great flat roof, where my uncles had watched for fires, Dick Shergold took me down the trim staircases, narrow as an ocean liner's, from floor to floor, first through the offices of a giant advertising firm with its open floor plan. Light through the high, well placed windows bathed an antic grid of cubicles and, one floor down, fell on uncluttered desks of the corporate staff of an international travel firm. The women in slim jackets and trousers suits, helmets of hair hugging their heads; the men with longer hair and tieless, wearing the tapered shoes and loose draped jackets of the day—they all tapped at keyboards or cradled phones to their shoulders.

After seeing the modern renovation of London's "most hygienic" factory, we were back in Dick Shergold's world of operations, donning boots, and were descending . . . down . . . down . . . to a world untouched for half a century. Underground in the Carreras factory it was still 1940, the winter of the Blitz. All around bombs fell, but inside Carreras every day was fair weather.

War is good for cigarettes.

The Crimean War and the American Civil War had spread the habit among young men throughout the world, and by World War I generals had begun demanding that cigarettes be included with the other rations. Carreras had done its part and grown apace through World War I, packaging small French dictionaries inside packages to the Marne, and using waxed paper and then cellophane to protect a soldier's smokes from a soaking. Carreras's wartime advertising featured a comely nurse lighting a soldier's cigarette. And why not? What better comfort was there to offer a soldier than a smoke?

World War II was fought on cigarettes, which were the staple of every underground economy. By the fall of 1940, when the Blitz of London began in earnest, Carreras cigarettes had been designated a protected war industry and embarked on its own blitz of rolling, rolling, rolling. Bernhard Baron's amazing cigarette rolling machine was pushed to its limits and yet demand exceeded supply. Indeed, demand for cigarettes was so high—for the ground troops, the RAF, and the mothers, fathers, brothers, and sisters minding the home fires in England—that my great-uncle Edward converted the factory basement, once a tobacco storehouse, to a vast dormitory and bomb shelter, and upstairs the machines ran twenty-four hours a day.

"Must be the building's settled some," Dick Shergold mused, looking rueful as we descended. Tobacco would not have survived such damp as we now felt, and even employees happy to be protected from bombs would not have liked sloshing around as we were. No, the river must not have come up then, for the signs that say "Do not make water in the entries," still printed on the walls, suggest other kinds of water.

Some employees, smuggling flasks through the tunnel, may have had a bit too much fun in the bomb shelter. Dick Shergold had heard that the managers would lock the door to the tube station at a certain hour to keep the young folk from excesses of communal spirit. The tube functioned as a makeshift barracks, and Eddie applied himself to the task as wartime innkeeper. His concrete-lined shelter was equipped with showers, toilets, and washbasins, and each worker had his own bunk. Sleeping was difficult as the underground thundered overhead, yet what parents concerned for the safety of their children would not send them to work on Sunday and breathe easily until the following weekend? A parent might worry that socializing at the canteen would lead to socializing in the bunks, but the Baron brothers had supervisory controls in place. A certain "Mr. Campbell" whose official function was warden had his presence advertised on signs at every turn.

"Might be the building's settled some," Dick Shergold mused again. The floor sloped down. The round beam from Dick's flashlight kept dimming in murkiness.

After eighty years any building would settle, I tried to tell him. Certainly one so massive, constructed of reinforced concrete, with the largest floor plates in Europe holding up its floors but also compressing the earth, decade by decade.

Despite my reassurances, Shergold was not at peace. He worried about the river water oozing up past the old pilings; worried at the compromise of the building's foundations; about settling beams, cracking ceilings, mold, moisture, and nature's reclamation of the modern marvel of engineering he cared for and supervised. His great humming system of a building, heated and cooled, comfortable, well lit, epitomized the triumph of industrial know-how, but the river with its dark tang threatened it.

⌇⌇

I thought about Shergold a few years later as I watched the longshoremen load their trucks onto the ferry Yael and I had boarded for the overnight trip across the Baltic. His concern for the great building that was his charge came to my mind as, the sun setting, we observed how the longshoremen carefully locked their ten-wheelers onto the deck. When morning came, these strong longshoremen would turn the winches left, hop into the cabs of their trucks, and be on their way, conveying the goods of western Europe to the eastern hinterlands. Each trip they made recapitulated the history of commerce, from the present day back to the heyday of the Hansa.

Sure enough, the ATM we found tucked in the hallway of the Klaipeda port belonged to Hansa Bank, its logo the medieval vessel that once called at this German port, Memel. The Hansa logo invoked a profitable and orderly commerce that benefited western Europeans. It had given them honey, had supplied them with feathers, tar, leather, and bristles, and kept them alive through plague. This commerce reminded me of the welcome reverse, west to east, flow of enlightenment—of books and ideas and Haskalah and *Jugendstihl*, of machine technology, rationality, and *Wissenschaft*.

But it brought to mind too some of the bloodiest, cruelest invasions ever chronicled. For the route Yael and I had set out to follow belonged not only to commerce but also to conquerors—the route taken by the Teutonic Knights in the twelfth and thirteenth centuries and then by Hitler in the twentieth. Clearly it was not only trade that brought the Germans to the Lithuanian plains, but conquest. Hitler reached back to the twelfth century when he chose the name of a Crusader emperor, Frederick Barbarossa, for his invasion of the Soviet Union. His march toward conquest was called Operation Barbarossa.

A few hours travel into the old lands of the Prusses, the Lats, Livs, and Zemgallians helped Yael and me understand why both traders and conquerors found these lands irresistible. A couple boarding the ferry with us in Germany had brought with them nothing but bicycles and backpacks, since the lands to which they journeyed were so gently rolling and navigable one might walk across them all the way to the Russian border.

Thus as I watched the green, unbroken lands pass by, Alexejus and Yael chatting in front, I let myself feel it—the invaders' itch. Without mountains, the sparkling narrow rivers crossed in a twinkling, the sun dappling the ripening fields, these eastern plains seem literally ripe for conquest. Hitler found them irresistible, these Ostland miles he'd earmarked for growing room, as had the German Crusaders long ago.

The Lithuanian heartland is today just as verdant, as lovely, as it was, say, for a young Crusader knight marching eastward toward a first sortie. The clashes fought by this knight or his heirs would be deemed so memorable as to merit new genres of literature. In the German language, it was necessary to invent the "chronicle" to capture the valor and terror of the battles waged for Christendom. Whether the Church needed to vindicate losses in the Muslim east or simply raid lands too rich to ignore, the first decades of the thirteenth century saw the Knights of the Cross and then the even more ferocious Teutonic Knights arrive in the Baltic countries. Taking ten hostages at an encampment they called Riga, they quickly subdued the Estonians in the lands that now belong to Latvia, home of the Kurs, and by 1270 even the lands of the fierce Prusses had come under Bremen's sway. Why then would this region south and east of Riga not submit also?

The accounts offered in these chronicles and the poems—epic cycles—expand middle Europe's imagination and concentrate ideals of manhood in the Crusader. One cannot, thinking back on the first knight, but pity him. Pity the young man in a white tunic disembarking from a raft in a strange forest a few hours' march from the Baltic coast. On the raft, he'd have drifted pleasantly, dozing a little. Would he not have reason to think, as the raft touched the bank and his feet the yellow-pebbled sand, this green and flat land would be the site of triumph?

Indeed, one cannot blame this knight, marching with his comrades into the wooded hinterlands, for imagining that the conquest would be a short and glorious chapter, a triumphant one. Nothing thus far would have suggested that people of the plains, the Samogitians, would defend their belief in gods of thunder and oak to the death.

The poets loved this land. What is it—the magnetic darkness, a look of latency and ripening toward evening that makes the central

Lithuanian plains so compelling that there are songs, odes, epics written to it in German, Polish, and Lithuanian?

At dusk, all open ground seems the forest's vestibule.

As night drops, fog drifts around the doorjambs, the birds grow quiet.

Men step out of the fields to stand by the road.

Even today, driving the roads that press north along the Dubysa from the Neman, one feels the ancient throb.

The descendants of the Samogitians preserve a look of vigilance. The men have wide cheekbones; their faces are polished, planar, brown over strong necks. Their hair is ashy white, straight but full, growing in tufts. They work late burning grass. In the fall and spring, the whole plain flickers, dotted with small, smoky pyres of the turf from which ash is rendered to fertilize the next year's crop. Thus a twentieth-century poet, the German Bobroski, gives the history of these bloodsoaked lands, passing and lingering in my family's towns. "The first night," he writes, "you stop at Raseinen." Ambush. Vengeance. "People like no other, of joy! / People / like no other, no other, of death / People / Of smoldering groves / Or burning huts, green corn / Trampled, bloodstained rivers," he writes.

Song licks along the edges of the landscape till it catches flame. Thus poet Czeslaw Miloscz chimes in: "Through the meadow fields at night, / through the meadow fields of civilization / we ran shouting, singing, in a tongue not our own but one which terrified others."

Would-be conquerors would have to prove their readiness to butcher and be butchered in the quiet woods around the smallest villages—Raseinai, Ariogola, Telshai—of the remotest pagan stronghold. Who knew those villagers had warriors, their horses nimbly pivoting between the birches? The pagans were everywhere—behind stacks of hay, in oak groves, and hidden behind the embankments of high burial mounds.

What did these waiting in ambush care about the knights with pale hair beating over their temples? They killed them with swords and burning torches. They laced the knights to their horses in their metal breastplates and bucklers and helmets. They lifted knight and horse together into oaks and set them afire. Knights sent to conquer the Samogitians found opponents ready to drink the blood of their horses, to adorn their forts with animal skulls, to kill their own elderly, sick, blind, and lame. Reinforcements from all over Europe were brought in summer after summer to help beat back the most ferocious of Christendom's opponents, more ready than they to sacrifice all.

When fresh troops arrived in Vidukle, east of Raseinai, they found the Samogitians had stolen their vengeance. They had burned themselves alive or beheaded each other. But chroniclers identify a spot just outside a town known as Saule, Shaulev, or later, Siauliai, where the knights suffered their greatest defeat.

❧

This place is now Lithuania's greatest tourist attraction, the Hill of Crosses. A great, spiky promontory of heaped and piled crucifixes in wood, paper, gold, porcelain, clay, stone, steel, and straw, the Hill of Crosses was, Yael and I agreed, the kind of place where the human faculty for the most bestial terror, and also for the most mindful contemplation, somehow meet. The crosses look like limbs or arrows or tangled barbs; they suggest human will in its most violent, terrible guise. For most contemporary Lithuanians, the site marks resistance to the Soviets. The Hill of Crosses rose, as local legend tells, on the very spot where the Teutonic Knights were first repulsed, "Cut down like women," as they rode into the marshes, their blood fertilizing Samogitia's long history of sacred martyrdom.

Aside from the battle of Tannenberg in 1410, fought in the environs of Koenigsburg, no defeat for the invading Knights of the Cross is remembered in greater detail than the encounter of 1236 in which they were first repulsed. In the woodland coverts around the hill, in the hollows, the knights pressed valiantly and hard. But the Samogitians drove the Christians into the hollows between hills and down

The Hill of Crosses, Siauliai, Lithuania. Photo taken by Yael Levine.

into the rushes. As thunder gathered over these green plains, the clouds banking gigantic and forks of lightning hurtling to earth, the battle raged. Recorded in the Livonian Chronicles as a humiliating defeat for the Teutonic Knights, the battle site remains, to this day, a primeval, uncanny place. Some of that uncanniness, from my very first visit, was detectable in the way evening fell in that town so near the Hill of Crosses: Shavli.

Or Shavl, or Shawli, or Siauali, or Szawle, Schaule, Schaulens. The many spellings of my ancestral town reflect how many were its conquerors, how blood-soaked its history.

～∾⚜∾～

That morning in 2007, before Yael and I drove out to the Hill of Crosses, my old friend Vilius Puronas, Shavli's most serious archivist (a little balder than when I last saw him, his beard now wiry with gray) had welcomed me again into his office in the Municipality to share with me more Shavli lore. His book on this subject was now available in the local bookstore (mine, he beamed at me, soon to be there), but yes, there was more to say than he had thought necessary to share with a first-time visitor to Show-lay. He said the town's name so fondly, and I recalled, listening to Vilius form the syllables, the same fondness my cousin Moshe had expressed when he pronounced his town's name, a pronunciation different from that of Vilius, and yet warm despite what eventually happened there.

Moshe's pronunciation had a sound so poetic and tender I loved the place right then. The simple sound of it, *Shavli in Lita*, was, I thought, soothing. I heard in it: *shah shah*, Yiddish for "hush." And *shav*, the Hebrew root meaning "return." And *schav*, like the French *chou*: a little cabbage, a homey soup. The *li* at the end of Shavli, transposed into Hebrew, means "to me." For years the very sound of my ancestral town had been a shibboleth of blessing and belonging, a sound vouchsafed only to me.

But not only blessing. On cold nights, or sometimes when I smelled burning leaves or heard a sudden sound, or picked up the sound of sirens as they rose over cobbled streets, my town's more barbed and forbidding spellings came to mind. Its very name could scare me, quickening a sense—illogical but deep—that these *s*'s and *c*'s and *z*'s and these keening or moaning vowels were the burnt and black sounds of the the ashy ends of the alphabet. These were the letters reserved for sounds of terror. Schau, Shav, and Auschw, Auschv were aural cousins, and so, when I allowed myself to think these thoughts, was the fate of those snagged on their barbs.

For in the twentieth century the Jews of Shavli fell under the sword with stunning suddenness. Hitler's Operation Barbarossa, together with the quickened rage of locals caught between enemies, had in a matter of days reduced our family's number by half. But the identity of their killers, to this day, is not precisely known. It was the Lithuanians, the Samogitians, Leibe Lifshitz had told me before, who butchered the Jews in these parts. Although—and he said this with bitter mockery—they were too drunk, too crazed to do the job right and so the Nazis had to finish the terrible task.

Doubtless—and Vilius looked sorrowful—some of what Leibe said was right. If we preferred, Vilius was ready to tell us what he believed happened in Shavli in the summer of 1941. What he told me, he trusted, would only fill in what I'd learned from my reading or what the angry, righteous Leibe had told me on my last visit. I was lucky I'd met Leibe. Vilius missed him.

Leibe Lifshitz was the white-haired man who had shepherded us to the grave pits and then back to the Jewish Community Center, writing out for me in a careful hand the names of my family who, in 1942, were still alive. On my second visit to Shavli, Leibe had invited me to the home he shared with his daughter near the old Jewish graveyard. It was a cinder block box with a small kitchen along one wall and a tiny dining table; the remaining space was scarcely big enough for an old couch, two wooden chairs, and a space heater. All around the walls, stacked from the floor up to his belt buckle, was Leibe's personal "ar-*heev*," his documents on the fate of Shavli's Jews that, as he'd bitterly remarked, no museum was interested in having. There, for hours, he'd poured into a translator's ear stories of the ghetto he had survived. His hatred of the Nazis mixed with his rage, his burning sense of betrayal by his neighbors.

Yes, Leibe—Vilius told me—had died.

It had been in . . . hmm . . . 2002, just months after I'd seen him last. His death was a loss for Show-lay and for Vilius personally, for Leibe was the conscience of the city. And between them they served as the most assiduous historians of the region.

Angry? Yes, Leibe had suffered much. First under the Nazis and then for years and years, as they all had, under the Soviets.

But also, Vilius ventured, looking tentative, perhaps it was his nature? For even as Leibe told his story and the world heard his version of events, Leibe was not appeased. I remembered, when I met Leibe, that he claimed he had been rebuffed by memorial organizations, and I had, on returning to America, called the Holocaust Museum to tell them that they ought to get the archive of one Leibe Lifshitz.

Leibe's ar-*heev*—Vilius smiled fondly—the archive, which he'd sworn, angrily, bitterly, no one would ever care about—well, here it was. Vilius held up a thick volume, yellow, published by the Vilna Gaon Jewish Museum in the city of Vilnius, in Lithuanian, Russian, and English. Its publication date was 2002 and its acknowledgments included, as well as the Holocaust Museum, the Conference on Jewish Material Claims against Germany, the Foundation for Jewish Culture, and the Jewish Genealogical Society of Great Britain. Leibe's own narrative of the ghetto, in three languages, along with the narrative of a professional historian, was now between covers.

Vilnius suggested that Yael and I take the volume with us, to follow Leibe's maps and read Leibe's stories. They had been checked and were, all agreed, invaluable. Vilnius had little to add but to remind me of certain dates, for the calendar told so much of the story.

Then, taking out a magic marker and a piece of paper, Vilnius wrote, slowly and deliberately, two dates: June 14, 1941. June 22, 1941.

Eight days.

June 14, 1941, the day the Soviet Army annexed Lithuania, would remain forever stamped in the minds of Vilnius's neighbors: 30,000 of their fathers and brothers and sisters were taken away, some 700 to 800 from the center of Siauliai. The suffering relatives, many still alive today, saw their loved ones herded into the jail on Smallprison Street. They heard the screams of those tortured and the rattle of the trucks that took suspected anticommunists to Siberia. Yes, Leibe's book noted that some two hundred of those taken out of Show-lay by the Soviets were Jews. But this—Vilius shook his head—did not wash with those who felt Jewish communists had betrayed them. Was it not true, many Lithuanians bitterly agreed, that the Jews always curried favor with authorities, whoever they might be? In the 1914 war, the friends had been the Germans, and for this the Russians had

deported all the Jews. The Jewish friends of the Germans had operated, it was still believed, just a few miles away at Kuzhai. Then, in the
1940s, when they feared the Germans more, it was the communists
they propitiated. Had it not always been the Jewish way, as a certain
cartoon Vilius showed me depicted, to don the manners and even the
uniforms of those in power, and to sell out others, even when they
were your kinsmen?

Vilius wrote a second date, June 21, 1941. One week later.

The Soviets were in retreat, and the Nazis were pushing across the
plain from Klaipeda, occupied since 1939. It was a clever ploy. After
giving the Soviets, theoretically their allies, a week to remove thousands of troublemakers, the Nazis launched Operation Barbarossa,
fanning out across the plains in a matter of hours and killing Jews.

At first many reaching Show-lay thought that in escaping the villages they'd be safe. Jews from villages that lay in the Nazis' path
began to arrive panicked in town, their numbers adding to the hundreds of Klaipeda's Jews who had already been there for a year after
decamping to escape the Germans' 1939 arrival. Over a few days near
the end of June 1941, from the smaller towns west and south where
the German line caught up to the Russians, Jews arrived in Shavli,
telling terrible tales of the mobile killing squads, the *Einsatzgruppen,*
who rounded up prominent citizens first and then everyone else,
drove them into forests, had them dig graves, remove their clothes,
and then be mowed down.

And everywhere they had help.

The story coming out of every Jewish town was the same. The
Einsatzgruppen found large groups in every town ready to wreak
vengeance on Jews who had betrayed their own. Orders went out
from Berlin to use the locals whenever possible. Such Lithuanian
"volunteers" as wanted to help with the clearing of the Jews from
Ostland were most welcome.

Driving today through Max Levy's town of Raseinai (forty-five
minutes from Shavli, where the Germans appeared several days be-

fore they reached Shavli on June 26), I understand why he would have chosen to live there—and return there, even after spending World War I in exile. Looking down the lanes and down the alleys of tidy cottages, I glimpse open fields. Every driveway in Raseinai today boasts great pots of flowers, and behind every house there is a greenhouse. (Not excluding the centrally located 28 Mairones, which the Raseinai phone book of 1941 lists as Max Levy's home, nor the house next door that the phone book lists as his son Adolph's). Drive past today in late summer and the greenhouse windows are misty with condensation. Long green hoses disappear into the roses. In the summer of 1941, when they took Max Levy with the first group of prominent citizens, the town would have been as green as Yael and I saw it.

Seven years ago I asked Victoris Andrekaitis, standing in his driveway, how Raseinai's Jewish population got along with their neighbors, and I thought his answer had been unambiguous.

We had no problems with the Jews, Victoris said. We Lithuanians raised the wheat and rye, the cows and the barley. The Jews sold what we raised.

Thin faced, knobby elbowed, his face lively in the deepening dusk, he'd told me a story of how it used to be in Cow Alley before the Jews were "all gone." One particular story concerned—and I remember he smiled—how his father, no Jew, came to honor the Jewish dietary laws.

Victoris's father, he related, had begun life as a policeman. But robbers roamed the woods, drunkards and such, and his wife feared for him. Eventually his wife's appeals to find a more neighborly calling wore him down, and Victoris's father became a butcher.

In smaller towns without tanneries or fertilizer plants, Jews and Christians divided up not only the labor of processing the cow but the cow itself. Once established in his new trade, Papa Andrekaitis discovered that butchering in a town half populated by Jews had its distinct points. A clever butcher willing to work a bit off the books— help the Jews with the Korobka tax the government levied on kosher meat—could claim with his own cleaver the various toothsome portions forbidden the Jews—the sirloin, the rump, and all the nether quarters proscribed by their laws.

Better still, if by chance the Jews' rabbinic slaughterer slipped— his knife missing the carotid artery so that the beast choked on his own blood—then the front as well as the whole back quarter, rendered unclean for Jews, could be had at a deep discount.

This is how it happened that Victoris's father became a real stickler for rabbinic supervision. One couldn't be too careful. Nothing less than absolutely kosher meat would do for the Jews! Naturally, Victoris recounted, smiling, it was considered bad form to raise a genuine ruckus as the slaughterer made his cut. And in almost all cases, the slaughterer had the concentration of an athlete.

Yet one might occasionally hazard a bit of whistling. Or a sneeze. A father might look indulgently at the sudden romping of little Victoris, tagging along. It would not be neighborly to gloat. But that night the town's Christian housewives would grind into their cutlets—adding some dill, a little onion, and a bit of diced pork fat for moistness— -the saddle of a kosher cow.

Max Levy's photograph is still, to this day, on the wall of the Museum of Raseinai, and Victoris Andrekaitis remembers him. When I mentioned the name, Victoris pantomimed an old man, somewhat stooped, raking with his fingers his two points of beard, raising his polite bowler. And he tucked a cane under his arm—the cane he carried as real gentlemen did.

❧

The Schomberg translation of *Yahadut Lita*, the great Hebrew work on Jews of Lithuania, includes in the description of Raseinai, among "prominent citizens of the last generation," my great-grandfather's brother Max. An asterisk by his name indicates that he was among those killed by the Nazis. No other descriptions of what happened in

Raseinai survive, but Leibe's book describes the procedure. The men were led through the town's main street in suits and ties, loaded onto flatbed trucks, and driven into the forest, where they dug large pits, removed their clothes, and were shot dead. Sometimes the "volunteers" were more eager. Jews were set upon by their neighbors in the town square and fell in a melee of clubs and scythes. In Zagare, enthusiastic locals drove the Jews onto the green common lined with Jewish apartments, shops, law offices, and small industries, and dispatched them. Then they moved across the river into the houses of those now gone. A few weeks hence the German authorities chose Zagare to receive the "overflow" of Jews from Shavli, announcing that this overflow would be "resettled" there. The newly formed Jewish council made a convincing case that a second ghetto in Shavli would enable the Jews to help the war effort through the manufacture of shoes and leather goods. Thus the plan for Zagare's ghetto was abandoned, and some thousand of Shavli's Jews were taken there and killed.

Yael and I had asked Alexejus, now with us for the whole day, to find the spot. We stood respectfully, awkwardly, and then got back in the car. It was hard to know just how to pursue the grim itinerary. How many hours? How many turns into the forest to place stems on the monuments? To ask locals, "Where did they kill the Jews?" To search each town for its old Jewish graveyard.

Yael was a young woman now. Knowledgeable in the history of the region, speaking one of its languages, she pointed out signs and Alexejus turned off rutted roads. She reached her arm back to me for Leibe's book, I passed it over to her, and we followed across the dips and rises of the green plain the course of the *Einsatzgruppen*, the rapid, improvised, alcohol-fueled shootings of July, August, and September 1941: 148 men in the tiny hamlet of Juniskis in the last week of August; 46 at Gruzdzai; 300 women and children at Linkuva, all in August. Twenty minutes' drive this way, thirty-five that, took one to the copses and glades where the Jews of Kursenai, Pakurojis, Lygumai, Papile, and Saukenai fell; then those of Radviliskis, Bubai, and Seduva. It was August again. Thunderclouds piled up as the afternoon wore on. Leibe's book—his maps—oriented us, but we stopped to ask questions of locals.

What would they say?

Eight years before, driving back from the mass grave site at Kuzhai outside of Sedova, we had slowed to ask a woman wearing a kerchief if she knew where we could find the burial place of the Jews. Rearing back from the open car door, squeezing her face into a grimace, she let forth a stream of spit. Today nothing like that happened. A man on a tavern porch or on a tractor, or the woman leaning on her hoe, earth-crusted potato in hand; the girl in Capri pants stepping along the dusty road smoking a cigarette—all tried, politely, to point out where "they had killed the Jews." Turn right, here. Then left, then right. Then one finds the place in the forest where a sign points, and between the trees the next sign, explaining: The earth is "watered with the blood of approximately 1,650 people, children women and men by Nazis and their helpers."

Max Levy's old house in Raseinai has a shed behind it that looks seventy or eighty years old. A hiding place, perhaps, for the twenty-five family members captured in the photo of 1928, if they had time to imagine hiding would be wise. The prominent Jews of Raseinai had filed out the main street to the fields in an orderly procession. Victoris Andrekaitis, in his eighties, suggested by an uneasy, wincing smile that he had not forgotten the summer night when they killed the Jews, Max Levy among them, the summer breeze so soft.

❧❧

In London, Edward Baron (né Levy), director of Carreras cigarettes, announced the firm's biggest year ever at the annual shareholders meeting of 1941. Few who saw him at that meeting would be surprised when, later that year, he was knighted for meritorious service.

How modestly, at a shareholders meeting of early 1942, he dismissed unseemly talk of record profits. How lightly he passed over the matter of dividends, addressing the attention of the assembled rather to the matter of keeping production up for the valiant troops: "supplies to the Royal Navy and Merchant Service as well as all the other fighting and defense services which it is our privilege and duty to serve."

How gracefully too Edward announced a Christmas gift of three weeks extra wages to all who had served during the whole twelve months of the last terrible year. And with what equanimity he stated that, despite labor shortages "only natural in time of war," the company would soldier on.

It had perhaps struck some as odd, hearing his lush Baltimore vowels, when Edward, returning from a visit to America in 1933, announced, "Thank God I am an Englishman!" Asked for his "impressions of the United States" after a call on suppliers and a visit with his sisters, Edward had really poured it on, expanding on the notion that if "ten thousand of our young men could go over to the United States to study and assimilate American methods," the British "stolidity" could combine with American kick to make the ideal businessman. A decade later it all rang less false, for his whole family now threw itself into the fight against Hitler. His nephews Jerry and Earle, along with his new son-in-law, the air marshal's son Dickie Longmore, were all in the war—Jerry in the Middle East and Italy, Earle in London. And dear Dickie flying planes, just like his father, for the RAF.

Some Britons, less than enchanted with Edward and his petite adjutant, Bertha, may have raised an eyebrow at the bluff, unapologetic Englishness of the family's mien, and at how things always came out just as Bertha had devised. For no one who knew them did not see Bertha's hand, or rather her Italian-slippered feet, scrambling up the rungs of Anglo-Jewish society.

By a stroke of luck, Bertha was a well placed hostess in London at the moment the Prince of Wales fell for a Baltimorean, Wallis Simpson, who was exactly Bertha's age. Eddie and Bertha's Belgrave Square house was conveniently near Buckingham Palace, and they were happy to offer hospitality. The Belgrave Square sitting room made an excellent stopping place for a couple wanting privacy. Wallis's taste in clothes, in entertainments, in certain Paris spots, as well as her memories of finishing school in Baltimore and her comfort with clever American women, had brought her and Bertha together in the days before the war. Whatever latent anti-Semitism Wallis and the Duke of Windsor would eventually show, such Jewish families as the Barons and Sassoons did not regard themselves as inconvenienced by it.

Bertha too had learned much during the 1930s from Rose Henriques and her husband, Basil, who gave her lessons in that noblesse oblige that was natural among Jews to the manor born. The warden and his wife, resident at the Bernhard Baron settlement, helped Bertha understand, or at least act as if she understood, her social duty, the obligation of the fortunate.

While an Oxford undergraduate in 1911, Basil Henriques had visited the Oxford Mission, the first English settlement house, and then in 1913, at 23, he petitioned the heads of the wealthiest synagogues in London for their support. The year 1914, before Basil went off to war, saw the opening of the Oxford and St. George's Jewish Lads Club and then a Girls' Club, whose directress, Rose Loewe, he married on his return. Decorated for heroism, Henriques and his bride took up residence in the manager's flat in the East End Settlement and launched a campaign to provide social services for Jewish youth by winning the support of Bernhard Baron. Baron lived just long enough to lay the foundation stone of the settlement, but then left to his heirs—Eddie and Bertha—London's most visible and distinguished pet project. As an experiment in communal welfare it had no peer in Europe. But led as it was by Sir Basil Henriques, and supported by the young and handsome Barons, it became something more than merely where modern plutocrats bestowed charity. After the dedication ceremonies in 1930, the Duke of Gloucester presiding, the Bernhard Baron Settlement rehabilitated not only the Jewish poor but the Jewish rich.

While all around the East End families slept six to a room, twenty persons sharing one stinking overflowing toilet, at the same time all around Mayfair young heirs idled, gambled, squandered time and money. The "Gaffer," as Henriques was known, subjected poor and rich to the same wholesome regime.

The settlement magazine, *Fratres,* summed up its earnest creed.

Whether one's home was a dank tenement hung with diapers or a Belgrave terrace nursery; whether one became a tailor like one's father or a Baronet, one would never be more at the settlement than an oldest boy. With an atmosphere clever rather than earnest, jolly rather than serious, the Bernhard Baron Settlement House was where the Sassoon, Rothschild, Marks, and Baron children played and sang around a secondhand piano, where a "cottage" donated by the Rothschilds provided a place of retreat not only for the Warden Henriques but also, as the years went by, for "honeymoon couples and tired parents."

As Bertha and Eddie ascended to the upper echelon of society, their compatriots agreed that it must be Bertha who got Eddie's handsome face in the paper so much. He was featured as a lion of industry, a regular on the business pages, but also featured in John Clennel's "Faces of Destiny" series, where Edward S. Baron was described as having a "high head above his ears, indicating firmness . . . nose of the business type . . . nostrils wide and curved showing sensitiveness and pride."

Likewise it must have been Bertha who managed his brothers' marriages to show the family to best advantage: Theo, introduced by Bertha to a niece of Sir Hugo Hirst; their presentations at court reported in the press. And happy-go-lucky Paul: Bertha found for him the languid beauty Elizabeth Defries and then, Defries making him miserable, another. These excellent matches paled, of course, beside the one she managed for her own daughter Millicent to the handsome son of the RAF air marshal, Sir Arthur Murray Longmore.

In photos Bertha, always by Eddie's side, seemed to preserve the look of a bride on a wedding cake. Here she was in a smart suit, an orchid corsage tucked under her pointed chin. Here as avatar of evening, her gown a dazzling waterfall of sheen and float. Bertha went to pains to be captured always epitomizing luxury *comme il faut*, and with the photographer arranged for in advance, she was not to be caught discomposed. But neither was she caught neglecting her social duty.

From the flat in Belgrave Square and even from the country house at Fulmer Chase, Bertha's chauffeur brought her several times a month to the Bernhard Baron settlement, from which vantage point she engineered a knighthood for her husband, Edward S. Baron.

Thus it happened that in the spring of 1942, my aunts Fanny, Myrtle, and Jean each received a letter, clippings enclosed, from Eddie.

> *Bertha Continues her Work at the YMCA Canteen at Victoria and the running of an Officer's Club, which she does well and enjoys.*

> *Betty, as you no doubt know, has just received her commission as an Officer in the Woman's Auxiliary Air Force. She is very much interested in her work, and after roughing it for a year, she well deserved to be commissioned.*

> *Dick, at the moment, is abroad and a little while ago had the pleasure of sinking a U boat.*

> *Jerry is still in the Middle East and was made a Major, which is most pleasing.*

> *Earle, still in this country and is a Captain.*

It is, however, to the two clippings enclosed that Eddie directs his sisters' special attention. For they will notice that he writes not from the square but from the "cottage" at Fulmer Chase. He and Bertha have donated the house itself as a lying-in hospital for officers' wives.

Some, of course, will see this donation, this loan, of Fulmer Chase as just the quid pro quo—a country home for a title—that clinched the deal. Some will shake their heads, not without admiring, at Bertha's determination, at her managing to get Clemmy herself, the very wife of Churchill, to choose Fulmer Chase for her own pet project.

My aunts Fanny, Myrtle, and Jean did not, needless to say, have these reactions.

A knighthood! For someone in our family!

They put not only the cuttings but Eddie's charming and modest letter into their albums and kept them preserved there next to the picture of the family in Raseinai in 1928.

"I am enclosing herewith," Eddie wrote, "some newspaper cuttings which will convey to you some of the reasons which occupied my time for a while."

> A former American, who went to England 32 years ago, was among those made a Baronet yesterday by King George of England. He is Edward S. Baron, now Sir Edward Baron, who was born in Baltimore 50 years ago. Three sisters are living there, Mrs. Edward I. Goldman, 1721 Georges Lane, Mrs. Harry Rosenstein, 1733 Georges Lane, and Mrs. Charles Jaffe of Melrose Court. Sir Edward went abroad to continue a musical education, but stopped in England and became so interested in a cigarette factory owned by an uncle that he stayed there. He turned his estate over to the British government for use as a maternity hospital for the wives of men in the Royal Air Force and Royal Navy.

FOURTEEN

Yellow Star, Gold Star

In the late summer of 2007, when Yael and I were on our way out of Berlin to catch the ferry at Sassnitz, our taxi driver made a wrong turn.

As the car sat stalled in the left lane, Yael and I glanced to the right and saw, across the idling traffic on the handsome avenue, a field of brokenness: Berlin's Holocaust memorial.

A plain of uneven stumps, the memorial forces a stumble of eye, of foot. To walk through it, even to look from the window, is to feel both balked and overtaken. These halted risers of granite gather anonymous history into Berlin's center—towns, lives, stories, nations—all mustered into one sorrowful admission. The field of stumps proffers no explanation. Civilization's cogency, its confidence, restored? Enlightenment? The monument yields none of this.

As we made our turn and drove away, I took Yael's hand, pale with its lovely small bones and trace of veins, not sure what I was doing, what story, what sequence would ever contain even my own family's lost ones or its survivors, who'd never known enough to grieve for any but their own children.

Not from us your peace of closure, say the stumps.

And not from us your tale of continuity.

By 1941, with both Jacob and his brother Paul Levy recently dead, the places on Jacob's cane and the people still living in these places had been mostly forgotten. And so from the time I first saw the cane, and read on it an obligation to learn and then to tell its story, I'd begun to collect, to keep, and to hold sacred more or less everything.

My files, if you could call them files, were unruly and eclectic, the pages a thicket of places and languages, and the folders full of odd, knobby, bulky, crumbling things—a strip of pale birch bark from the glade at Shavli, a small diamond-shaped piece of purple carbon from the YIVO archive that had once passed through Max Levy's typewriter. I'd taken myself to every one of Jacob's addresses and to factories and machine shops, and I was saving, in little plastic baggies, small bits of masonry, architectural drawings, scrawled notes on envelopes. I kept in my office a box top full of tobacco, now crisp as December underfoot, but yellow still. And, also, a pack of stale cigarettes with Carreras Rothmans stamped on it. And countless gray Xeroxed clippings and smudged carbons, my materials for a book, now become a mad Geniza like the cellar of sacred books found in Cairo.

❧

It had been a problem for me from the start: how to pay honor and to whom. Years ago, with Yael, I'd stumbled trying to recite the *Kaddish* over the mass grave at Shavli, embarrassed at the contrivance of the act, so embarrassed before my daughter and Leibe and Chaim that I did not know all the words.

I felt unsure, looking up at a carved figure, a sort of pieta it seemed, that Christians had erected over the gravesite, whether the very place was not somehow desecrated by Christian guilt. I'd had that experience before. Research over the years had gotten me used to a method comprehensive if not entirely comprehensible, even to me.

My research had made clear that nothing, no one, ever dies out of this world alone, that every event is kin to every other. In Berlin the field marking cities burned and graves defaced makes no separation between sacred and profane, monument and macadam, so that in effect around this plot all Europe spreads in one unbroken field of brokenness. One never reaches the end. How then could I?

For instance. Just the night before, strolling the Friedrichstrasse, the rain shower of the afternoon making the lights of the boulevard soft and lambent, Yael and I had walked west to east. Past Checkpoint Charlie and along the muraled time line of the twentieth century, we'd found Berlin's Opera House, its doors open to the generous cobbled plaza, and past it, the pillared Humboldt Institute, and then hailed a cab for Oranienburg. My map showed that here Jewish civilization had its last, and some thought greatest, flowering.

The soaring Neu Synagogue, of which the Moorish synagogues of Baltimore's Eutaw Place were copies, stood at the junction, and a few doors down was the salon where the Jewish Enlightenment's great sage, Moses Mendelssohn, held court. In his parlor conversations, free thought exposed Jewish boys to newer ways. Few took long to exchange their rustic clothes for frock coats, for why else had they come—running west from their fathers, fleeing eastern mud to soak up Enlightenment's spirit, to learn Emancipation's German accent. It was from here, here in Berlin, that the books flooding the ports of Klaipeda were dispatched, and from here that the newly trained architects, ripened on *Jugendstihl,* retraced their steps east to Riga, to rebuild it in a German image. It was from here that giddy tidings came of emancipation, modernization; from here the spreading railroad networks connecting west to east. And from here all the ideas that taught Jacob's brother Max to believe in the law as an instrument of emancipation, his brothers Paul and Isaac to believe in scientific agriculture, and Jacob himself to carry to Baltimore his faith in industrial progress as the engine of civilization.

And from here too, German Jews were transported eastward and deposited in Riga. To make room for the new arrivals from Berlin,

Jews already in Riga, too much including my relatives, were ushered to the grave pits first.

Where better, as plans evolved in late 1941 for the disposal of Germany's own, than Riga, so long hospitable, so long convenient, reasoned Hitler's planners. Where better to send them than to the Ostland, the Baltic states that had long given Germany an easy field for conquest, plus scope for commerce. And now Germany wanted "living space," *Lebensraum*, as soon as the Ostland could be "cleared."

There, far from the prying international press or protestations from the tenderhearted, Berlin's Jews might be unloaded without fuss. If the human contents of trains did not arrive "intact" and "fit to work," they did at least arrive where "operations" had reached improved efficiency. Operation Barbarossa had been ragged at first, operation scattershot. Just months before, in the summer and fall of 1941, what with resistance and the unpredictability of local militias, the killing squads sometimes passed two or three times through the same little hamlets, each time doing reconnaissance for a suitable site to execute the identical mission, killing the Jews.

Far better, urged the commander of the Ostland, to commandeer whole districts, enclose them, and use them as mustering grounds and staging places, dispatching unnecessary laborers and those no longer fit for labor. In this way those in charge had already achieved the desired results. Commanders in the Ostland were proud of the systems they were devising, eager to test them on larger populations.

Impatient to dispose of Berlin's Jews and also Frankfurt's, in late 1941 Hitler had them shipped from Charlottenburg and Oraienburg to Riga, as if that city's environing forests were nothing but the leafy outskirts of Berlin's suburbs. Jews loaded on trains at Berlin disembarked directly to a place where techniques and a certain infrastructure were ready to receive them.

The area selected for the ghetto was no more than half an hour's walk from the Riga railroad train station. For Jews who had journeyed many days without food or water—and were still capable of walking—the walk to the ghetto took about an hour. Those who could not walk, those so famished, frozen, and disoriented from standing in the unheated cars for several days with nothing in their mouths but snow chipped off the cars, were taken directly to the forest in lorries.

Ironically, there was work, plenty of it, as factory supervisors clamored for workers in the beet processing factories and in bricks and peat. Those among the German Jews who were reasonably healthy were kept in the so-called Large Ghetto recently cleared of Riga's resident Jews.

German Jews who could not work would follow Riga's Jews to the grave pits at Rumbula.

❧❧

In Riga, when I first stopped there, I went as far as the graveyard fence and then halted, deciding not to walk into the forest where the condemned from the train were sent. It was my second trip to the Baltics, this time without Yael.

The day before I'd gone to the city archive and had gotten my shy translator, Valtis, to help negotiate permission to rummage in the stacks. There we had found the addresses, first 28 Kalnu Iela in the city center, where Isaac's daughter Sarah, listed as Zarah, had kept house through the 1920s. According to the city directory, Zarah was still at this address in July 1941. Leaving the archive, I'd made my way to 28 Kalnu Iela, glad to find Sarah's flat so central, on so distinguished a street, proud of this handsome address—the curved elegant building, its shallow, dove gray steps rising out of the softly lit vestibule. To this flat, I was pleased to realize, my great-grandfather Jacob had taken himself on foot, during his visit in June 1928, from his hotel, the Petersburg, near the president's house. Sarah's brother Avram, a jurist living on Lachplesa, and her sister Betti, living on

Stabu, were also listed in the 1941 Riga directory and would likely have been there in the fall as the storm troops perfected their methods and readied the town to receive Berlin's Jews.

These family members, I surmised, would not have died in the first roundup. They may even have preserved a measure of calm, confident as Riga's Jews tended to be, that the luck and prosperity they'd long enjoyed, courtesy of German trade, would make them different.

Many years later, in 2000, Riga's remaining Jews, an audience of whom I'd spoken to a few days before, were not shy in reminding me of how distinguished, how special, their Jewish community had been. They had agreed with my hunch that as longtime residents of the city, Sarah, Avram, and Betti and Minna—although Lithuanian born—would have not been among the Lithuanian Jews who sought sanctuary in the Gogola Street synagogue only to be trapped inside when the great wooden reading desks were covered with benzine and the whole building burst into flames. Most of the dead were Lithuanian Jews fleeing from Zagare and other border towns, not longtime residents of the city like my distinguished relatives.

No, Zarah would have remained unmolested until the whole plan was in place. Kalnu Iela was not even a predominantly Jewish district that in a day or week could be emptied of its inhabitants wholesale. Noisy shouting and gunfire, the inevitable concomitants of a massacre, were to be avoided in this neighborhood. Near the city center, steps from the elegant hotels and the foot traffic, it was fitting that a certain quiet discretion prevail, at least until the processions had passed the railroad station. There were plenty of fugitives and poor Jews to round up before notifications, edicts, and other appeals calculated to quell an uproar would result in Riga's more prosperous Jews gathering in the courtyards wearing yellow stars, one stitched on the breast and one on the back. Then there was the headache of transporting Riga's Jewish elite, the most educated and prosperous in the Baltics, to the derelict part of the city between the old graveyard and the railroad tracks, which in any event had space for only 13,000.

Some days movements of Riga's Jews were complicated by the arrival of trainloads from Berlin. Overcrowding in the fall of 1941 meant more and more of Riga's Jews were marched to labor camps to clear mines or dig peat. Thus room was made for newly arriving German Jews. Despite the outflow to labor camps, it was obvious by late November that clearing much more space, rapidly, would be necessary.

Communiqués to Berlin had a boastful note. In the days between November 29 and December 8, 1941, *Einsatzgruppen* units, aided by Latvian volunteers, marched 25,000 of Riga's Jews into the Rumbula forest and shot them in mass pits. By the opening months of 1942 only five thousand Jews survived in the Riga ghetto. Childless and thus unencumbered, a woman in her forties, Zarah Levy would have been unlikely to survive the last weeks of 1941. Competition between the two ghettos for the choicest labor assignments, pitting German Jews and their Baltic cousins against each other, kept factory quotas filled, but it was hard on those who were not young and strong. And thus despite a high demand for slave labor—a paradox that there was work for as many as the Nazis managed to keep alive—Zarah was not, I think, one of those spared past the first weeks of 1942.

That day in 2000, I paced a dusty track through the Large Ghetto, the German one, and the Small Ghetto, reserved for surviving Riga Jews. Zarah Levy and her brother Avram and sisters Betti and Minna—whom I'd followed as far as the ghetto—I left there. But I have their photo. These Riga cousins of mine, Isaac's children, looked like my great-grandfather Jacob's children—Avram with the prominent Levy ears; Minna with my Aunt Fanny's look of kindly, second-string brains plus beauty; Sarah, or Zarah, sporting a decorous string of pearls and a smart little jacket.

꧁꧂

So much work needed doing at the Frankel Leatherworks that, while other towns had been purged of their Jews outright, it appeared possible that modern industry would once again revive the fortunes of the Jews of Shavli. Frankel's Leatherworks, the largest in eastern Europe, and Nurok's shoe factory too, were considered industries of the first importance. Capable of supplying boots and packs and other leather goods to Wehrmacht forces on the eastern front, the factory was a great boon to Shavli's Jews as well as to the Germans. Its efficient maintenance and unimpeded production schedule even merited keeping necessary Jews alive.

The fierce, uncompromising Leibe told me that his father had been an accountant to Frankel, and his family was among those exempted from deportation to Zagare and the various *Aktionen*. Sitting on the sunken couch in his cold, small house, with its corrugated iron roof and chipped walls, a few days after I stopped at the edge of Riga's Jewish ghetto, I talked for the last time with Leibe.

For hours he turned the pages of his ghetto notebooks, guiding me through the edicts: *Jews may not walk on sidewalks. Jews may not wear fur. No shoelaces for Jews. No milk.* Yes, he'd nodded his head, he'd been there from the beginning, from 1941 when the ghetto was formed until the few hundred survivors, including apparently one Solomon Levy, were taken to Stuthoff and then Dachau. As Leibe had told me before, it was because Solomon could register as a "specialist in metals" that he'd been preserved in one of the ghettos. On Smallprison Street, now a derelict neighborhood of workshops, was the house in which my great-grandfather Jacob had been born. It was still standing and, as late as 1941, still owned by the Levys. Solomon had paid the taxes on the house, but I surmise that in 1942 it was someone else's home and castle.

As a relatively valued ghetto inmate, Solomon and his family enjoyed nicer accommodations, the authorities even winking at the "usefulness" of young mothers such as Fanja for the sake of her husband, Solomon. One can understand how hopes might have risen in Shavli, since the first years in the ghetto were bearable, even for the least "essential" inmates. For instance, until 1943 the Nazis winked and happily exploited Jewish women whose "essential" skills maintained luxury workshops for embroidery, furs, and lace. Nazi wives had tablecloths and even stoles of fox and ermine made by the widows of murdered Jews. Later, of course, their faith in assignments of this kind was used against these women. Those who volunteered, eager to prove themselves skilled at needlework, were the first shot. Wiser ones were allowed to board barges for Stuffhoff, where they hauled sandbags in grit and frozen rain.

One of the women who filled Shavli's definition of usefulness—by working in embroidery—was a Levy bride. Born in Ekaterinburg, Russia, she, like Solomon's lovely Fanja, had married in Russia and then come west after World War I, enjoying a period of independence and prosperity with her westernized husband. That husband gone, shot I presume in one of the earlier *Aktionen*, she and her eldest child took themselves to work in the morning, leaving the little ones to get through the day on their own. There were no children in the ghetto, one commentator mourned, "only little Jews."

At least through 1942 an effort was made to preserve a semblance of childhood. "Children's corners" were a proud feature of the Shavli Jewish council's organization. There younger teenagers were kept busy (the better to keep their thoughts from possibly joining the partisans). The three little Levy girls whose mother did embroidery were, I infer from Leibe's ghetto census, among those released at lunch (such as it was) to spend the afternoons alone. Before he was shot, their father had kept his father's store, the Brolai Levy, going, and so I imagine that Rocha, Sora, and Aliza would have played store, using a stick to spoon out "rice" and "cocoa" and "coffee." Naturally, none of the children could be prevented from playing war, though it made their parents anxious. All children played games based around food, for the precious onions, potatoes, and field greens hanging in sacks over the mother's bed were all there was to eat. There was no milk for babies. Their mothers told them to be glad they had teeth.

It is against Jewish custom to name a child after a living person; the practice is considered bad luck and for some tantamount to a curse. I think of this when I look, as I do now, at pictures of my Aunt Myrtle's son Jack, whom she named (out of excess of sentiment, solicitude, desire to salve the feelings of the man who'd lost his own sons?) after her living father, Jacob.

The picture I am looking at was taken, as best I can tell, in the summer of 1942 before Jack enlisted in the U.S. Army. Given to me by Fred, his brother, the image shows Aunt Myrtle peeping between the shoulders of two tall boys, both lanky, grinning, one shirtless, one with a girl—a girlfriend—at his shoulder. Myrtle is in her early forties here but looks younger. Her hair looks damp in the summer heat, but I can tell it is still black. Her sons lean toward her in a familiar way. Years before, when I'd looked at this photo in the album, I called Aunt Myrtle over and she pointed the sons out to me, though I already knew that the one on the right was Fred and the shirtless one on the left was Jack, her Jack, who "died in the war." And then Aunt Myrtle smiled, holding my shoulders, and asked me if I could guess who was the young child whose little black bob frizzed in the heat. Aunt Myrtle squeezes my shoulders and rolls her eyes at me, for the little girl in the picture has been given, like the boy, the liberty of going without a shirt. It is, of course, my mother who pokes out her narrow nippled chest above the narrow shoulders of the laughing boys. It is from her age in the picture, six or seven, that I date the photo to 1942, the summer before Jack's letters began.

❦

War begins a game.

Jack, age nineteen, writes to his mother, Myrtle,

> *Today was the first day I really started to enjoy this man's army.*
> *I have all of my clothes and some field equipment. I receive the*

rest of the latter after I'm shipped. The helmets are quite novel, being in three pieces: a wool cap, a plastic helmet for protection against the heat and finally the familiar metal piece which encloses the latter two quite snug. The long underwear is swell, but those g . . . d . . . shirts still itch me so I wear the top of the underwear almost continually. . . . please excuse the bad handwriting but I got my injections yesterday and my left arm is pretty stiff and sore. Those are the only bad effects. All the veterans (two days!) called us needlebait when we first arrived. . . . believe it or not, every bit of my clothes fits me perfectly.

She would want his clothes to fit perfectly. He knows this. To his mother Jack writes the letter of a boy dressing up. His first letter to his brother Fred, eight days into his basic training, is overlong with the excitement of playing real soldier.

Our training is very strenuous, as you can presume from my letters. Particularly brutal is the bayonet drill and close combat training. Brutal in the moral sense, as I am getting accustomed to all other phases of our routine. They teach us to use no mercy and all idea of fair play is forgotten. When a man is down, you butt him in the head with your rifle to bash out his brains. When he attacks you, you first jab him in the throat with a long thrust of your bayonet, You follow up with a short thrust into the midsection, and if he still lives, jab upward with your bayonet being carried and forced with your entire body through his lower jaw into his skull.

When you are both disarmed and he tries to grasp you, push his head back by applying your hand and forcing it against his chin. Surprisingly effective. Raise your foot as high as possible and, with the edge of your heel, bring it down sharply on his kneecap. This rips it off, and, when carried through, will tear most of the skin off his shin. Continue the downward action and smash all of

your weight on the top of his arch, twisting at the same time. This
will break every bone in his foot.

Another is to bring your knee sharply up into his groin and to
inactivate his family jewels. When his head is close to you, and is
held by you, put your fingers into his eyes and pull down sharply.
This will blind him, and also rip his face off.

Swing from your opposite shoulder putting all your might be-
hind the stroke. Choice spots are the Adams apple, guts, heart,
back of ear. The striking force is terrific.

All of the latter is what your kid brother has been learning these
past weeks."

With war still far away in 1942 and the situation stateside not com-
parable in any way to what Eddie, Paul, and Theo had seen in London the prior year, Aunt Fanny's diary entries are, like Jack's letters,
not too discomposed. Detailed accounts of table settings, birthday
gifts, and small purchases fill Fanny's pages along with a record of
days logged at the plant—business picking up with wartime orders—
and the routine visits the aunts made to my grandfather, Emil, in the
Inst-*ee*-tution. No change, the doctors shook their heads. No change
expected.

The big news comes from London. The Carreras factory makes it
through the Blitz without a "speck" of damage. Bertha busies herself
at the London canteen, and when they are lucky enough to get to the
country, she and Eddie write from the humble quarters of Fulmer Cottage. Eddie does not need to tell his sisters that his star has never shown
so brilliantly, with Carreras profits going through the roof, and he and
Bertha swept completely up in His Majesty's Great Effort. He says as
much to stockholders at annual meetings (clippings enclosed), and
Bertha now is sure to send her own clippings, these full of the latest on
the Fulmer Chase Lying-in Hospital. The reason they write from the
"cottage" is that the large main house, Fulmer Chase, has been converted into a hospital. Bertha and her committee of concerned ladies,

Clementine Churchill among them, can't do enough for these wives of the brave officers of the RAF and Royal Navy.

From the pictures and clippings thoughtfully enclosed one can see just how splendidly Bertha brings off the day on which Clemmie herself shows up to salute the Barons: She adopts the Officers Hospital at Fulmer Chase as her own particular project. A clipping relates:

> Mrs. Winston Churchill visited the hospital recently and was delighted with all she saw. Fresh fruits and vegetables are being sent from adjoining country houses, and with the increase in the number of patients, further gifts of this kind and of such things as a freshly caught salmon would be appreciated. Grateful letters are constantly arriving from mothers who have been at Fulmer Chase. They all speak of the great kindness shown to them and of the happy atmosphere of the house.

In the *Guardian* a breathless reporter catches the spirit of the day:

> In the afternoon, Mrs. Churchill, Miss Brooks and Lady Portal took us to see a maternity hospital which they have organized for junior officers wives in a house lent to them by Lady Baron. They can take 22 patients at a time and I must say that the whole atmosphere was pleasant and happy. The babies were the loveliest I have ever seen—healthy, placid, and beautifully cared for. Those young mothers live through anxious times, with their husbands missing or off in some distant part of the world, and most of them going through their own ordeal for the first time. Yet everyone could show her baby with pride.

That same spring of 1942, in the Shavli ghetto, official tolerance of so many unproductive mouths to feed—the elderly and children—wore thin. The plan for thinning the ghetto to essential personnel began with babies.

In the spring of 1942, a notice, *skelbimai*, went up: "Births are permitted in the ghetto only up to August 15th 1942." The edict continues:

> After this date, it is forbidden to give birth to Jewish children either in the hospitals or in the homes of the pregnant women. It is pointed out, at the same time, that it is permitted to interrupt pregnancies by means of abortions. If they do not comply with this order, there is a danger that they will be executed along with their families.

On March 24 the Shavli Jewish council, the Judenrat, agonized through the night. Despite the edict, there were at least twenty pregnant women in the ghetto, some in the early months and some willing to undergo abortions. But a few women in their second trimester resisted abortion, including one who would be in her eighth month by August. Delivery of this child risked implicating doctors in a live birth or killing a live child, "which would be murder."

As August 15 approached, the SS posted warning signs throughout the ghetto:

> The time is over. It is the last minute. The 15th of August is not far. Remember Jewish women, after the 15th births will be forbidden even in private homes. A strict examination of private dwellings will be conducted. Physicians, midwives and nurses will be forbidden to assist Jewish women.

In case any mistook their meaning, the notices made clear that live births meant death: "All will be punished with the utmost severity. Do not forget the danger you might bring upon yourself or your children."

❧❦

Leibe Lifshitz remembered the relative calm between the fall of 1942 and 1943. Working in the Frankel factory and returning home to the ghetto, Leibe had found a former shopkeeper, a gentile still working in the factory, who sometimes slipped him food. Leibe had no younger siblings, but those who did managed to keep most of them alive. For more than a year, from August 1942 through November 1943, young children survived in the ghetto.

But the morning of November 3, 1943, as Leibe told me and then wrote in his correct, slow hand, had brought the infamous *Kinderaktion*. Their parents at work, the smaller children of the Shavli ghetto were at home alone when the Nazis pulled trucks playing gay music into the ghetto. Those under twelve could not resist the roundup.

Bulletins sent to the nearby Jews of Kovno inspired terror, fear that the terrible crime against children perpetrated in Shavli augured a similar action in Kovno. Especially terrifying were the reports of the calm with which the *Aktion* was carried out. No one bothered with the time-consuming sadism. The children were relatively easy—small, underfed as they were—to get into trucks. By fall of 1943, thinking that the war was going their way and having already killed so many Jews, the German professionals scoffed at wasting excess effort on an easy task. More than five hundred children were taken away that day. Solomon and Fanja's young son Isaac, named after his grandfather Isaac the Tanner, was taken, as well as all three Levy children in the other ghetto, Sora, Rocha, and Aliza.

I will remember all my life the look in Yael's eyes as she watched Leibe, on our first trip, write the names of those children twelve and under taken on November 3. As she watched his face under its shock of white hair, he lifted his head to explain. What with the wounds some children, especially the older ones, received in the "scuffle," and allowing for the cold and hunger of the trip to Auschwitz, the parents never knew which of the children arrived there "safely."

Historians of the ghetto admit that after the *Kinderaktion* the parents of Shavli went a little crazy. Hitherto they had prided themselves that tight organization and the Frankel factory permitted a hopeful outlook. But as order began to break down, many parents gathered for séances, seeking to communicate with their little ones. The generation gap widened, and what influence parents had over their teenagers dissipated. With half of the adults already gone, and now all the little children, the teenagers believed the adults were incapable of saving anyone.

Now began the period of the secret underground meetings where the young pledged to find their way out of the ghetto. "Vengeance" was the name of their cell. They had organized in 1941, but their organization had the character of a youth group. Now they told each other the story of Masada, of the brave Judean resisters who held off the Roman army on a mountaintop fortress in 70 ce. Now they received and carried messages, slipping through fences, and planned and replanned escapes. Now they communicated with bands roving in the forests. While their grieving mothers tapped at tables, while their elders communed with the dead, the teenagers poured gas into lightbulbs, recited directions through the forest to each other, practiced German phrases. The teenagers did not trust their parents, who had lost faith in themselves.

If the Levys were at all representative, the teenagers were right in thinking that their parents would be able to do nothing. For aside from Moshe's brother Solomon, preserved all the way to Dachau because his metalworking skill made him useful, the only survivor of the family shown in the photos of 1928 was a young girl. Her name was Riva. And I actually found a letter from her in my Aunt Jean's files. She wrote,

> *If you have heard something from Max Levy and his family, who lived once before the second world war in Lithuania, then you must know that he had a daughter Sonitscha, and five sons, Grisha, Salamon, Adolf, Nathan and Saul. Nathan is my father! He, my*

brother Elinka and my mother Sheina were killed in the terrible
war. I was in ghetto, then a partisan in the forest.

I read and reread this letter, looking from it to the 1928 family portrait showing Max seated beside Jacob, the cane under his curved
knuckles. I find Nathan, and then the girl who must be Riva. Standing in front of her father and mother, she is only a youngster, five or
six years old. She stands in a ruffled dress with her hand on the hand
of her mother. Her younger brother, the one in a little boy's sailor
suit, still has his baby fat.

The letter, written by Riva, a woman born in the 1920s, had neither envelope nor return address. I have wracked my brains in vain
for ten years, thinking how to find this Riva.

I know that I never will.

I sometimes like to think, though I know it couldn't be true, that
Jack, 21, somehow saved Riva, also 21, and that his death in the snows
of Alsace hastened to its end the "terrible war" that consumed every
person but two in the family photos of 1928. It is fantasy, I know, but
spinning tales counteracts the sense that nothing fits, that the ends are
all unknown, that history's bitter strands unravel. In my mind I let
Jack ride slowly to the east to find and rescue Riva; he, as Jacob's
American namesake, would try to keep one person in his grandfather's European family alive.

Jack writes from Camp Breckenridge, Kentucky, in April 1944, two
months before D Day,

> *The invasion is more gigantic than most people realize. Latest re-*
> *ports state that there are twenty divisions in the battle area and*
> *that is plenty of men. Just to see this one division ship from Camp*
> *Polk up here and then magnify that by twenty times would stag-*
> *ger the imagination. I was on a detail loading the vehicles and*
> *thought I would never see the end of the long line of jeeps, half*
> *tracks, tracks of all sizes, anti tank guns, field pieces and other*

stuff too numerous to go over. It sure must have been a sight to see
all of that equipment moving down towards the Dover Coast.

He does not mean to be callous, does not mean to hurt his mother, yet it is clear from his tone that the impressions made by the war, the sheer scale of the enterprise of which he is a part, dissolve his nearer vision. He declines—though she begs—to assure her that he will apply for further training to keep him safe at camp. He neglects to thank her and her sister Fanny for the packages they scrimp to send. Mothers at a loss for what else to do assemble packages of food for their boys at camp; my Aunt Fanny's diary shows weekly excursions with Myrtle to buy "pineapple juice, Shaeffers' candy, cookies with raisins, giant Hershey bars, potato sticks, figs and prunes, sugar coated peanuts, liverwurst, plantation dainties."

And also, though I can well imagine what the effort must have cost them, pictures of pinup girls.

Still, Jack cautions her, "don't let our initial success stir you into believing we have won the struggle. Hitler is playing a shrewd game and will put up a strong fight before Victory is even in sight."

Then he adds an analysis of his own division that was hardly comforting: "We are going to hear more and more reports of casualties and replacements but—the division . . . is certainly not ready for combat. The men are rugged and trained, but to be frank, the majority of officers aren't worth a damn, being too inexperienced."

And worse, from his mother's point of view:

Maneuvers are drawing closer and plans are being completed.
Where or when I couldn't tell you for obvious reasons, or how we
will travel. You know how I am about such things but can tell you
that we will probably leave Camp Breckenridge for good around
the first week of next month [March 1944]. After that, it is hard
to tell what is in store for us. I hate to see this Division go over as
it is certainly not prepared for Combat Duty. . . . The Officers are

almost all green at their job and the enlisted men are disgusted with their assignments.

Nevertheless, in September Jack is still in the United States, "champing at the bit" and determined to join the "titanic struggle." He tells his mother flatly that he is "only too glad to return to the Mortar Platoon even if it means remaining a lowly Private First Class." By October he is finally moving east, bound for Europe:

> *The only thing I am permitted to tell you is that I am somewhere on the Eastern Coast . . . I know that your chin will slip a little at times but keep it up as you have done all these years. Fred's and my past conduct attest to the result of your work. I shall never forget, where I may be and whatever I do, to be all you expect. . . . Take care of yourself, honey, it won't be too long, and that grand day which we are all continually praying for will come very shortly.*

Having arrived in Europe, Jack is overjoyed. His V-Mail quotes a popular ditty on censorship: I'm Mum, Hun/Can't tell where we sail from.

Late in the early winter of 1944, Aunt Myrtle's son Jack spends his last leave in London.

> *After getting settled at a Red Cross center, I began a two hour search for Carreras. The factory is rather prominent, which decreased the difficulty of finding it. I was invited to eat dinner with the Board of Directors later and so went back to the Red Cross— got a bit cleaned up which included a full hour session with the barber and went back to Carreras at about one o'clock. The dinner was very good, and then I was shown through the factory, which took about four full hours. It is truly a "wonder house of machinery" boasting a very complete Air Raid Shelter for all of some*

3000 workers, cafeterias on each of the floors and then the most modern methods.

After Uncle Ted finished up, we went over to his "flat" which had been damaged slightly during the "blitz." Had a few drinks and picked up Aunt Doris at sort of a Private Night Club. A delicious dinner followed at the Barclay, and proceeded to the train station about twelve midnight. A few hours journey brought us to a small town north of London where we picked up another car of Uncle Ted's and drove out to his country home.

That home is the most beautifully furnished I have ever seen— complete with big oak rafters, large open fireplaces and just about the best in everything to make a home comfortable and tastefully furnished. . . . I didn't get up till eleven thirty the following morning—fairly wallowed in a hot bath and had breakfast in bed at Aunt Doris's insistence. After dressing, I walked around the house, put on a pair of Uncle Ted's boots and took a stroll through the grounds until two o'clock.

With a "swell goodbye and the gift of a cigarette lighter and a couple of tins of pipe tobacco," Jack returns to the front. "I was certainly the downcast soldier, going back to Camp after such a splendid leave."

❧

I think it was reading a poem from a newspaper, a yellowed cutting my Aunt Myrtle kept in her album along with photos of her father's 1928 journey to Europe, which suggested to me that I would someday have to follow the trail of my family's history.

As a child I'd been made to understand there were reasons why our whole clan comported themselves as though we were persons to whom nothing untoward ever happened. It was made clear—not in so many words, but clear—that we lived by a different standard from everybody else, and that the family's caretakers, its wardens, were my aunts.

If I'd asked directly what made us so special I think they'd have said that, naturally, as we'd come from industrialists, or even *may*-jer man-*ahfack*-chrs from Balt-ee-mewer, our higher quality than, say, mere New York Jews went without saying. We left to them, New Yorkers, the pushcarts and the retail trade; to them the rutted *shtetl*, the dirty boots; to them the traces of accent and the consciousness of gentiles.

Our well-dressed children, our candy dishes nestling chocolates in brown frills, proved our membership in a gentler world. Proved we'd eradicated, or at least transcended, cold and want and struggle. My aunts' environs proved it. Those delicate cups and cake servers, those crystal-hipped bottles on the silver trays—these objects which my aunts disposed around their rooms—were like emanations of the women themselves.

Still, long ago, in one of Aunt Myrtle's albums, I had read that poem. It had the stylized quality I associated with her, but it introduced notes darker than one heard in her delicate precincts. "There's a Gold Star in my window," the poem began, "And an ache in my heart." My mother whispered to me that Aunt Myrtle was a gold star mother, which meant she had lost a son in The War: my mother's cousin Jack. Mothers whose sons had been killed switched the blue star in the front window, meaning they had a son in the service, for the gold star, revealing that the son had been lost. While the sentimentality of the poem was not out of place in Aunt Myrtle's world, there was something almost unbelievably discordant about the facts the poem memorialized, facts one could not square with the deep carpeting, the candy in frills. Sharing a carefully protected page with a telegraph from the War Department, a booklet narrating certain events of February 1945, and various telegrams from England, the poem admitted into my aunt's world, and mine, winter and the death of children.

When I finally began to follow Jack's story, taking Yael to drive along the borders of eastern Belgium and Alsace, I was trying to bring the death of this American boy into focus. I was trying to visualize what Jack might have gone through as he faced Hitler's Panzers in the last violent months of the war.

But the vibrant green of the countryside passing by the car windows made it hard to envision.

In summer, overlooks in the Ardennes provide sweet views down to dells where cows bend their large heads into the flowery grass. Every switchback props a tiny cobbled town—one church, five or six open doorways at the crooked X where the town's two lanes meet, and then the two or three blocks of flats—voices from the window, bicycles leaning against the stucco—before the town gives way to another mountain view of uncropped grass and the cemetery. Most towns in this region of Belgium have these World War II cemeteries. The monuments are often larger than any of the town's dignified edifices, for they have been quarried in far places, then brought and placed here by the British, French, and Americans. Despite the profound calm of these towns with their staid and settled names—Grandmenis, Vielselm—they are names on a bloody itinerary.

The roads past the cemeteries were the site of tanks turning over and over down the hillside, and of trios and quartets of men found encased dead in new snows, an accidental glimpse of a reddened garment all that had discovered them. The wooden posts that display clustered company insignias, each with its symbols, its numbers and code, break the peace of these towns. When one faces them, reading the fervent inscriptions on the posts, it is 1944, winter, but when one turns, all again is summer, trees rustling overhead, sun pooling in the squares, sound of children, clank of dishes, rich smell of lavender, crust, cheese.

Near Colmar to the south, where Jack and other survivors of the Battle of the Bulge were sent, it is the same. The villages have been rebuilt, their facades fresh but in the same Alsatian style, and looking as if nothing ever jarred their tranquil lookouts over the vineyards that coil in semicircles around the frontage of every hill. Stopping in these towns, I drink pale wines—heady, but so softly fresh they quench the thirst. The waiters pour them into small straight-sided glasses that might fit in a child's hand. Certainly Yael is big enough now, and I say nothing when they fill her glass along with mine as she chooses from the heavy plate of paté and bread. Our guides are two Frenchmen in their seventies who interrupt each other, press paté on her, and the local onion tart. She nibbles at what they recommend, enjoying the courtly attention they pay her.

We are glad to have found these men, and I am grateful for Yael's French, so much more recent than mine. Our guides remember the war. They were little boys then, and they tell us that during the winter of 1944–1945 their mothers were eager to billet American soldiers and perhaps receive their protection. But these Frenchmen use many words we do not understand, so we compose labored sentences to get them to help us picture those wartime days. We carry a booklet with the insignia of Jack's division, the 75th, in which we keep his letters and other testimonies of that awful winter, the six weeks between December and February when Jack's division was thrown into the worst of the battles.

Combat-hardened veterans named Jack's outfit the "Diaper Division," brought to these regions to break the German line in December 1944. Overtrained yet inexperienced, some of the raw soldiers landed on the steep frozen hills of Belgium too fast for their minds to adjust. Jack's letters show a mother's son transformed into a soldier, a man for whom home and family, worry and comfort have become provincial in the cold light of what he sees. The letters he sends he actually writes to himself, to keep his bearings. The tone shows me how Jack increasingly claims an adulthood he never had achieved as his mother's son. He prays to God that all the misery of war will end soon: "I want to forget the roar of artillery, the men huddled in mudholes and wretched civilians wondering which side is going to trample through their houses next." And yet there is a stark worldliness, as well as an enormity, in what he writes that is his alone and that his mother, helpless at home, must simply receive and absorb.

It was the coldest winter Belgium had seen in decades, and the new recruits were in as much danger during lulls and at night as in battle. It must have been fearsome to these boys fresh out of camp in Kentucky, Jack only a week past his leave in London, to find themselves dug into a hole on a hillside where darkness fell purple across the snow in the late afternoon and the temperatures steadily dropped for the next twelve hours. Exhausted boys who'd spent the day crawling through snowfields sometimes fell asleep in foxholes not deep enough to protect them from the wind, and they woke to find their fingers unusable, frostbitten. They could not make fires and so they ate their C rations—meat and beans, meat and vegetable hash, meat and vegetable stew—cold out of the cans.

Back in the states Jack's mother and her sister Fanny had shopped together and made up parcels to ship overseas. Aunt Fanny's diary records one day's purchase of Marshmallow Fluff, Uneeda Crackers, Clark Bars, Velveeta cheese, sandwich cookies, Good and Plenty, strawberry jam, peanuts, licorice, Jordan almonds, pistachios, turkey spread, and pretzels, but on roads slicked with ice the packages from home rarely got through. Jack's letters are sporadic, interrupted for days when fighting is fierce and then coming every day, sometimes two a day.

"I was up at the front on Christmas and New Year's and can't boast a very good time." Sometimes he remembers to share news of comfort to his mother: "One woman in a house we stayed at made me a pair of mittens out of a blanket and a small hood that covers my whole head." Good son that he is, sometimes he remembers how his mother must be feeling: "Glad you are staying at Aunt Jean's now and hope it rids you a bit of your loneliness." But as the days go by his letters reveal details that must make his mother wild:

> *Life is certainly a change now—dull and monotonous with only the sounds of our own artillery and the debris of War lying around to tell us war is not too far away. It leaves us taut with tension waiting for reports to roll in.*

And in a letter to his brother:

> *It is almost too cold to write. . . . the men run wild in the evacu-*
> *ated towns. . . . All one sees here is half torn buildings with gap-*
> *ing holes from artillery, bloated dead corpses in the ditches,*
> *isolated civilians walking down the road not knowing exactly*
> *where they are going . . . Occasionally a few POWS pass by,*
> *hands on their heads, looking less like soldiers than bedraggled*
> *civilians. We all wonder why they aren't just shot instead of being*
> *sent home for an easy life of chopping wood and cleaning PX's.*

Moved south to Colmar, in Alsace, late in January, Jack receives a
package. The terrain is more accessible and the Allies have traction.
A parcel including Log Cabin syrup, salted nuts, liverwurst, cheese,
taffy, chicken paste, and other treats gets through on January 21, but
Jack betrays agitation at not receiving items from a list of basic needs.
His tone is not sharp but impatient: "I managed to get a flashlight.
Could you send me batteries, please." And then he adds, "After looking around a bit, I am thoroughly convinced that the individuality of
our men is what is winning this war. When the chips are down they
do the best work, and although they complain about the army that is
as normal as civilians grumbling about rationing. I guess that is what
is called the American spirit—something the jerries don't have. Keep
your chin up. Devotedly, j."

Jack's last letter, dated February 2, 1945, arrived days after the War
Department's telegram informing Aunt Myrtle of his death.

> *Tomorrow my life of ease ends as I have been called up to the*
> *Company and assigned to the Mortars, my old position. I doubt I*
> *will go as a gunner, probably assistant gunner—due to my long*
> *absence from the weapon. The boys have done a splendid job with*
> *the cost not being too high, but there are many faces I will never*
> *see again. Many of the fellows are changed—they are quiet. All*
> *very high strung and nervous to a certain degree. I hope I shall*

not change too much but already I have seen enough sorrow and
brutality, destruction and waste to sober my youth earlier than nor-
mal. All of us are just plain sick and tired of battle, but there is a
job at hand to complete. Please send small packages of soap, cig-
arettes, candy, V-Mail, batteries. I don't carry much with me but
my rifle and my bedroll so they must be small.

❧❧

It is the end of a long day of driving, but Yael and I travel through the
town of Wolfgantzen, where Jack died a few days before his unit
crossed the Rhine at Neuf-Brisach. It could never have been a large
town and isn't now, and so we go slowly, especially through the patch
of woods throwing shadows on the low houses, as I read the letter
Aunt Fanny received from Jack's friend in late February. By this time
Fred, furloughed briefly for his brother's death, had left Aunt Myrtle
in her sisters' care. A "wreck," as Fanny's diaries confessed, Myrtle
was too distraught to write for details, and so the letter came to Fanny.
Jack's friend described the situation to Fanny and Myrtle:

> *It was Feb 4th, and though the temperatures were considerably*
> *warmer than those he'd seen in the Ardennes, and the terrain itself*
> *easier to traverse, fighting here was brutal.* [A record 3,000
> rounds, Yael and I read in the pamphlet issued by the 75th,
> were fired by the unit into the town of Wolfgantzen.] *The Ger-*
> *mans resisted fanatically, because only by defending Wolfgantzen*
> *could they hope to keep open the escape route to the Rhine.*
> *Crouched in concrete dugouts around the town, they put up a de-*
> *fense that was equal to their savage reputation.*

Our car passes through a vertical stand of trees as Yael and I continue reading from the letter:

*They attacked from the woods Northwest of Wolfgantzen but the
battalion received heavy mortar and artillery fire. . . . The 291st
infantry, advancing through the woods encountered strong enemy
position . . . The advance of the 3rd Battalion toward Wolfgantzen
was halted by intense artillery, mortar and small arms fire. . . .
Jack died quickly. . . . Please tell his mother that he didn't suffer.*

After we passed through Wolfgantzen, proceeding to Neuf-
Brisach, where the American, English, and French finally broke
through, I stood looking at the straight choppy band of the Rhine and
thought about crossing over.

I felt just as I had at Riga when there was nothing more to pursue,
no promising lead to follow, and like the other time when I had turned
into a café for lunch, declining to follow the trail out to Rumbula
where they shot the Jews. What should I do now, having found the
spot, more or less, where Jack died? Cross the bridge and press across
the Black Forest to Dachau? In a few hours we could be there and
next morning could tour the place where the family's one male survivor, Solomon, along with other tenants of the Shavli ghetto, had
clung to life.

Or perhaps we could proceed east along Germany's southern border, find the source of the Danube and ride it east through Jacob's falsified birthplace, Austria, and thence back to Rostov-on-Don and the
Crimea, where the young Bernhard Baron had, or so I thought, seen
the boy conscripts of the Crimea piled in the ditches and, as I'd imagined, observed begrimed survivors pinching handmade cigarettes.

Or we could even follow the straight chop of the Rhine to its outlet in the North Sea, there to hail a steamer. It vexed me that I had
never gone to Bremen to see the town from whence so many emi-
grants (perhaps including my ancestors) sailed for America, though
I had twice planned to do so. How could I square this, or the fact that
while I made my way across the Baltic, I'd omitted the North Sea leg
of the journey that perhaps Jacob had made.

I thought of other skeins of the story that I had not unraveled to the end. I never managed to get to Eddie's Fulmer Chase, the estate with its lawns and dogs he'd swapped for a knighthood, or even to the "humble" house in Hove where Uncle Baron lived modestly while his adopted sons climbed London's social ladder.

I did find and pace the lawn of the house on Bond Avenue in Glyndon, Maryland, where the young boy Theo, longing for England, would spin fantastic plans with his younger brother, Emil. I went in summer, and so it was not hard to see the small boys in my mind's eye, sweating, glowering at their foolish father and more foolish uncle speaking their German twaddle on the porch. But I never did make it to Paul's grave, nor to the Hanover Street house in Baltimore where Jacob and Paul went courting, one to marry Baron's sister, another his niece.

For a time, in the first years after seeing Jacob's cane, I maintained the strictest sense of sacred and profane. With file folders and plastic tabs, color coded, I sought to quarantine and cordon off Baltimore from Shavli, Shavli from London, Brest from Rostov, and Germany from everything. My files were grouped by place of settlement, then surname, assigning Jacob to Baltimore, Bernhard to London, and then just letting the children fight it out. As in a fashion, they had.

The shortcomings of such a system were obvious. Luck made Myrtle, Fanny, and Jean's brother Edward Levy, notwithstanding his birth in Baltimore, into the most glittering of the Barons. But not even burial in a North London tomb, mingling dusts with his great benefactor, Bernhard Baron, could make him a real Londoner or into the man his mentor was. He and his brothers never understood that it was the beautiful machine, the labor-saving, lung-preserving Baron cigarette rolling machine, that made the difference between them and a man with a touch of greatness. What Baron had seen in Brest-Litovsk, in Rostov, and in cramped, choking New York and Baltimore, had driven him to try to improve the world he lived in. The London papers called him a "Prince of Benefactors." I know now that the three Levys-turned-Barons were not like him, not the great men Uncle

Baron promised he'd make them. He had a touch of greatness; they were just lucky—they were mere members of the monied class.

I tried for a few years to work chronologically. But convergences and divergences of fates across the globe—terrible ironies of simultaneity—arrested this plan. How would it look, turning the pages, to see that just as Eddie sent his first postcard from London, his uncle Max fled from Raseinai after Lithuania's entire Jewish population became subject to expulsion?

Or that in the very months that my great-grandmother Amelia began to show clear signs of derangement, her uncle Baron was launching his first smash hit in advertising. The lucky Londoner who identified the Black Cat van cruising the Strand would win a sack of gold sovereigns.

Or that, worst of all, in the same month Eddie received one of England's highest honors—being, as my aunts wonderingly put it, knighted-by-the-Queen (though it was of course the King)—his nephews, cousins, and remaining uncles were being herded into grave pits and ghettos.

The terrible irony of it did not mean that Eddie bore guilt for the enormities perpetrated on his relatives. He surely didn't. Someone— I can't remember who—once swore the family had "tried" to find out what happened to the European relatives, had tried to help by looking for them in Austria. Was guilt therefore to be laid at Jacob's feet (he was of course dead by then) for falsifying facts? Still, I do not know whether Jacob might have passed through Austria and for that reason wrote Austria on his naturalization documents, anymore than I can be sure the cousins who shared the story of Aunt Jean's out-of-wedlock child had had some motive, all too easy to imagine, for bringing down queenly Jean a notch or two.

How could I know whether it had been in Bernhard Baron's mind all along, on meeting the Levy brothers, to make them caretakers of his sisters in Baltimore and then breed from their loins his management team? Perhaps Good Uncle Baron was no less than the Rumpelstiltskin my great-grandfather took him for. What will ever tell me where and how the mysterious Riva survived, or whether, in his last minutes at Wolfgantzen, Jack had pain.

⤞⤝

Black dust powders the personal effects and mementos I once regarded under sconces swagged with silk, the album's heavy pages lifting slowly and dropping heavily.

History is a random business, made out of wanderings, guesses, luck, and old glue. Pity the investigator who ignores the glue or picks off the old scabs, banishing falsehood, curse, rhetoric, and rhyme. What but the story of a promise (*"Send me your sons and I'll make them great men"*) followed by a curse (*"May you never have sons"*) is there, in the end, to keep the page, this page, from disintegration?

For sentimental reasons, I buy a fresh pack of Craven A each time I visit Jamaica, where it is still manufactured. I don't smoke it; I just look at it. The brand J. M. Barrie called the Arcadia mixture is still popular in former outposts of the British Empire, and the black cat on the pack remains the same as it was in the 1920s. The lipstick red is the same as the lipstick red of the Carreras sign that is still seen any day as one ascends from the Mornington Crescent tube.

On a display shelf in a cabinet I keep my aunt's sweet cameo mounted on black velvet, and a hand-painted plate with maidens disporting. I remember looking at both as a child. I keep there too, behind the cabinet's miraculous curved glass, my grandfather Emil's deco silver cigarette case, a page from Aunt Fanny's diary, and a picture of a chicken coop on Paul Levy's farm.

But I keep in a drawer the plastic bag of gray-green borders sliced from the photographs taken in Shavli, Raseinai, and Riga in the summer of 1928. Produced in the old-fashioned way with rounded corners, the photos gave me anxiety, for no framing store I found could accommodate rounded corners and I could not bear the thought of some anonymous person slicing the edges off. Eventually I cut borders off myself with a razor and inserted behind each frame's backing a little fan of cuttings. The drawer holds too the birch peelings I collected at the mass grave at Kuzhai and the photo of the monument next to the tree from which I peeled the bark.

I do not display the photo of the monument but I keep it close at hand, for I think my aunts would have liked its refinement, the woman's eyes drawn down, the rope of carven beads around her neck. And I think of it always when I look at the last photograph I've hung there, the one showing my little-girl mother sitting on Jack's shoulders the summer before he went to war, both of them with shirts off, and Aunt Myrtle looking younger than she would ever look again.

We Expand from Shrinking

I don't know why I didn't think of searching the Yad Vashem database for family survivors earlier.

A few months after completing the manuscript for this book, I made one more startling discovery: Riva, the partisan fighter, Max Levy's granddaughter and my great-grandfather Jacob's niece, was still alive in 2008.

Failing to find Riva earlier made me wonder how much else I'd missed. Riva had written to Aunt Jean in 1984, shortly after arriving in Israel from the Soviet Union, but the scrap I had said simply "Riva," no last name. Finding a Riva, or worse a Riva Levy, in Israel seemed like a needle in a haystack, especially given her age.

Nevertheless, in the summer of 2008, Yael's younger sister Maya at my elbow, I tapped the names of the family dead—Max Levy first—into the database at Yad Vashem in Jerusalem and up popped the old pictures. And more. Probable date of death. The occupation and standing of the persons in the picture. And more still. On an information screen was the name of the person who had completed the data; it also showed our own familiar photograph and the date of this person's visit. It turned out that Riva, now Rivka, Levy had made a visit to Yad Vashem in 1999, about the same year that I first heard of her. Three minutes more at the information desk and we had her address in Holon, Israel. The next morning we stood at her door.

Seventy years older than the child in the picture, Rivka could still be recognized as the little girl with square knees in a flounced dress, a bit of lace around her chubby neck. Yes, she had been in Raseinai that summer of 1941; she had been there when they took the men away, her grandfather Max at their head. As a community leader, Max had been singled out. Soldiers had stood him up in a wagon and tortured him before the crowd, yanking out the long hairs of his divided white beard in clumps before, half dead, he was taken with the others to the pit. He'd shouted at his tormenters, though, Rivka said, and called them fascists, and told his townsmen, his fellow Jews, not to be afraid.

Had it actually happened this way? I wondered, watching Maya's face and thinking of other stories I'd heard of this day. I remembered how Victoris Andrekaitis, standing in his driveway, had helped me see the line of men marching into the twilight in their coats and trousers. He did not mention the torture, but smiled in that odd embarrassed way people have when what they have experienced is not, will never be, processed. All day at Yad Vashem, watching the survivors testify on film, I'd seen that smile flicker at the corners of people's mouths, and some version of it wreathed Rivka's lips as she explained to Maya that she and her mother were fortunate enough to get out of Raseinai by running to Kovno (Kaunas) and the temporary safety of the ghetto there.

Talking about her time in the ghetto, Rivka spoke Hebrew with me—in part to make things easier for her but also, I thought, to let me filter the stories for Maya. Maya wanted Rivka to know, and she told her in English, that her sister Yael spoke Russian—what a shame Yael was not there to talk to her. But Rivka assured her in English it was not a shame; how pleased she was, how overjoyed, to meet Maya herself. But yes, Maya was right, knowing languages was important. Many people were killed in 1941, she explained, for missing an order, mistaking a word, but she had learned some German from her grandfather Max, and she emerged as a leader among the younger persons in the ghetto. Later, after the war, after her time in the forest, she stayed in Kovno (Kaunas) and became an engineer, training in the Soviet Union and remaining there until the 1980s, when the Soviets began to let Jews leave for Israel. She had known Moshe and Tanya in Israel, yes, and was sorry I wouldn't be able to see them again. She loved them. They had died a few years before.

"But what happened to your mother?" Maya asked. Rivka looked at me for permission to explain. I nodded. Rivka said that when the teenagers heard about the *Kinderaktion* in Shavli, they knew it would soon be their time too. She was among those who decided to flee to the forest and join the partisans. Her mother, like all the other mothers, had begged her not to go. And yes, after she left, her mother was killed. Maya was silent.

Too much! Rivka announced. Too much terrible talk for one morning. Would you like an apple, a cracker? Look at some pictures perhaps? Then Rivka led us into a small, neatly arranged guest room with pictures we'd never seen of persons we'd come to know.

By this time we were not surprised at the pride of place Rivka gave the family photo I'd first seen in Myrtle and Fanny's album, the photo in which Jacob holds the cane given to him by Max. That photo was taken not in Austria but in Lithuania. The same white scrawl, the name Raseinai that Moshe had pointed out to me ten years before was in the photo on Rivka's wall. We pointed at it and marveled.

Returning to the living room, before we all tired of the emotions of the morning, Maya and I began to tell Rivka all about how the uncle from America had moved to London, and about the marvelous opening of the Carreras cigarette factory.

Cigarettes are bad for you.

Despite ads claiming that Carreras cigarettes were "better for the throat," recommended for "business and scholarly concentration," and sundry other testimonials to tobacco's desirable effects, Uncle Eddie and his brothers would surely have known well before Eddie began to receive ominous documents in the 1950s that the habit they'd helped spread around the world was toxic.

Even if workers wore masks and marvelous machines protected the tendons of the wrists and hands; even if a Craven A was capped with a cork filter from Portugal, or a Black Cat was wrapped in hygienic cellophane, it was hard to deny that the "bewitching vegetable" shortened life, caused cancer and heart disease and emphysema. Smokers themselves, my uncles all died about the age of seventy, a good twenty-five years before their nonsmoking sisters.

With the great Carreras plant no longer in the family, all of them, even Eddie, lived out their lives more humbly than they could have foreseen, and they became angry at each other for how it all came apart. Myrtle and Fanny didn't doubt that Eddie "sold his brothers down the river," and maybe this was so.

I never met any of the uncles myself. By the time I began reading about them, looking at their pictures in my aunts' albums, they were all dead. My own guess, which I know my aunts would reject, is that Eddie, Bernhard Baron's handpicked Levy successor, always bore more of the Carreras burden and probably deserved more of the spoils. Arriving in England several years before his brothers and serving for forty years as the company's public face, Eddie took on the heaviest responsibility. His correspondence of 1955–1957 with officials of the British medical establishment, and with the various Royal offices once so encouraging to the tobacco trade, has the sound of a man marking time, looking for an out. In 1958 he found a way out by selling Carreras to Rembrandt Tobacco Corporation of South Africa, which had taken a controlling interest in Rothmans in 1954. Then in 1999 Rothmans was acquired by British American Tobacco.

One summer afternoon in 2007, I got myself to British American Tobacco's archive in London and read through the three hundred or so memos recording the postwar decline of the company fortunes. The documents seemed to lead only one way. The war years were the company's last hurrah. By 1948, 1949, and 1950, management experts were being called in to help the directors increase profits while preserving worker protections, and by the mid-1950s Uncle Theo was sending back reports on new and perhaps cheaper sources of leaf tobacco in Bulgaria. Newspaper clippings of that time show a division in the ranks of directors as pressures mount to streamline the operation and eliminate bonuses and the elaborate worker benefit schemes that had once made employment at Carreras so desirable. Workers Uncle Paul relocated to a new plant in Basildon wrote to complain of long trips on unheated coaches, the quick trip to work on the tube now only a memory. The final sellout had the look of a rout, with the millionaire South African mocking the old-fashioned methods of the Baron brothers and promising a more glorious future for their signature brands.

The brands themselves, including the one J. M. Barrie loved so well, endure. The great art deco monument built by Bernhard Baron looms today massive and splendid as ever at the top of Regents Park. Recently restored and filling a commuter's whole field of vision as he emerges from the Underground, Carreras is home now to hip advertisers and Internet groups. Smoking is allowed in its halls, but the building is no longer redolent with the scent of Chesapeake weed or the whish of long knives slicing six-foot lengths of wrapped tobacco into sticks. One would never know, passing through its halls, that it had once been hailed as a Temple of Tobacco; its builder, Bernhard Baron, as a Prince of Benefactors; or that his heirs were scions of a great tobacco concern.

Until she died, Aunt Jean clung to the grandeur that her sons had enjoyed and the "sacrifice" she'd made to give them their big chance.

Rising up, imperious, in her chair, Jean would repeat Bernhard Baron's promise, "Send me your sons and I'll make them great men!" But Myrtle and Fanny would just purse their lips, leaving it to their own loyal boys, Dan and Fred, to rebut Jean's foolishness and to tell again the story of Jacob's famous curse pronounced on any who did not keep faith with him. I remember Dan and Fred roaring, lifting a finger to mime the old man's wrath and then laughing, leaning back in their chairs, reminding each other how—without exception!—Eddie, Paul, and Theo's marriages produced only daughters, and then their daughters produced more daughters.

I don't recall anyone ever taking up my mother's case—the fact that her father, Emil, was deprived of sons too, his meager issue the one daughter born before he was taken off to the inst-*ee*-tution, there to spend the rest of his days. It was always the family line that had Emil not "taken sick," as Aunt Fanny put it, he would have had Levy's International Shrinking Company on a silver platter. But he had never wanted it, never believed he was destined to be a shrinker. His silver cigarette case, bought at Aspreys in London in 1928, convinces me that had he been well he'd have followed his brothers to strut the streets of London until the firm went bust. Thus it seems right he had just one daughter, my mother, and he shared the curse with the brothers who went away. "Still, how *brilliant* that there should have been a *curse!*" chortles Uncle Paul's daughter Paula, in England, as, finishing our lunch the day after I visited British American Tobacco, we toast each other, toast our dear dead aunts, and Jacob and Uncle Baron too.

Paula and I have become friends. I visit her in Bath where she lives, and we lunch and chat between her exits from the restaurant for a quick cigarette. She is my best informant, the one who had confided to me the news that Aunt Jean's firstborn, Earle, was (as he'd told her himself) a *bastard*. And Paula is the person who helped me work through the one failure of the curse—the contradictory fact that Aunt Jean's younger son, Jerry, was allowed a son.

After all, Paula reasons, was it little Jerry's fault his mother bustled him off to be taken care of by Eddie and Bertha? Not at all. It made sense, Paula insisted, that the older son, Earle, should have taken the curse on the chin. Remaining in Britain, dying as an Englishman, he would naturally have had only girls. But dear Jerry, who never wanted to go, who cried himself to sleep for months after being sent to London—for him it was only proper that the curse should fail—that after Carreras was gone Jerry would return, his English wife with him, to his birthplace in America—three sons in tow.

As for us, mere women, Paula and I enjoy agreeing with each other during lunch that, between not being the object of a curse and being one, we would choose being cursed (so much more interesting!). When Paula returns from smoking her cigarette in the restaurant garden, we begin to discuss Jacob's legacy and his company, Levy's International, which still, to this day, expands from shrinking.

The Philadelphia plant that Jacob opened shortly after losing his run for Congress survived the twentieth century and is now, at a new location, one of five owned and operated by Jacob's male heirs. Jacob spent the last decade of his life pulling it through the worst of the Depression and giving Jean the management training he would have given Emil or Theo, Paul or Eddie. At the end of the Depression, when so many other businesses had gone under, Levy's International Shrinking was still afloat.

Through World War II, Jean sat in the boardroom and Myrtle and Fanny stoked the furnace and rolled piece goods for the war effort. After Fred and Dan (but not Jack) came back from the war, Myrtle and Fanny's sons scraped together enough cash to buy and customize machines capable of treating the fabric used for car seat covers, and then expanded into other variations on this activity, branching out from woolens and cottons into synthetics of all kinds, wovens and nonwovens, fabrics for domestic and a vast number of other uses.

Walk through one of The Synthetics Group's factories with either Dan or Fred, or with Dan and Fred's sons, Jack and Jeff, or their sons, now in the family business as well, and you will hear the unselfconscious rhapsodies of the machines, those beautiful machines that transform ordinary woven cloth into miracle fabrics that repel odors and wick moisture, that stay supple when suppleness is what's needed and go stiff if that's what's called for. Once, in his factory space on Lombard Street, Jacob treated, inspected, rolled fabric for menswear, rainwear, and the odd shop awning. Now his grandsons' and great-grandsons' and great-great-grandsons' machines do much more than shrink. They keep the wallpaper in your kitchen from smelling like stir fry and the batting around the smoked trout from absorbing oil. These beautiful machines keep the sateen on the box spring from sagging, the gauze from sticking to the toddler's knee, and the drink you spill over the Atlantic from soaking your airplane seat. Nonwovens are as profitable for Jacob's heirs as wovens were for him. The blue drapes on your doctor's examining table and the padding around your hard drive. All of these have likely passed through TSG.

The last time I visited one of the plants I was shown Jacob's original machine, still performing the tasks of cold water shrinking that Jacob patented a hundred years ago. Every time I visit I see military khaki running through, since uniforms, as Fanny's son Dan explains, must breathe and be flexible in all weathers without stiffening or stretching out of shape. Some of what the company does is complex and modern, but I'm told that there's still a call for old-fashioned shrinking and Levy's is the last American company still doing it.

In other words, it is fair to say that the tortoise beat the hare. Bernhard Baron's Carreras is gone, but Jacob's firm continues to expand from shrinking, and even the boast of Jacob's "international" has been vindicated. "Levy's International" may have started as a few dunking tubs and drying rods in Jacob's Lombard Street basement, but in its modern incarnation The Synthetics Group is one of the largest independent textile processors in the world.

Buddy, who ran the Baltimore plant and whom I visited years ago with my young daughter, died this year. His wife, Myra, keeps Jacob's cane still. I have not seen it for a while, but I like to think the cane is

Advertising card, 1923, for Levys International Shrinking Company, Baltimore and Philadelphia. Gift to the author from Alvin "Buddy" Levy.

safe in Baltimore, standing up in a closet on a cushion of carpet, the letters of my great-grandfather's initials, and Max's, and Isaac's, and Paul's gleaming through the louvers.

What does it mean that I let this cane seize me, let it bear me for nearly a decade of my life, carrying every day in my mind the gleam of those initials, the straightness of the cane's dark length and graceful crook, carrying the cane as a pointer and a talisman?

I had just turned forty that fall when I first saw my great-grandfather's cane, and last year I turned fifty. I realize that now I have followed this object, clung to my need to know about it, from the tobacco coast of North America to the Belarusian town of Brest-Litovsk, from Berlin to Baltimore, drawing my daughters after me to stand at gravesites and factories, farms and archives, and to a copse of trees in Alsace where Jack fell.

Just this year I've been to Jacob's grave in Baltimore, and to that of his three sons who lie with Bernhard Baron in a stately London cenotaph, and I've been to the Shavli ghetto, where I held my daughter Yael's hand as we absorbed the death of the Levy children in the *Kinderaktion*.

Every endpoint was a grave—all endpoints are—but I know that my great-grandfather Jacob's cane is now mine as well. It has taken me somewhere I had to go, to a place where I needed to spend part of my own Jewish life. The cane took me into the hopeful heart and workshop of my great-grandfather's civilization, into that worldly, cosmopolitan, emancipated Jewish century that ended in 1945. It taught me to love, honor, and pass down the breathtaking vision of modernity my forebears cherished. I keep it and press it into this book.

ACKNOWLEDGMENTS

I am immensely grateful to the many people who have helped me keep on writing *Jacob's Cane*. First thanks must go to my three daughters, Yael and her sisters Orli and Maya, who have made real to me the commandment "Teach it diligently unto your children." Their curiosity and faith have kept my diligence alive. Ronald New and Joan New, my parents, have been my first, best, and most constant fans. My wonderful husband, Larry Summers, has inspired me as the face of my ideal, though impatient and elusive, reader. This book has been part of all their lives for a very long time.

Many members of the extended Levy and Baron families shared their stories, their archives, and their time and hospitality. My three inimitable great-aunts, Jean, Myrtle, and Fanny, although they died before I began this book, left our whole family the example of civilization at its highest and most generous. I did not miss them while writing the book, but I shall now. Their children and grandchildren and great-grandchildren carried on for me in their stead.

On Cape Cod, in the months before he died, Jerry Adler told me stories of his mother, my Aunt Jean, of his childhood in London, and of the tobacco business in the 1940s and 1950s. In Philadelphia, my Aunt Myrtle's son Fred Rosenstein and daughter-in-law Anita Rosenstein, and Dan and Lenora Goldman, Aunt Fanny's children, told me stories, photocopied documents and letters, and let me riffle through their albums and file drawers. They welcomed me to their company house in North Carolina and gave immeasurable support and help along the way. Jack Rosenstein and Jeff Goldman, now principals of The Synthetics Group (formerly Levy's Shrinking Company), gave me tours of the factories in Philadelphia and North Carolina and provided news items and memorabilia. Carol and Joel Silver gave me support as well as a glimpse of the one book remaining from my great-grandfather Jacob Levy's library—fittingly, *Don Quixote*.

In Baltimore, Buddy (Alvin) and Myra Levy and Anita Abrams, as well as Joyce and Louis Kaplan, gave me access to the cane that belonged to Jacob Levy, for which I'm eternally grateful, and also shared with me their stories, their cache of turn-of-the-century photographs of Baltimore, and on several occasions, their spare room. Donald Abrams showed me his short film of Levy's Shrinking Company. In Baltimore, I was lucky enough to meet with Nancy Katz, of Pollan-Katz umbrellas, and with Abraham and Naomi Cohen, who told me stories and gave me leads.

In London and Bath, Paula Baron and Vanessa Baron Stopford talked to me for long hours, telling wonderful stories and also sharing their archives of clippings about the glory years of Carreras Cigarettes. Also in London, Elizabeth Luard shared memories of her grandfather, Eddie Levy, and in particular of his wife, her grandmother, the indomitable Bertha. Her memories of these grandparents can be found in her wonderful memoir with recipes, *Family Life.*

Of those thanked above, Buddy Levy, Jerry Adler, and Naomi and Abraham Cohen have all since died. Moshe and Tanya Levy, of Givat Ram, Israel, have also died, as I learned after the manuscript of this book was finished. Rivka Levy's firsthand account of her grandfather Max Levy, and of life in a Lithuanian ghetto, also came to me after the book was completed. I am deeply grateful to her for seeing me, along with my daughter Maya, on such short notice and for opening up her store of painful memories.

This book took me on three research trips to the Baltics, three trips to London, and many to Baltimore. I thank the University of Pennsylvania, Harvard's Clark Cook Foundation, and the Robinson Rollins Funds for monies that proved crucially helpful in defraying the expenses of these trips.

Over the years, I had numerous drivers and guides in Eastern Europe, especially in Siauliai; each of the guides was superb in a different way. I thank Chaim Bargman for being an excellent mentor to a first-time Jewish traveler; he not only took me to key sites of interest in Siauliai and Kaunas but also drove me around the Lithuanian countryside. Had not Chaim known enough to take me to see Leibe Lifshitz and Vitalija Gircyte, chief archivist of the Kaunas Ethnographic Museum, this book would not have gotten off the ground. On my second trip, the superb Viktorija Urbanovicuite provided not only guidance in English but also translations from Russian and Lithuanian, plus introductions to Vilius Puronas (in

Siauliai) and Victoris Andrekaitis (in Raseinai). I also want to thank Nerija Gulbinaite of the Tourist Information Center of Siauliai.

On my third trip, in 2007, my daughter Yael's Russian language skills replaced Viktorija's. Previously, Yael's French, so much better than mine, had made my badly planned 2003 trip through the Belgian and Alsatian battlefields of 1944–1945 a great success. When we visited Belarus, Yael's Russian made all the difference, as it did on the Baltic ferry *Vilnius*.

Over the course of researching Siauliai and its history, both Leibe Lifshitz (now deceased) and his friend and colleague, Vilius Puronas, chief architect and planner of the Municipality of Siauliai, went from being informants and guides to becoming characters in their own right. The year before he died Leibe invited me to come to his home, where he showed me his personal archive of ghetto documents and artifacts and allowed me to make copies of many of them. Vilius provided hours and hours of time, crucial documents, and access to and use of images from his archive. I am grateful to both for representing, between them, the best of Jewish and non-Jewish Siauliai.

I am grateful to Victoris Andrekaitis for sharing his memories of Raseinai between the wars as well as his personal reminiscences of Max Levy. I would not have found Victoris but for the efforts of Raimenslos Petrosevicius of the Raseinai municipality.

My descriptions of Riga owe a very great deal to Valtis Alpinis, who took me around Old Riga, into the Jewish ghetto, and also helped me find the apartment where my relatives had lived on Kalnu Iela. I am also indebted to Galina Baranova and to Reuben Ferber, of the Center of Jewish Studies, University of Latvia, and Marger Vestermanis, director of the Jewish Museum of Riga, and his assistant, Svetlana Bogojavlenska. Rita Bogdanova, at the Latvian State Archives, and Karmella Skorika also provided much-needed guidance and orientation. Access to and help in the Central State Archives of Lithuania were provided by Irena Gruenberg and Jovita Vainelidene.

My third trip to the Baltics, by far the best organized, was managed by MIR Travel, of Seattle, Washington. I thank Douglas Grimes and Annie Lucas for their expert planning and management of the trip, and especially for securing for me the guidance of our driver and friend in Lithuania, Alexejus Zobov. My guides to Belarus, and especially Jewish Brest-Litovsk, were Rabbi Haim Rabinovich and Natalia Padalko, and my driver was Vladimir Padalko.

Research in Baltimore would not have been nearly so fruitful without the assistance of dedicated curators and archivists of that city. The most important archival collections, and most valuable help, came from the Jewish Museum of Maryland; the Enoch Pratt Library, Central Branch; the Baltimore Museum of Industry; the Maryland Historical Society Library; and the Special Collections at the Milton S. Eisenhower Library of Johns Hopkins University.

I am immensely grateful to Avi Decter, Virginia North, Abby Lester, Robin Waldman, Jennifer Vess, and other staff members of the Jewish Museum of Maryland, my home base in Baltimore. Nancy Perlman of the Baltimore Museum of Industry was generous with time and advice, and Francis O'Neill, of the Maryland Historical Society Library, helped me untangle the election of 1912. The archivist in the Special Collections of Johns Hopkins University helped me get my bearings, not only on the socially progressive traditions in Baltimore but also on the ambiance and feel of residential life on Eutaw Place. Francis O'Neill spent several days with me, helping me to understand tobacco commerce and the politics of the industrial center, and gave me a crash course in early photography. Thanks also to the staff of the microforms room in the Enoch Pratt Free Library, the reference room of the Maryland Genealogical Society, and the Baltimore City Archives. Gilbert Sandler, author of *Jewish Baltimore*, shared observations and encouragements.

I am indebted to Ann B. O'Neill of the Glyndon, Maryland, Historical Society for her insights and access to her archives as well as for a day of great talk about Glyndon. I am especially grateful to her for sharing with me and my superb research assistant, Orli Levine, the minutes of the Pomona Grange, circa 1914. And I am grateful to Christian and Mary Profacis for allowing me to tour Paul Levy's old house, now theirs, on Bond Avenue, which allowed me to imagine what it might have been like one hundred years before.

In London, Richard Knight, at Camden Local Studies and Archives Center, and Aidan Flood, senior librarian, were helpful in sharing with me the history of Carreras Cigarettes, especially the effects of the factory on the neighborhood. The manuscript versions of the History Project of Camden collected there were especially useful. I am grateful to Susan England of Southampton University, where the Basil Henriques papers are housed; to Brian Darmand, archivist of the Bernhard Baron Settlement; and to Miriam Sopel, past warden of the Bernhard Baron Settlement, who kindly shared memories and materials of Basil and Lady Henriques and of

Eddie Baron and family. The archivist of the Liberal Synagogue of London was generous with time and information, as was the staff of the British Newspaper Library.

The staff of Greater London House on Hampton Road—formerly the Carreras Cigarette Factory—could not have been more generous. Jeff Shergold, facilities manager, and Robert Hossen, assistant manager, showed me original plans, pointed out architectural features, and even took me in rubber boots into the waterlogged basement, once the Carreras air raid shelter.

John Casey, of British American Tobacco, gave me access to the papers of the Baron family still extant. I am also grateful to Jan De Plessis, Philip Scourfield, and Robert Rubin for making this possible.

In North Carolina, I was helped by the staff of the Tobacco Life Museum, especially Melody Johnson in Kenley, and also by Grethel Boyette. Joey Scott, of Wilson County, taught me about the growing of tobacco, from seed to curing barn. He gave me insight into the long history of tobacco cultivation in the Carolinas during the period I was writing about, as well as into the ethical complexities of raising tobacco.

In New York City, three libraries were important to my research. The staff at YIVO has always been immensely helpful. I was also helped by the staff of the Arents Collection at the New York Public Library, Main Branch, as well as archivists at the Science, Industry and Business Branch of that library. Suzanne Wasserman of the Gotham Center, CUNY, provided much-needed support.

Several Boston area libraries have been important research and work spaces. The curatorial staff at Harvard's Baker Library was kind to me for years, bringing out the same volumes of Duns Register for me to look at again and again and allowing me to set up shop in their basement stacks. The reference staff of the Hebrew College Library, especially Shalva Segal and Harvey Bock, provided crucial assistance, as did that of the Brookline Public Library. I made each of these places my study and home for weeks and months on end.

University and academic audiences at Harvard and elsewhere provided useful feedback as these chapters emerged. It was in John Demos's class in my freshmen year at Brandeis that I learned enough historical method to interview my three aunts, and others, with tape recorder running. I spoke and read to audiences at the University of Latvia, Brandeis University, Stern College for Women, the American Literature Association, Southern Jewish Historical Society, Harvard Americanist Colloquium, the Harvard

English Department Faculty Colloquium, Harvard Summer School, and the University of Pennsylvania Kelley Writers House. I am especially grateful to Steve Whitfield, Eric Sundquist, Larry Buell, and Al Filreis for invitations to present materials not ordinarily delivered from an academic rostrum. In addition, I know I've benefited from questions and comments from Edward Serotta, Wendy Steiner, Paul Hendrickson, Peter Conn, Rebecca Bushnell, Ben Shen, Werner Sollors, John Stauffer, Peter Sacks, Marc Shell, Stephen Greenblatt, Ramie Targoff, Jared Hickman, Jason Puskar, Lara Scales, and Jim von der Heydt.

I owe deep thanks to Fred Levine for his faith in and support of this project, and me, through the years when the project was gestating silently and then beginning to put down roots. His listening and notetaking skills, especially at times when I was too emotional to write, have proven invaluable.

Editors and literary professionals who asked the hard questions that helped the book develop include Jake Sagalyn, Loretta Barrett, Albert La-Farge, David Black, Alane Mason, Jo Ann Miller, and finally my superb agent, Andrew Wylie, who knew just what to do with the manuscript of this book and when to do it. I owe deep thanks to Luke Menand for putting me in touch with Andrew. I'm grateful to Lara Heimert and to the wonderful Amanda Moon and Whitney Casser at Basic Books. Michelle Welsh-Horst was cheerful, patient, and meticulous in producing the book, and Jennifer Carrow, the jacket designer, turned tattered and faded artifacts into vibrant art.

Bill Chapman provided crucial help with images at the last stage. Sol Kim Bentley, faculty assistant in Harvard's English department, did the hard work of inputting corrections to chapter drafts, draft after draft, translating my thickets of pencil edits into readable copy again and again. Her cheer and intelligence, and her dispatch, have been so important.

My two greatest writerly debts are to Sarah Potvin and Charlotte Maurer.

Sarah, now a professional archival librarian, showed her gift for research early on. She worked on this book as my research assistant from 2000 to 2004, all through her four years at Harvard and beyond. I owe to her the discovery of Jacob Levy's and Bernhard Baron's patents, my understanding of the importance of Norddeutscher Lloyd, and much detail about Baltimore socialism and the importance of H. L. Mencken.

Charlotte Maurer, my dear friend and cherished editor, came to my rescue at the moment it became clear that I may have written a book, but I had not yet told a story. Without Charlotte's firm common sense and candor, her steady work and kindness, this book might never have been finished.

SELECTED FURTHER READINGS

JEWS IN EASTERN EUROPE

Abramowicz, Hirsh. *Profiles of a Lost World: Memoirs of East European Jewish Life Before World War II*. Detroit, MI: Wayne State University Press, 1999.

Appelbaum, Anne. *Between East and West: Across the Borderlands of Europe*. New York: Pantheon, 1994.

Ascheim, Stephen S. *Brothers and Strangers: The Eastern European Jew in German and German-Jewish Consciousness, 1800–1923*. Madison: University of Wisconsin Press, 1983.

Baron, Salo. *The Russian Jew Under Czars and Soviets*. New York: Macmillan, 1974.

Bilmanis, Alfred. *A History of Latvia*. Santa Barbara, CA: Greenwood, 1970.

Dawidowicz, Lucy. *The Golden Tradition: Jewish Life and Thought in Eastern Europe*. New York: Holt, Rinehart & Winston, 1967.

Dubnow, Simon M. *History of the Jews in Russia and Poland, From the Earliest Times Until the Present Day*. 3 vols. Philadelphia: Jewish Publication Society of America, 1916–1920.

Eliach, Yaffa. *There Once Was a World: A Nine-Hundred-Year Chronicle of the Shtetl of Eishyskok*. Boston: Little, Brown, 1998.

Gorky, Maxim. *Untimely Thoughts: Essays on Revolution, Culture, and the Bolsheviks, 1917–1918*. New Haven, CT: Yale University Press, 1995.

Greenbaum, Masha. *The Jews of Lithuania: A History of a Remarkable Community, 1316–1945*. Jerusalem: Gefen, 1995.

Hundert, Gershon David, ed. *The Yivo Encyclopaedia of Jews in Eastern Europe*. New Haven, CT: Yale University Press, 2008.

Jacobson, Dan. *Heschel's Kingdom*. Evanston, IL: Northwestern University Press, 2002.

Katz, Jacob. *Out of the Ghetto: The Social Background of Jewish Emancipation, 1770–1880*. Cambridge: Harvard University Press, 1973.

Levin, Dov. *The Litvaks: A Short History of the Jews of Lithuania*. Jerusalem: Yad Vashem, 2000.

Lohr, Eric. *Nationalizing the Russian Empire: The Campaign Against Enemy Aliens in World War I*. Cambridge: Harvard University Press, 2003.

McLachlan, Gordon. *Lithuania*. 2nd ed. Old Saybrook, CT: Globe Pequot Press, 1999.

Mendelson, Ezra. *The Jews of East Central Europe Between the World Wars*. Bloomington: Indiana University Press, 1983.

Nathans, Benjamin. *Beyond the Pale: The Jewish Encounter with Late Imperial Russia*. Berkeley: University of California Press, 2002.

Palmer, Alan. *The Baltic: A New History of the Region and Its People*. New York: Overlook, 2005.

Raisin, Jacob. *The Haskalah Movement in Russia*. Philadelphia: Jewish Publication Society of America, 1913.

Schoenburg, Nancy, and Stuart Schoenburg. *Lithuanian Jewish Communities*. New York: Garland, 1991.

Vital, David. *A People Apart: The Jews in Europe, 1789–1939*. Oxford History of Modern Europe. New York: Oxford University Press, 1999.

Wisse, Ruth R. *The Modern Jewish Canon: A Journey Through Language and Culture*. New York: Free Press, 2000.

GERMANY: HISTORY, ECONOMIC DEVELOPMENT; JEWS

Alon, Amos. *The Pity of It All: A Portrait of the German Jewish Epoch, 1743–1943*. New York: Holt, 2002.

Bach, Hans I. *The German Jew: A Synthesis of Judaism and Western Civilization, 1730–1930*. Published for the Littman Library of Jewish Civilization by Oxford University Press, 1985.

Berend, Ivan T., and Gyorgy Ranki. *Economic Development in East-Central Europe in the 19th and 20th Centuries*. New York: Columbia University Press, 1974.

Blumenthal, Michael. *The Invisible Wall: The Mystery of the Germans and the Jews*. Berkeley, CA: Counterpoint, 1998.

Braudel, Fernand. *The Structures of Everyday Life: The Limits of the Possible*. New York: Harper & Row, 1979.

Craig, Gordon. *The Germans*. New York: Putnam, 1982.

Doblin, Alfred. *Journey to Poland*. New York: Paragon, 1991.

Dollinger, Philippe. *The German Hansa*. London: Macmillan, 1970.

Fudge, John D. *Cargoes, Embargoes, and Emissaries: The Commercial and Political Interaction of England and the German Hanse, 1450–1510*. Toronto: University of Toronto Press, 1995.

Gay, Peter. *Schnitzler's Century*. New York: Norton, 2002.

Hanak, Peter. *The Garden and the Workshop: Essays on the Cultural History of Vienna and Budapest*. Princeton, NJ: Princeton University Press, 1999.

Higgonet, Patrice, David S. Landes, and Henry Rosovsky. *Favorites of Fortune: Technology, Growth, and Economic Development Since the Industrial Revolution*. Cambridge: Harvard University Press, 1995.

Hoerder, Dirk, and Jorg Nagler, eds. *People in Transit: German Migrations in Comparative Perspective, 1820–1930*. German Historical Institute. Cambridge: Cambridge University Press, 1995.

King, Wilson. *Chronicles of Three Free Cities: Hamburg, Bremen, and Lübeck*. New York: Dutton, 1914.

Landes, David. *The Unbound Prometheus: Technological and Economic Development in Western Europe from 1750 to the Present*. New York: Cambridge University Press, 1969.

Levine, Bruce C. *The Spirit of 1848: German Immigrants, Labor Conflicts, and the Coming of the Civil War*. Urbana: University of Illinois Press, 1992.

Lloyd, T. H. *England and the German Hanse, 1157–1611: A Study of Their Trade and Commercial Diplomacy*. Cambridge: Cambridge University Press, 1991.

Meyer, Michael, and Michael Brenner. *German Jewish History in Modern Times*. New York: Columbia University Press, 1998.

Pollard, Sidney. *European Economic Integration: 1815–1970*. London: Thames & Hudson, 1974.

Robertson, Ritchie, ed. *The German-Jewish Dialogue: An Analysis of Literary Texts, 1749–1993*. New York: Oxford University Press, 1999.

Roy, James Charles. *The Vanished Kingdom: Travels Through the History of Prussia*. Boulder, CO: Westview, 1999.

Schorske, Carl E. *Fin-de-Siècle Vienna: Politics and Culture*. New York: Vintage, 1980.

Stern, Fritz. *Gold and Iron: Bismarck, Bleichroder, and the Building of the German Empire*. New York: Vintage, 1979.

Seward, Desmond. *The Monks of War: The Military Religious Orders*. New York: Penguin, 1995.

Taylor, A.J.P. *The Course of German History*. London: Routledge, 1988.

Urban, William. *The Baltic Crusade*. DeKalb: Northern Illinois University Press, 1975.

TOBACCO, BALTIMORE, AND THE CHESAPEAKE

Berlin, Ira. *Many Thousands Gone: The First Two Centuries of Slavery in North America*. Cambridge: Belknap Press of Harvard University Press, 1998.

Breen, T. H. *Tobacco Culture: Mentality of the Great Tidewater Planters on the Eve of Revolution*. Princeton, NJ: Princeton University Press, 1985.

Brooks, Jerome E. *Green Leaf and Gold: Tobacco in North Carolina*. 2nd ed. Raleigh: Division of Archives and History, North Carolina Department of Cultural Resources, 1997.

Brooks, Neal A., Eric G. Rockel, and William C. Hughes. *A History of Baltimore County (Maryland)*. Towson, MD: Friends of the Towson Library, 1979.

Brugger, Robert J. *Maryland: A Middle Temperament*. Baltimore: Johns Hopkins University Press, 1988.

Byrd, William. *The Prose Works of William Byrd of Westover: Narratives of a Colonial Virginian*. Edited by Louis B. Wright. Cambridge: Belknap Press of Harvard University Press, 1966. Originally published as *The Westover Manuscripts*, 1841.

Clemens, Paul G.E. *The Atlantic Economy and Colonial Maryland's Eastern Shore: From Tobacco to Grain*. Ithaca, NY: Cornell University Press, 1980.

Cooper, Patricia A. *Once a Cigar Maker: Men, Women, and Work Culture in American Cigar Factories, 1900–1919*. The Working Class in American History. Urbana: University of Illinois Press, 1992.

Davis, David Brion. *Slavery in the Colonial Chesapeake*. Williamsburg, VA: Colonial Williamsburg Foundation, 1986.

Douglass, Frederick. *The Oxford Frederick Douglass Reader*. Edited with an introduction by William L. Andrews. New York: Oxford University Press, 1996.

Genovese, Eugene. *The Political Economy of Slavery: Studies in the Economy and Society of the Slave South*. New York, Pantheon, 1961.

———. *Roll, Jordan, Roll: The World the Slaves Made*. New York: Pantheon, 1974.

George, Christopher T. *Terror on the Chesapeake: The War of 1812 on the Bay*. Shippensburg, PA: White Mane Books, 2000.

Johnson, Charles Richard, and Patricia Smith. *Africans in America: America's Journey Through Slavery*. New York: Harcourt Brace, 1998.

Kolchin, Peter. *American Slavery, 1619–1877*. New York: Hill & Wang, 1993.

Kulikoff, Allan. *Tobacco and Slaves: The Development of Southern Cultures in the Chesapeake, 1680–1800*. Chapel Hill: University of North Carolina Press, 1986.

Mencken, H. L. *Happy Days: Mencken's Autobiography: 1880–1892*. Buncombe Collection, vol. 1. Baltimore: Johns Hopkins University Press, 2006.

Morgan, Lynda J. *Emancipation in Virginia's Tobacco Belt, 1850–1870*. Athens: University of Georgia Press, 1992.

Morgan, Philip D. *Slave Counterpoint: Black Culture in the Eighteenth Century Chesapeake and Lowcountry*. Chapel Hill: University of North Carolina Press, 1998.

Olson, Sherry H. *Baltimore: The Building of an American City*. Baltimore: Johns Hopkins University Press, 1997.

Rawick, George P., ed. *The American Slave: A Composite Autobiography*. Westport, CT: Greenwood, 1972.

Scharf, J. Thomas. *History of Baltimore City and County*. Introduction by Edward G. Howard. Baltimore: Regional, 1971.

Wennersten, John R. *Maryland's Eastern Shore: A Journey in Time and Place*. Centreville, MD: Tidewater, 1992.

Whitehorne, Joseph A. *The Battle for Baltimore: 1814*. Baltimore: Nautical and Aviation, 1997

Zunz, Dieter. *The Maryland Germans: A History*. Port Washington, NY: Kennikat, 1972.

CROSSING THE ATLANTIC

Bowen, Frank. *A Century of Atlantic Travel, 1830–1930*. Boston: Little,
   Brown, 1930.
Drechsel, Edwin. *Norddeutscher Lloyd Bremen, 1857–1970: History-
   Fleet-Ship-Mails*. 2 vols. Vancouver: Cordillera, 1994–1995.
Fox, Stephen. *Transatlantic: Samuel Cunard, Isambard Brunel, and the
   Great Atlantic Steamships*. New York: Harper Perennial, 2004.
Norddeutscher Lloyd. *Seventy Years North German Lloyd: Bremen:
   1857–1927*. Berlin: Atlantic-Verlag, 1927.
Roebling, Johann August. *Diary of My Journey from Muehlhausen in
   Thuringia via Bremen to the United States of North America in the
   Year 1831*. 1832. Translated by Edward Underwood. Trenton, NJ:
   Roebling, 1931.

AMERICAN IMMIGRATION AND
AMERICAN JEWISH CULTURE

Birmingham, Stephen. *Our Crowd: The Great Jewish Families of New
   York*. Syracuse, NY: Syracuse University Press, 1967.
Cohen, Naomi W. *Encounter with Emancipation: The German Jews in the
   United States, 1830–1914*. Philadelphia: Jewish Publication Society
   of America, 1984.
Dinnerstein, Leonard, and Mary Dale Paulson. *Jews in the South*. Baton
   Rouge: Louisiana State University Press, 1973.
Fein, Isaac. *The Making of an American Jewish Community: The History
   of Baltimore Jewry from 1773 to 1920*. Philadelphia: Jewish
   Publication Society of America, 1971.
Glanz, Rudolf. *Studies in Judaica Americana*. New York: Ktav, 1970.
Howe, Irving. *The World of Our Fathers: The Journey of the East
   European Jews to America and the World They Found and Made*. New
   York: New York University Press, 2005.
Levin, Alexandra Lee. *The Szolds of Lombard Street: A Baltimore Family,
   1859–1909*. Philadelphia: Jewish Publication Society of America, 1960.
Raphael, Marc Lee. *The Columbia History of Jews and Judaism in
   America*. New York: Columbia University Press, 2008.
Sanders, Ronald. *Shores of Refuge: A Hundred Years of Jewish
   Immigration*. New York: Holt, 1988.
Sandler, Gilbert. *Jewish Baltimore: A Family Album*. Baltimore: Johns
   Hopkins University Press, 2000.

Sarna, Jonathan. *American Judaism: A History*. New Haven, CT: Yale University Press, 2004.

Silberman, Lauren R., and Avi Y. Decter. *The Jewish Community of Baltimore*. Mount Pleasant, SC: Arcadia, 2008.

Wenger, Beth. *The Jewish Americans: Three Centuries of Jewish Voices in America*. New York: Doubleday, 2007.

Whitfield, Stephen. *American Space: Jewish Time: Essays in Modern Culture and Politics*. Armonk, NY: Sharpe, 1996.

PROGRESSIVISM, LABOR, SOCIALISM

Argersinger, Joann. *Making the Amalgamated: Gender, Ethnicity, and Class in the Baltimore Clothing Industry, 1899–1939*. Baltimore: Johns Hopkins University Press, 1999.

Banta, Martha. *Taylored Lives: Narrative Productions in the Age of Taylor, Veblen, and Ford*. Chicago: University of Chicago Press, 1993.

Chace, James. *1912: Wilson, Roosevelt, Taft and Debs: The Election That Changed the Country*. New York: Simon & Schuster, 2004.

Crooks, James B. *Politics and Progress: The Rise of Urban Progressivism in Baltimore, 1895–1911*. Baton Rouge: Louisiana State University Press, 1968.

Dick, William M. *Labor and Socialism in America: The Gompers Era*. Port Washington, NY: Kennikat, 1972.

Diner, Steven J. *A Very Different Age: Americans of the Progressive Era*. New York: Hill & Wang, 1998.

Ely, Richard T. *The Labor Movement in America*. New York, Macmillan, 1905.

Fried, Albert. *Socialism in America from the Shakers to the Third International*. New York: Columbia University Press, 1992.

Gompers, Samuel. *Seventy Years of Life and Labor: An Autobiography*. Edited by Philip Taft and John A. Sessions. New York: Dutton, 1957.

Hofstadter, Richard. *The Age of Reform: From Bryan to F.D.R.* New York: Vintage, 1955.

Kloppenberg, James T. *Uncertain Victory: Social Democracy and Progressivism in European and American Thought, 1870–1920*. New York: Oxford University Press, 1986.

McNeil, George E., ed. *The Labor Movement: The Problem of To-Day*. Milwaukee: Hazen, 1892.

Pike, E. Royston. *Human Documents of the Lloyd George Era*. New York: St. Martin's, 1972.

Pratt, Norma Fain. *Morris Hillquit: A Political History of an American Jewish Socialist*. Westport, CT: Greenwood, 1979.

Riis, Jacob A. *How the Other Half Lives: Studies Among the Tenements of New York*. 1890. New York: Penguin, 1997.

Rodgers, Daniel T. *Atlantic Crossings: Social Politics in a Progressive Age*. Cambridge: Belknap Press of Harvard University Press, 1998.

———. *The Work Ethic in Industrial America, 1850–1920*. Chicago: University of Chicago Press, 1979.

Rose, Edward J. *Henry George*. Twayne's United States Authors Series. New York: Twayne, 1968.

Steffen, Charles G. *The Mechanics of Baltimore, 1763–1812: Workers and Politics in the Age of Revolution*. Urbana: University of Illinois Press, 1984.

Steffens, Lincoln. *The Autobiography of Lincoln Steffens*. New York: Harcourt Brace, 1951.

ANGLO-JEWRY AND THE ANGLO-AMERICAN
CIGARETTE WARS

Alford, B.W.E. *W.D. and H.O. Wills and the Development of the UK Tobacco Industry, 1786–1965*. London: Methuen, 1973.

Aris, Stephen. *But There Are No Jews in England*. New York: Stein & Day, 1971.

Bermant, Chaim. *The Cousinhood: A Vivid Account of the English-Jewish Aristocracy*. New York: Macmillan, 1972.

Brandt, Allan M. *The Cigarette Century: The Rise, Fall, and Deadly Persistence of the Product That Defined America*. New York: Basic, 2007.

Buruma, Ian. *Anglomania*. New York: Vintage, 1998.

Corina, Maurice. *Trust in Tobacco: The Anglo-American Struggle for Power*. New York: St. Martin's, 1975.

Cox, Howard. *The Global Cigarette: Origins and Evolution of British-American Tobacco, 1880–1945*. Oxford: Oxford University Press, 2000.

Croad, Stephen. "Changing Perceptions: A Temple of Tobacco in Camden Town." *Transactions of the Ancient Monument Society* 40 (1996): 1–16.

Great Britain, The Monopolies Commission. *Report of the Supply of Cigarettes and Tobacco and of Cigarette and Tobacco Machinery, 1948.* London: HMSO, 1961.

Heimann, Robert K. *Tobacco and Americans.* New York: McGraw-Hill, 1960.

Klein, Richard. *Cigarettes Are Sublime.* Chapel Hill: Duke University Press, 1993.

Kluger, Richard. *Ashes to Ashes: America's Hundred-Year Cigarette War, the Public Health, and the Unabashed Triumph of Philip Morris.* New York: Vintage, 1997.

Middleton, Arthur Pierce. *Tobacco Coast: A Maritime History of Chesapeake Bay in the Colonial Era.* Edited for the Museum by George Carrington Mason. Newport News, VA: Mariners' Museum, 1953.

Parker-Pope, Tara. *Cigarette: Anatomy of an Industry from Seed to Smoke.* New York: New Press, 2001.

Percy, Alfred. *Tobacco Rolling Roads to Waterways: Tobacco, Incentive to Early Science.* Madison Heights, VA: Percy, 1963.

Tate, Cassandra. *Cigarette Wars: The Triumph of "The Little White Slaver."* New York: Oxford University Press, 1999.

THE BALTICS DURING WORLD WAR II

Cohen, Rose, and Saul Issroff. *The Holocaust in Lithuania, 1941–1945.* Jerusalem: Gefen, 2002.

Ehrenberg, Ilya, and Vassily Grossman. *The Black Book.* New York: Holocaust Library, 1980.

Eisen, George. *Children and Play in the Holocaust: Games Among the Shadows.* Amherst: University of Massachusetts Press, 1988.

Eksteins, Modris. *Walking Since Daybreak: A Story of Eastern Europe, World War II, and the Heart of our Century.* New York: Houghton Mifflin, 1999.

Faitelson, Alex. *Heroism and Bravery in Lithuania, 1941–45.* Jerusalem: Gefen, 1996.

Friedlander, Saul. *Nazi Germany and the Jews: The Years of Extermination, 1939–1945.* New York: HarperCollins, 2001.

Hilberg, Raul. *The Destruction of the European Jews.* New York: Holmes & Meier, 1985.

Levin, Dov. *Fighting Back: Lithuanian Jewry's Armed Resistance to the Nazis, 1941–1945.* Translated by Moshe Kohn and Dina Cohen. New York: Holmes & Meier, 1985.

Mangulis, Visvaldis. *Latvia in the Wars of the 20th Century.* Princeton Junction, NJ: Cognition, 1983.

Ofer, Dalia, and Lenore Weitzmann. *Women in the Holocaust.* New Haven, CT: Yale University Press, 1999.

Porter, Jack Nusan. *Jewish Partisans: A Documentary History of Jewish Resistance in the Soviet Union During World War II.* Washington, DC: University Press of America, 1982.

Trunk, Isaiah. *Judenrat: The Jewish Councils in Eastern Europe Under Nazi Occupation.* New York: Stein & Day, 1977.

United States Holocaust Memorial Museum. *1945: The Year of Liberation.* Washington, DC: USHMM, 1995.

———. *Historical Atlas of the Holocaust.* New York: Macmillan, 1996.

Vilna Gaon State Jewish Museum. *Siauliai Ghetto: Lists of Prisoners.* Vilnius, 2002.

BELGIUM AND FRANCE, 1944–1945

Martin, Ralph G. *The G.I. War, 1941–45.* New York: Little, Brown, 1967.

McKee, Alexander. *The Race for the Rhine Bridges.* New York: Dorset, 1971.

Pictorial History of the 75th Infantry Division, 1944–1945. Army and Navy Publishing Company. 1946.

Walsh, Albert C. *A G.I. Remembers.* Baton Rouge, LA: Help of Christians Publications, 1991.